The ID CaseBook

Case Studies in Instructional Design

Second Edition

Peggy A. Ertmer
Purdue University

James Quinn
Oakland University

Merrill
Prentice Hall

Upper Saddle River, New Jersey
Columbus, Ohio

Library of Congress Cataloging-in-Publication Data

Ertmer, Peggy A.
    The ID casebook : case studies in instructional design / by Peggy A. Ertmer, James
Quinn; with a foreword by David Jonassen.–2nd ed.
      p. cm.
    Includes bibliographical references.
    ISBN 0-13-094321-5
    1. Instructional systems–Design–Case studies. I. Title: Instructional design casebook.
II. Quinn, James III. Title.

LB1028.38 .E78 2003
371.3–dc21   2002022714

Vice President and Publisher: Jeffery W. Johnston
Executive Editor: Debra A. Stollenwerk
Editorial Assistant: Mary Morrill
Production Editor: Sheryl Glicker Langner
Production Coordination: Lea Baranowski, Carlisle Publishers Services
Design Coordinator: Diane C. Lorenzo
Cover Designer: Linda Sorrells-Smith
Cover art: Index Stock
Production Manager: Pamela D. Bennett
Director of Marketing: Ann Castel Davis
Marketing Manager: Krista Groshong
Marketing Coordinator: Tyra Cooper

This book was set in Times Roman and Christiana by Carlisle Communications, Ltd. It was printed and bound
by Maple Vail Book Manufacturing Group. The cover was printed by Phoenix Color Corp.

Pearson Education Ltd.
Pearson Education Australia Pty. Limited
Pearson Education Singapore Pte. Ltd.
Pearson Education North Asia Ltd.
Pearson Education Canada, Ltd.
Pearson Educación de Mexico, S.A. de C.V.
Pearson Education—Japan
Pearson Education Malaysia Pte. Ltd.
Pearson Education, *Upper Saddle River, New Jersey*

10 9 8 7 6 5 4 3 2 1
ISBN 0-13-094321-5

In gratitude to the five pillars in my life: Dave—support, Mark—wit, Emilie—cheerfulness, Laura—intensity, and Scott—playfulness

PE

To my parents, Charles and Carmel Quinn, and to the memory of Elvis Presley

JQ

Foreword

by David Jonassen

The case method of teaching began at Harvard University well over a century ago, first in the medical school and later in the law and business schools. While case-based teaching has not been unknown in the instructional design field, this book, now in its second edition, has made the practice more feasible.

Instructional design is an archetype of design problem solving. How do cases support learning how to be an instructional designer? Unlike historical conceptions of the design process, design problems are among the most complex and ill-structured kinds of problems that are encountered in practice. Design problems are ill-structured because they usually have an ambiguous specification of goals, no predetermined solution path, limited or delayed feedback from the world, and frequently irrational biases for solutions. Given any design problem, there are an infinite variety of solutions. The real difficulty in solving design problems is determining what the nature of the problem is, a process that usually involves a lot of constraint analysis. Designing almost invariably leads to a product, but the criteria for evaluating that product are seldom known or clear. The effectiveness of being a designer is largely a function of design experience. But there's the rub. That is exactly what instructional design students lack.

Historically, instructional design has been taught as a hierarchically organized set of discrete skills, if the students were lucky. Too often, however, instructional design courses, like most university courses, teach students only about the instructional design process. Students seldom learn how to do instructional design in an authentic context; however, that is changing. Why?

A decade or so ago, instructional design, as a field, began a paradigmatic journey. In the past, the teaching/learning process was thought to be a matter of communication efficacy. The more effectively that we communicate an idea to the students, the more likely they will learn. Nearly all of our research focused on how to better design instructional messages. All we had to do was tell students about the world, and they would learn—that is, they would "acquire knowledge." Contemporary theories and methods of learning are more concerned with what learners know how to do. Why? Because, in everyday and professional contexts, people do things. The purpose of their learning is to use what they learn. They solve problems, such as designing instruction, so how can we teach learners how to design instruction?

In general, there are three ways to teach learners how to do things. The easiest, and most decontextualized, way of teaching "how" is to teach skills. Instructional design consists of a number of skills: how to conduct a needs assessment or task analysis, how to sequence instructional interactions, how to write assessments, and so on. And, so, we offer courses on these topics in which we (hopefully) require students to conduct a needs assessment, write test items, and so on, rather than take a test about how to do those things. These experiences are useful but often lack coherence because there is no consistent context.

Contemporary theories and their methods offer two additional ways to approach teaching: practice fields and practice communities (Barab & Duffy, 2000). Practice fields, microworlds, constructivist learning environments, and cases, are simulations of a contextualized reality. Practice communities, like apprenticeships, are real-world contexts in which learners are fully participating members, so the learning issues are emergent; they co-evolve. Many of us believe that these are the most meaningful experiences and the most epistemically reliable; however, because practice communities are the most logistically problematic, cases provide an effective middle ground between isolated skill teaching and real-world apprenticeships.

This book is full of cases that tell stories about real design projects. That makes them more authentic than decontextualized skills development. Analyzing what designers did and making conjectures about what they should have done engage learners vicariously in many of the activities that designers do. Cases are meaningful learning activities, and this book makes a major contribution to that goal.

How closely does case analysis cognitively and socially replicate the design process? That depends on the nature of what is being learned. For example, analyzing cases, preparing briefs, and defending judgments are all authentic activities for law students. Instructional designers design. There is a lot of analysis, but it usually involves analyzing the context of the client. Analyzing the process is also a reflective and metacognitive activity.

Case studies are excellent practice fields for learning about how to do instructional design. This second edition has added to the breadth and depth of cases and therefore to the breadth and depth of experiences that design students can have. The cases all represent ill-structured design problems for which there are multiple solutions. The contexts, processes, and problems vary, just as they do in professional instructional design contexts. These problems cannot be appropriately solved using any single collection of boxes and arrows. I believe that *The ID CaseBook* provides an invaluable resource supporting the teaching of instructional design as well as promoting innovation in the instructional design field.

REFERENCE

Barab, S., & Duffy, T. (2000). In D. H. Jonassen & S. M. Land (Eds.), *Theoretical foundations of learning environments* (pp. 25–26). Mahwah, NJ: Lawrence Erlbaum Associates.

Preface

> It is possible that a person who is good at learning something from the book will not know how to deal with a realistic situation. Like some of the designers in the cases we discussed, we may have a master's or doctoral degree in instructional design, yet still not deal with a situation well. We need the opportunity to practice what we learn in our books.

So began a graduate student at the end of one of our instructional design (ID) courses, when asked to describe the value of analyzing and discussing ID case studies. This student's comments summarize our primary purpose for this text: to provide students with opportunities to practice what they learn in class, to bridge the gap between the complex reality of the design world and the foundational principles taught in traditional textbooks.

Although ID educators have recognized the potential of the case method of teaching in the education of instructional designers for a number of years, there have been relatively few materials available that help ID educators actually implement this approach in their courses. Most educators do not have the time or expertise to create ID cases for their courses yet would use such cases if they were available. The *ID CaseBook* offers ID educators a rich resource of authentic design problems that can be used in either introductory or advanced design courses, as well as in more specialized courses related to any of the specific design steps or issues. Because of our commitment to the case method of instruction, we felt a sense of urgency to make case materials readily available, so that ID educators can begin to use cases in their classes, immediately as well as relatively easily.

CONCEPTUAL FRAMEWORK

Our book arises out of a view of ID as a complex, ill-structured domain of knowledge, for which there is a methodology and a set of guidelines but not a single set of procedures that will guarantee success. This view of ID recognizes that professional ID competence requires more than technical expertise. Although some design situations may involve well-structured and clearly defined problems that will benefit from the application of a set of technical procedures, many more situations are ill-structured and poorly defined. In addition to the necessary technical skills and knowledge, such situations depend on the artistry and skill of ID professionals to operate creatively and effectively in these ambiguous, uncertain, and open-ended contexts. Given the constraints of time and other resources, how does an instructor convey the complexity and ill-structured nature of ID while teaching the technical skills that are prerequisite for ID practice? We believe, as do many others, that the case-teaching approach has the potential to help bridge this gap by situating the learning of technical ID skills within authentic contexts.

There are probably as many definitions of case-based instruction as there are ways of implementing it. In this text, we use an approach to case studies that is based on the business school model—that is, case studies are problem-centered descriptions of design situations, developed from the actual experiences of instructional designers.

The cases in this book are designed to be dilemma oriented—that is, each case ends before the solution is clear. Students are expected to evaluate the available evidence, to judge alternative interpretations and actions, and to experience the uncertainty that often accompanies design decisions. In particular, we hope that, by analyzing the cases presented in this book, ID students will learn how to identify ID problems and subproblems, to recognize the importance of context in resolving such problems, and to develop, justify, and test alternative plans for resolving ID problems.

ORGANIZATION

The ID CaseBook is divided into three parts. In the introduction (Part I), we provide students with suggestions and strategies for how to approach *learning* from case-based instruction. Although it is our experience that students are typically excited about using case studies in instruction, because of their unfamiliarity with this approach, they often feel a little apprehensive as well. We have found that, by providing helpful suggestions up-front, students' initial concerns are considerably lessened.

Part II includes 36 cases, situated in a variety of educational and business contexts. Case titles bear the name of the instructional designer in the case and are arranged alphabetically, by title, to avoid alerting students to the nature of the issues addressed. This decision was based on our belief that students need to be able to identify and define presenting problems before they can begin to solve them. To ease the selection process for instructors, however, a matrix is provided in the *Instructor's Guide* that outlines the primary and secondary issues of each case, as well as the specific content and context of each.

In Part III, we invite students to reflect on their own case-learning experiences, and, as beginning instructional designers, on the usefulness of the case method as a teaching and learning strategy. In addition, we invite students to explore some future possibilities for case-based instruction—in particular, the use of the World Wide Web as a delivery medium.

FEATURES OF THE SECOND EDITION

The second edition of *The ID CaseBook* consists of 36 ID case studies, representing 20 new cases as well as 16 of your favorite cases from the first edition. The increased number of cases in the second edition allows us to present a broad range of issues, content, and contexts. For example, there are several new cases dealing with issues related to the design of instruction for online delivery, reflecting current emphases in our field. In addition, we have significantly increased the number of cases that focus on the selection of appropriate instructional strategies. Other issues that receive increased attention in this edition include contextual analysis, project management, change management, evaluation, and ethical decisions in the design of instruction.

The increased size of the second edition also allows us to include a greater range of case contexts. For example, as requested by some reviewers and adopters of the first edition, we have significantly increased the number of cases situated in K–12 settings. In addition, the number, as well as the range, of cases set in corporate environments have increased. As in the first edition, each case is based on a real experience encountered by the case authors. By compiling these experiences into one book, we offer students the combined professional experiences of some of the best scholars and practitioners in our profession.

As in the first edition, each chapter begins with a case narrative. The *case narrative* includes relevant background information for the case, including the problem context, key players, available resources, and existing constraints. In addition, each case includes *relevant data,* presented in a variety of forms and formats. In this edition, however, we have added two sets of discussion questions at the end of each case to stimulate students' thinking and to provide a focus for class discussion. The first set of questions—"Preliminary Analysis Questions"— asks students to identify and discuss issues, to consider the issues from multiple perspectives, to develop a plan of action to resolve problems, and/or to specify possible consequences resulting from their recommended plan. The second set of questions—"Implications for ID Practice"—requires students to think more broadly about the issues presented in the case from the point of view of ID theory and practice.

ANCILLARIES

The updated *Instructor's Guide* accompanying the second edition includes the following key features:

- *Case matrix:* expanded for the second edition, a summary matrix that allows instructors to see, at a glance, the primary and secondary issues of each case, as well as the context in which the case is set
- *Teaching suggestions:* ideas for instructors regarding the different ways cases can be used with different levels of students
- *Case overview:* a brief description of each case, including the "big idea" students should glean from the case
- *Case objectives:* the specific focus of the case (the supporting concepts and principles learners should use in analyzing the case issues); the knowledge, skills, and/or attitudes students should gain from their case analyses and discussions
- *Debriefing guidelines:* suggestions from the case authors regarding how to think about the case
- *References:* a list of references related to the issues presented in the case

We have been very pleased by the response to the first edition of our text. It is our hope that this expanded edition of *The ID CaseBook* and the *Instructor's Guide* will continue to provide both students and instructors with challenging and rewarding learning experiences. We continue to view this whole venture as a work in progress. If instructors or students have suggestions for future editions, we'd love to hear them! Our e-mail addresses are

pertmer@purdue.edu
quinn@oakland.edu

ACKNOWLEDGMENTS

Since the publication of the first edition, we have been greatly encouraged by the comments and suggestions from both instructors and students who have used *The ID CaseBook* in their courses. In fact, some of those instructors and students are now authors in this new edition. We very much appreciate the positive response to the first edition and are glad to have had the opportunity to develop the second edition.

Of course, this work would not have been possible without the support, advice, and encouragement of a number of individuals, including the contributing authors, supportive colleagues, patient family members, insightful students, careful secretaries, an outstanding editor, and exceptional reviewers.

We are gratefully indebted to the more than 50 authors who contributed to this volume. They made our work both interesting and enjoyable. Having never met many of our contributors, we feel fortunate to have had the opportunity to work with them at a distance. We firmly believe that each author has added something unique to the text and sincerely appreciate the time all of them gave to develop and revise their cases.

Our former reviewers, current adopters, and current and past students have been influential in shaping many of the details of the text, particularly in making suggestions for how to think about the case-learning process. We are grateful to our colleagues who have used the cases in their courses and who have provided valuable feedback regarding numerous aspects of the cases.

We especially would like to thank our editor, Debbie Stollenwerk, and the rest of the production crew at Merrill/Prentice Hall. Debbie has tirelessly supported our efforts during the development of this new edition, bringing an enthusiasm to the revision process that few can equal. Finally, we wish to acknowledge a number of reviewers who assisted in the development of this edition through their insights and suggestions, including Bonnie H. Armstrong, Florida State University; Robertta H. Barba, San Jose State University; Gayle V. Davidson-Shivers, University of South Alabama; Khalid Hamza, Florida Atlantic University; Linda L. Lohr, University of Northern Colorado; and Sara McNeil, University of Houston.

In sum, we are grateful to all who have played a part in making this second edition both bigger and better than the first. We hope you enjoy it!

Contents

Note: Every effort has been made to provide accurate and current Internet information in this book. However, the Internet and information posted on it are constantly changing, so it is inevitable that some of the Internet addresses listed in this textbook will change.

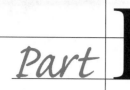

Part I

Introduction

BY PEGGY A. ERTMER AND JAMES QUINN

Although case methods have been used in business, law, and medicine for over 100 years, it is likely that this will be one of your first experiences with the case approach. This may give rise to a wide range of feelings—excitement, nervousness, curiosity, intimidation. In addition, you'll probably have a lot of questions: How do I analyze a case? How will I know if I've done it right? Where will I find the information and resources I need to solve the case problems? Although it is our experience that students are typically excited about using case studies in instruction, because of their unfamiliarity with this approach, they often feel a little apprehension as well. We've written this part, addressed to you specifically, because we have found that initial concerns can be lessened by describing, up front, the types of tasks you will be expected to complete, as well as some of the adjustments you may need to make in your current learning mindset. As one of our former students noted:

> In my opinion, if students were told up front that this style of learning [case-based instruction] feels slow and cumbersome at first, and that they should read and re-read the information in the case a couple of times, do what they need to visualize and better understand the scenarios—it might be easier to adjust to. I think case-based learning is a valuable and interactive method that just takes a different mindset than most students are used to.

We think this student makes two excellent suggestions: Tell students what this approach "feels" like and tell them how to actually do it (i.e., analyze a case). Although we don't really believe that we *can* tell you exactly how it feels to learn from cases or how you must go about analyzing a case, we offer a few thoughts and suggestions related to these two elements of the case-learning experience. We begin with suggested strategies and procedures for analyzing a case and then provide suggestions on how to adopt a "facilitative" mindset, so that you get the most from your case-learning experience.

STRATEGIES FOR ANALYZING A CASE

There are probably a variety of ways to analyze a case study effectively. We offer the following sequence as one possibility:

1. **Understand the context in which the case is being analyzed and discussed.** If your instructor is using this text to supplement another, then the cases will probably be used to provide real-world examples of the content or design steps you've discussed. This context can help focus your attention on relevant issues, questions, and concerns related to your readings and other coursework. Also, each case includes two sets of focusing questions at the end. You may want to read these questions first, as a way to "prime the mental pump." Reading case questions before you read the case may help you read more meaningfully and more effectively.
2. **Read the case.** Your first reading should be fairly quick, just to get a general sense of what the case is about—the key players, main issues, context, and so on.
3. **Read the case again.** Your second (and subsequent) reading(s) should be much slower: taking notes, considering multiple perspectives, and thinking about

alternative solutions and consequences. The benefits you reap from your case analysis will relate to how much time you spend—not necessarily reading but, rather, reflecting on what you have read.

4. **Analyze the case.** This is probably the fuzziest and thus most overwhelming step of the whole case-analysis process. Assuming that you have already identified the facts of the case, relevant information, key players, context, and resources and constraints, we recommend that you complete the following steps during your analysis:
   a. Identify the key issues in the case.
   b. Consider the main issues from the perspectives of the key players.
   c. Generate a list of potential solutions related to each issue.
   d. Specify possible consequences of each solution.
   e. Weigh the advantages and limitations of each solution and make a recommendation for action.

5. **Actively participate in class discussion.** The case class is a learning community— together, you, your instructor, and your peers are working to gain a more complete understanding of the case situation and possible solutions. It is important that you be an active participant as well as an active listener. Listen carefully to what others are saying, so that your questions and contributions can move the discussion along. Coming prepared to class is critical to your ability to participate in, and benefit from, the case-learning experience.

6. **Reflect on the case-learning experience.** Boud, Keogh, and Walker (1985) stated that, in any learning experience, reflection is needed at various points: at the *start,* in a preparatory phase when you start to explore what is required of you, as you become aware of the demands of the situation and the resources you bring to bear; *during* the experience, as a way of dealing with the vast array of inputs and coping with the feelings generated; and *after* the experience, as you attempt to make sense of it. The case method provides fertile ground for facilitating a reflective approach to learning. Starting with the first step in the analysis process, as you consider the context in which you are studying a case, you engage in a reflective process. As you implement your analysis approach, you complete four activities that Noordhoff and Kleinfeld (1990) stated are inherent in a "reflective approach" to design:

   ■ Naming and framing situations and issues
   ■ Identifying goals and appraising their worth
   ■ Sorting images, selecting strategies, and spinning out consequences
   ■ Reflecting on effects and redesigning one's practice

Finally, at the end of a case analysis, reflection helps you make sense of your experiences with the case and deepen your understanding. By reflecting on both the products and the processes of your learning experiences, you gain insights essential to improving future performances. Reflection can link past and future actions by providing you with information about the strategies you used (learning process) and the outcomes you achieved (learning products). It allows you to take stock of what has happened and to prepare yourself for future action.

Developing a Facilitative Mindset

In all forms of professional education, a fundamental goal exists: to help a novice "think like" a member of the profession (Shulman, 1992). Kitchener and King (1990) indicated that reflective thinking matures with both age and experience. They listed the following qualities as characteristic of mature reflective thinkers: viewing situations from multiple perspectives, searching for alternative explanations of events, and using evidence to support or evaluate a decision or position. These qualities form an essential part of the mindset that we believe facilitates learning from case studies. The following additional guidelines have been gleaned from our own experiences and those of our students, as well as from the results of an exploratory research study conducted by one of us (Ertmer, Newby, & MacDougall, 1996).

There is no one right answer. If you enter the case-learning experience with this idea firmly planted, you are less likely to be frustrated by the ambiguity inherent in the case-study approach. There are many answers to the issues in each case. The solutions you propose will depend as much on the perspective you take as on the issues you identify. Sometimes it may help to know how the designers in the cases "solved" the problems, but not always, and probably not usually. Being frustrated by a lack of answers can actually be very motivating. If you're left hanging after reading a case, chances are you'll continue to ponder the issues for a long time to come. As one reviewer noted, "After reading the first few cases, I felt that this is 'hard work' and it was going to take some time to work through—but they [the cases] made me stop and think about potential solutions. Some time after reading them I still found myself contemplating potential answers."

Accept the fact that you will not know how to solve each case. Furthermore, if you have no clue where to begin, give yourself permission not to know. Then begin the analysis process by paying attention to how others analyze the case based on their own personal experiences.

There is more than one way to look at things. One of the advantages to participating in case discussions is that you get the chance to hear how others analyzed the case and to consider multiple points of view, thus gaining a more complete examination and understanding of the issues involved. Listening to others' ideas *allows* you to see the issues from different points of view as well as *forces* you to consider exactly where you stand. By paying close attention to what others have to say, you can evaluate how that fits with your own views. Thus, you learn more about who you are, where you are coming from, and what you stand for. Your views of others, as well as of yourself, may be broadened.

Keep an open mind; suspend judgment until all ideas are considered. This suggestion builds on the previous one. It is important to come to the case discussion with an attitude of "Let's see what develops." Begin by regarding your initial solutions as tentative. Listen respectfully to your peers; ask questions to clarify and gather additional information, not to pass judgment on ideas different from yours. As one of our students recommended, "Be flexible and open-minded. Remember that problems can be attacked from many different angles." Use the case discussion as a means to gather additional data. In the end, your final recommendation should be informed by the collective wisdom of the whole class yet reflect your own best judgment.

Be leery of assumptions and generalizations; avoid seeing things in extremes. If data are ambiguous or there is little evidence to support why case players acted as they did, be cautious of the assumptions you make. Be especially careful to state your assumptions tentatively, suggesting uncertainty. Along the same lines, be careful not to generalize your observations beyond the data provided. Avoid using labels or slogans that lump people together. If you're inclined to see things in black and white, all or nothing, stand back and look at the words you use in your analysis. It is fairly safe to say that you should avoid words such as *always, never, everybody,* and *nobody.* Stick close to the facts when describing the issues, drawing conclusions, and making recommendations.

Expect to get better; focus on the analysis process. At the beginning of a case-based course, you may feel overwhelmed with the challenge of trying to solve case problems. It is important to recognize, first, that this is not uncommon. Many students initially feel overwhelmed and apprehensive. Second, it is equally important to recognize that, as with most skills, design skills and knowledge improve with practice. Furthermore, most students actually start to enjoy the challenge involved in analyzing problem situations. If you maintain the mindset that you learn as much, if not more, from the analysis process as you do from identifying a potential solution, then your case-learning experience will be less frustrating. The analytical process is at the heart of the case method. Pay attention to the progress you make in analyzing the cases. Judge your success not by how many you "get right," but by your approach to the analysis process. Did you consider all the issues? Did you look at issues from the varying perspectives of the key players? Have you based suggestions on available data? If your skills are improving in these areas, you're gaining in precisely the ways promoted by the case approach. And remember that learning is a lifelong process. You'll never know all there is to know about designing, yet each experience with design situations should move you closer to thinking and acting like a professional designer.

Take time to reflect. Reflection has been a recurring theme in our discussion of how to approach a case study. Quite simply, that's because we believe that reflection enhances everything that happens in the case method. According to Rowland (1992), "Reflection is critical to understanding experiences and to developing skills. Students must engage in reflective conversations with themselves and with others in order to make sense of experience and deepen their understanding" (p. 38).

It's true that a case analysis takes more time to complete than traditional course assignments, yet there is little to be gained by trying to rush the process. Acting or responding impulsively decreases the chances that you will gather all the relevant information, examine all the potential courses of action, and consider the many possible ensuing consequences. Take time to think. Ask questions of yourself, your peers, and your instructor. Hills and Gibson (cited in Grimmett & Erickson, 1988) describe how reflective practitioners might go about their work. The development of this type of reflective mindset can begin with your work on these cases:

> As you go about your work responding to phenomena, identifying problems, diagnosing problems, making normative judgments, developing strategies, etc. think about your responses to situations and about what it is in the situation, and in yourself, that leads you to respond that way; think about the norms and values

on which your judgments are based; think about the manner in which you frame problems, and think about "your conception of your role." "Surface" and criticize your implicit understandings. Construct and test your own theories. (p. 151)

Enjoy yourself. As indicated earlier, the case method may at first feel like a strange and difficult way to learn. Yet, even when students indicate that learning from case studies can be frustrating and unnerving, they also admit that it is exciting and valuable. Being actively involved, working with stimulating case material, having a chance to express your ideas and hear those of others—these are all enjoyable aspects of case learning. We think one of our students summed it up wonderfully: "I like how cases challenge you and frustrate you. My advice is to relax. Let the ideas flow. Don't say 'This isn't possible.' And, most of all, be confident that what you are doing now will pay off in the future." We echo these sentiments: Relax, enjoy, and get ready to learn!

REFERENCES

Boud, D., Keogh, R., & Walker, D. (Eds.). (1985). *Reflection: Turning experience into learning.* New York: Nichols.

Ertmer, P. A., Newby, T. J., & MacDougall, M. (1996). Students' approaches to learning from case-based instruction: The role of reflective self-regulation. *American Educational Research Journal, 33*(3), 719–752.

Grimmett, P. P., & Erickson, G. L. (1988). *Reflection in teacher education.* New York: Teachers College Press.

Kitchener, K. S., & King, P. M. (1990). The reflective judgment model: Ten years of research. In M. L. Commons, C. Arman, L. Kohlberg, F. A. Richards, T. A. Grotzer, & J. Sinnott (Eds.), *Adult development: Models and methods in the study of adolescent and adult thought.* (Vol. 2, pp. 63–78). New York: Praeger.

Noordhoff, K., & Kleinfeld, J. (1990). Shaping the rhetoric of reflection for multicultural settings. In R. T. Clift, W. R. Houston, & M. C. Pugach (Eds.), *Encouraging reflective practice in education: An analysis of issues and programs* (pp. 163–185). New York: Teachers College Press.

Rowland, G. (1992). What do instructional designers actually do? An initial investigation of expert practice. *Performance Improvement Quarterly, 5*(2), 65–86.

Shulman, L. (1992). Toward a pedagogy of cases. In J. H. Shulman (Ed.), *Case methods in teacher education* (pp. 1–30). New York: Teachers College Press.

Part II

Case Studies

Jackie Adams

BY MELISSA J. DARK

PART ONE: CREATING AN EVALUATION PLAN

Upon graduating with a master's degree in instructional design, Jackie Adams accepted an instructional design position with a federally funded project at a large university. As the instructional designer on the job, Jackie's main responsibilities were to work with technical subject matter experts in the development, delivery, and evaluation of in-service faculty education. The Advanced Manufacturing Technology Education (AMTE) project was a new venture, which meant that Jackie would be clarifying her job at the same time she developed the in-service faculty education program. The first thing Jackie did was read the grant proposal and talk with her new boss, Ray DeMilo.

Jackie learned that the AMTE project was one of many projects funded by the Advanced Technology Education (ATE) program. The goal of the ATE program was to improve science and engineering technician education at the undergraduate and secondary school levels. The ATE projects focused on curriculum development, instructional materials development, teacher/faculty enhancement, and/or student recruitment. The AMTE project focused specifically on teacher enhancement as a means of advancing technology education. The rationale behind AMTE was to provide educators with state-of-the-art knowledge in their technical disciplines, so that their students, in turn, would benefit from the most current advances in technology. Over the life of the three-year grant, the AMTE project was to provide faculty development to 100 science, math, and engineering technology educators each year.

Over the course of the next several months, Jackie worked with several subject matter experts to plan in-service workshops in high-tech areas, such as computer numerical control, programmable logic controllers, robotics, electro-mechanical controls, lasers, solid modeling, and rapid prototyping.

Jackie had been on the job about four months when Ray asked to discuss her progress to date. Ray told Jackie that he was pleased with the progress of the project and that her skills in instructional design had significantly contributed to this progress. Jackie felt great. He went on to explain that he had just received a bulletin announcing new legislation that was going to have an impact on all federally funded projects, including AMTE. The new legislation required greater and more stringent performance assessment of all federally funded projects. Jackie asked Ray what that meant for AMTE. According to Ray, they needed a more detailed evaluation plan to assess the performance of their project. Ray delegated the evaluation to Jackie and asked her to submit a detailed plan for evaluating the project in a month. He also told her that the evaluation plan would need to be submitted to the funding agency and filed in the grants office at the university.

After Ray left her office, Jackie worried about how to approach this task. She had never written an evaluation plan before. Jackie thought that she and the subject matter experts she was working with had been making good decisions in designing the instruction for the target audience and establishing the goals and objectives of the in-service workshops. However, because they were just getting started, Jackie did not feel ready to think about measuring outcomes of the teacher in-service workshops.

Concerned, she remembered reading a little bit about evaluation in the grant proposal. She pulled out the proposal and reread the section on project evaluation that Ray had written for the grant (see Figure 1–1).

Jackie read the section several times, trying to make sense of it. However, she did not have a background in quality. The most that she understood was that the "quality system" was supposed to provide a standard for evaluating and continuously improving AMTE's operations. There was no information in the section about how this was to occur. She pondered this for a few days and finally wrote down some thoughts (see Figure 1–2).

As she looked at what she had written, Jackie reflected on what she needed to do with the evaluation plan: (1) give it to her boss, Ray DeMilo; (2) send it to the funding agency; (3) file it with the university grants office; and (4) use it to conduct the evaluation.

PRELIMINARY ANALYSIS QUESTIONS

1. Use Jackie's questions (in Figure 1–2) to decide what she needs to do to complete this evaluation.
2. How can Jackie determine whether the short- and long-term outcomes are being achieved? What evaluation data does she need to collect?
3. How should Jackie design the instruments for this evaluation?

IMPLICATIONS FOR ID PRACTICE

1. How is evaluation important to the theory of instructional design?
2. How is evaluation important to the practice of instructional design and at what point(s) in the ID process should it be considered?
3. Evaluation is sometimes compared to quality management. How does this comparison apply in instructional design?

The focus for the AMTE evaluation plan will be the development of a quality system that will provide a well-defined and agreed-upon standard for evaluating and continuously improving AMTE's operations. The use of standards to establish quality systems in industrial and education settings is growing rapidly and provides an excellent framework for the development of AMTE's evaluation plan.

Quality systems based on such standards typically include the development of both a program for assuring an organization's quality and all the activities and operations required to implement it effectively. AMTE is proposing to establish a comprehensive quality system, which will cover elements such as documentation, implementation, review and correction for all activities having a bearing on the quality of the information, and services and activities supplied by AMTE.

A key factor in the management of AMTE's quality system will be the development of a quality audit, which will be used to provide the data for evaluating and improving the effectiveness of its quality system. The objectives of AMTE's quality system audits will be to a) maintain or improve efficiency of its operations and image, b) determine how disciplined and effective the organization's operations are, and c) meet an appropriate level of quality assurance as specified by an agreed-upon standard or contractual agreement. The standard for the AMTE quality system audits will define its policies, lines of responsibility and accountability, and procedures, in addition to work instructions, and recordkeeping requirements as appropriate. Audits will be conducted periodically by internal AMTE auditors in order to maintain and improve the quality system, as well as external reviewers who may provide a more objective assessment of the project.

FIGURE 1–1   AMTE Evaluation Plan

Evaluation Planning Notes

According to the grant proposal, the mission of the center is to

"improve significantly the educational experiences and opportunities of students preparing for careers in manufacturing and distribution by keeping teacher enhancement as a major focus."

Tie evaluation to mission.
Answer the following questions:

Why evaluate?
Evaluate what?
How should the evaluation be conducted?
Who should be involved?
When should it be done?

FIGURE 1–2   Jackie's Evaluation Planning Notes

PART TWO: CONDUCTING A META-EVALUATION

The AMTE project had been operating for a year and a half. Ray DeMilo, the project director, came in to see Jackie Adams, the project instructional designer. Ray shared with Jackie a letter that he had received from the funding agency regarding an upcoming meeting. The funding agency would be sending out a six-member team to review the project's progress and impact. This was a routine practice on large grants to ensure that the money was spent as intended and that the project was meeting its goals, as well as having the intended impact.

According to Ray, this meeting was very important. Upon conclusion of the review, the six-member team would report the success of the project to key administrators at the university and the funding agency. The review team had asked to meet with Ray's boss, Ron Bentley, the dean of the school, and Ron's boss, Bruce Stingel, the vice president for academic affairs.

Since the beginning of the grant, Ray and Jackie had talked about the importance of a good plan for project evaluation. Ray and Jackie knew that if they had a good evaluation plan they could accurately measure the impact of the project and identify areas where the project could be improved to increase impact. The upcoming review session would examine how well AMTE had achieved its goals and how goal attainment had been measured and reported. Ray told Jackie, "Well, kid, that evaluation plan is going to be important now. We will get to show the agency, my boss, and my boss's boss what we are all about. I know you did a good job." Jackie appreciated Ray's vote of confidence but didn't feel quite so confident herself. She did not feel comfortable having a lot of people review her work. Furthermore, the stakes seemed high. If she did a good job, it would reflect well on everyone, and they would have a better chance of securing additional funded projects in the future. If she did a poor job, it would not bode well for the institution and future projects.

As the meeting kicked off, Ray and Jackie became acquainted with the review team. The team included four post-secondary educators with a background in science, engineering, and technology and two engineering practitioners from industry. Each person on the review team was responsible for reviewing and documenting a different aspect of the project. Hank Lundstrom, an engineering technology professor, was the lead team member. Hank's job was to assess Jackie's evaluation plan. Hank had served on accreditation teams in the past, thus giving him more experience in evaluation than his fellow team members.

During the two-day meeting, Hank spent the entire first day with Jackie. At the beginning of the meeting, Hank explained to Jackie that the team would be reviewing the project's progress and impact. He went on to explain that the impact of the project would be assessed using data gathered from the project evaluation plan. According to Hank, the value of data gathered would be directly related to the evaluation plan methodology, and his job was to document this. The team would then get back together, report their findings, evaluate the project, write a report, and present it to the dean, the vice president, and the program officers at the funding agency.

Jackie shared the AMTE evaluation plan in detail over the course of the first day. During the time they spent together, Hank asked a lot of questions and listened intently as

Jackie explained the evaluation plan. Hank had a very factual and impersonal manner throughout the meeting. He did not comment much on the information that Jackie shared, making it hard for Jackie to determine if he thought it was a good plan or not. By the end of their meeting, Hank had detailed what he had learned from Jackie about the AMTE evaluation plan in a summary report. He thanked Jackie for her time and let her know that he would be sharing his summary with the rest of the team in order for them to write an evaluation report. (See the instructor's guide for a copy of Jackie's evaluation plan.) As Hank walked away, he felt confident that he had enough information to start on his review.

PRELIMINARY ANALYSIS QUESTIONS

Part A: Questions Related to the Evaluation Plan

1. What are the main evaluation questions Jackie appears to be addressing?
2. What are the strengths and weaknesses of the evaluation design for answering the questions?
3. Given the goals stated in the ATME proposal, are these questions sufficient?

Part B: Questions Related to Instrumentation

1. How appropriate are the instruments for the goals of the evaluation?
2. Are the evaluation questions answered in enough detail, or are other instruments needed?
3. What, if anything, would you change about the instruments and why?

IMPLICATIONS FOR ID PRACTICE

1. What is meta-evaluation? How is it important to instructional design?
2. In what kinds of situations is it appropriate to conduct a meta-evaluation? What are the challenges and advantages to conducting one?
3. How do issues related to measurement instruments impact the practice of instructional design?

Sam Bell

BY JACQUELINE L. DOBROVOLNY
AND ROBERT J. SPENCE

Sam Bell sat in his office, staring out the window and enjoying the calmness of the early morning. He came in early, since he didn't sleep well last night. He kept reflecting on the discussion he had yesterday during lunch with his long-time friend, David Townsend, a marketing executive with a local manufacturing company. Sam received some advice from David that seemed simple enough, but he just wasn't sure it would work. As he drank his coffee, he reviewed the chain of events leading up to his current dilemma.

As the training manager for NorthCentral Bank (NCB), Sam was responsible for implementing a new computer-based training (CBT) curriculum in 2,000 branch offices, which employ 37,000 people. He was very conscious of the responsibility and keen to make a success of what all the officers of the bank saw as a significant project. If he were successful, it probably meant a promotion and significant raise. If the CBT project was not successful, he figured he would have to look for a new job. The stakes were high.

Sam recalled two significant events that had precipitated this whole situation. First, over the past 18 months, the competition had increased significantly. As a result, the bank needed to reduce costs and to operate as efficiently as possible. Second, NCB had always emphasized on-the-job training within each branch. In some cases, this training had been supplemented with group-paced courses at centralized locations. Three years ago, NCB began replacing the group-paced courses with paper-based, self-paced instructional materials, which were designed to teach specific, procedural issues and teller skills.

Sam was in charge of all of this training and found that the amount of maintenance required for the paper-based materials was tremendous. It was time-consuming and costly because thousands of pieces of paper had to be updated annually. Competitor pressures and the need to reduce costs, together with the expense of maintenance, helped convince Sam that CBT was an attractive solution. Along with the accounting department, he performed numerous cost-benefit analyses that demonstrated how CBT would reduce costs significantly. Sam and two of his trainers also conducted an extensive evaluation of the major CBT authoring systems. They purchased the system that rated highest in their evaluation. They also purchased a compatible graphics development package.

Sam selected 12 developers from NCB's training department. All of them volunteered for this project and all were subject matter experts; that is, all began their careers as tellers with NCB. The CBT development team currently consists of two instructional designers, four writers/subject matter experts, two graphic artists, two authoring systems programmers, one editor, one evaluation expert, and Sam, the project manager. The graphic artists have received training on the use of the graphics software, and the authoring systems programmers have received training on the use of the authoring system.

The CBT development team established standards and procedures for courseware production. They decided to deliver the courseware via CD-ROM and PCs connected to NCB's proprietary intranet.

The teller training course is currently under development. Assuming no major problems, it should be ready for beta test in approximately six months. The beta test is scheduled to take three months, and revisions, on the basis of the beta test, are scheduled to take two months. Thus, the teller training course will be delivered to the 2,000 branches in approximately 11 months.

The development of the CBT teller course has been great fun for the development team. Everyone on the team is excited about the project and confident that trainees will receive it enthusiastically. Everyone who has seen the CBT has been impressed with the quality of the graphics, animations, and video clips.

Early last week, Sam visited some branch offices to select those that would participate in beta testing. To his surprise, rather than encountering enthusiasm from the training supervisors at the various branches, the mood was, at best, skeptical. Even Jane Harris, a friend of his who is well known and whose opinions are respected, was cautious. Her parting comment when Sam left her office was "Sam, I really am concerned that we aren't ready for this technology stuff."

On the flight home that day, Sam felt as if someone had let all the air out of his balloon. He pondered Jane's comments. He was mystified and could not understand why she and the other training supervisors didn't share his enthusiasm for the CBT. The more he thought about it, the more panic he could feel rising up from his gut. He believed the skepticism of the training supervisors could lead to the rejection of the CBT teller training.

The day after that trip, Sam began searching for anything he could find on the introduction of new technology, resistance to change, and implementation problems specific to the use of technology. His reading led him to believe that the training supervisors were likely to resist CBT because of the following:

1. Most of the training supervisors took teller training at a centralized location in a group-paced format. Those who took the self-paced, paper-based training were generally not happy with that format.
2. The training supervisors have little experience with PCs other than through their banking work, which is done via PCs connected to a local-area network within each branch. When there is a problem with the banking software, the training supervisors

turn it over to a software expert. If there is a problem with the CBT, the training supervisors will have to solve the problem themselves.

3. The teller training course contains an extensive computer-managed instructional (CMI) component, which will track trainee performance. Training supervisors will be required to review those data to determine how individual trainees are performing and to upload those data periodically from the local server to the evaluation server.

4. There is no funding for an installation team to visit each branch and set up the teller training. Nor is there any funding to send the training supervisors to a group-paced course. Thus, each branch will receive a new PC that contains the teller training course, and each branch will "self-install" their own system, using documentation that will come with the PC.

These insights were heartbreaking! Sam could see his career at NCB coming to a quick and disappointing end.

Early this week, Sam received a call from David, who wanted to meet him for lunch to catch up on all that had happened since they had seen each other almost six months ago. At first, Sam declined, explaining he was just too busy and had too many crises to handle. However, David persisted, so they met yesterday at a restaurant close to Sam's office.

During lunch, Sam described his situation and his fears and concerns about the resistance to CBT. David listened attentively but at first had no suggestions. As the waiter cleared their table, David suddenly frowned and then, looking Sam straight in the eye, said, "This is a marketing problem, Sam! You are introducing a new product and you have to convince your users to buy it."

PRELIMINARY ANALYSIS QUESTIONS

1. Identify the people, resources, and factors that provide support for, and roadblocks to, CBT implementation at NorthCentral Bank.

2. Identify the decision to implement CBT at NCB as either a top-down or bottom-up decision. Provide a rationale for your choice. Given the type of decision exemplified in this case, how do you think the training supervisors might take ownership of the CBT? What strategies might facilitate ownership?

3. Develop an implementation plan that Sam can use to ensure that the CBT is accepted at NCB. Identify challenges to implementing your plan and describe how you would deal with these challenges.

IMPLICATIONS FOR ID PRACTICE

1. List at least three major reasons people resist the implementation of new approaches to training.

2. Explain the role and responsibility of a change agent in the implementation of a new approach to training.

3. Describe how sales and marketing strategies could be used to help people accept a new approach to training.

Case Study

Abby Carlin

BY MONICA W. TRACEY

Just a few short months ago, while sitting in her final graduate instructional design course, Abby Carlin, a master's student in instructional technology, believed that she had found her life's profession. However, now that she had graduated and was standing in the middle of the floor of the Fritz David Manufacturing (FDM) Steel stamping plant, she began to have doubts. FDM, a company that manufactures large steel car parts, had hired Learning Together Through Training, Inc. (LT3), the instructional design firm where Abby's former instructor, Dr. Joyce Abbott, was vice president of design. The contract was for the design and delivery of training on the use of steel blanker machines. These were large, 60-year-old machines used to stamp out car parts from flattened steel. Abby, who had never been in a manufacturing plant before, received a call from Dr. Abbott, asking her to come work with her on this project. "Abby, you will be perfect for the job," she explained, "and this will be a great experience for you." These words gave a nervous Abby little comfort as she approached her first real instructional design job. Abby wanted to make sure she followed all of the necessary steps and completed the project successfully.

Abby's main contact, Andrew Thomas, the plant manager, met with Abby while Dr. Abbott was wrapping up another project. Watching him approach, Abby recalled what Dr. Abbott had told her. "You will have to approach Andrew carefully," she had warned. "He is somewhat skeptical of the training process, since he has never had a reason to use it before. Most of his senior employees have been working these machines for the past 30 years, and he has never had to train anyone. However, now that they are all retiring due to the incentives offered by FDM, he is faced with hiring new employees who have no idea how to operate this equipment. Andrew is just beginning to realize how much help he needs in this transition. That's why he's called us. He knows something must be done to keep production on track."

Andrew approached, holding out his hand. "Welcome to FDM," he said. "Why don't we go to the break room to talk?" They headed toward the break room located on the plant floor, and, after settling down with a cup of coffee, Andrew laid it on the line.

"This is the situation," he began. "Over the next 90 days, I have three shifts of employees retiring and being replaced by young, inexperienced operators. All of my guys have been with me for 30 years and have never needed any training to operate this equipment. The way I see it, the only way to learn how to use this equipment is while you're using it, and we've always had a new guy follow an old guy. But this time it's different, since there are so many new guys. We have to figure out a way to get them trained so I don't lose productivity."

"I'd like to begin by asking a few questions, if I could," Abby said. "Fire away," Andrew replied. "First of all, can you tell me a little bit more about the plant floor where the blanker machines are located?" Abby asked. Pulling out a notebook, Abby began to take notes.

"I'll take you on a tour in a minute, but, for the most part, it's a typical plant. All employees are required to wear safety equipment, goggles, hardhats, earplugs, and hard-toed shoes. The noise levels are pretty high down there, so there isn't much talking, and the lighting is bad. If the employees need to talk, they use this break room." He pointed to the wall, where a large bulletin board was filled with papers. "There's a board over there. They all know to check it for messages and announcements at the beginning and end of every shift."

"Can you tell me more about the current employees who operate the machines?" Abby then asked. Andrew replied, "For the most part, my guys are ready to retire. They are a good group of men, but, once they knew they were leaving, that was it. They aren't really interested in training the new guys. The problem is, they are the only ones who know how to operate the equipment. I came in as the foreman from another plant. Abby, I don't even know how to operate a blanker machine the entire way through. I have watched, but a lot goes on there that I just can't understand. We also don't have anything in writing on how to operate them."

"Can you tell me about the new employees who you have hired?" Abby asked. Andrew informed her, "For the most part, the new guys don't have a clue how to operate the blanker machines. Some have been in plants before; we even have a few transfers from other departments at FDM. They don't know what they have to do, even though all of them want to be here. We've had many applications, and we were able to pick the best of the best, which was great. The pay is good. We offer a lot of overtime and this is known as a great plant to be in."

"Is it possible for me to meet one of the retiring employees now?" Abby asked. Andrew, pleased with Abby's eagerness to learn more about the plant, replied, "Sure, let's go down to the floor now." The first stop was the safety area, where Abby received a pair of safety goggles, earplugs, and a hardhat. After putting on all of the equipment, she had difficulty hearing Andrew as he directed her to the stairway to the floor. Everything sounded muffled and looked darker due to the safety glasses.

The first stop on the tour for Abby and Andrew was the blanker machine operated by "Big Jon." She glanced at his name on his hardhat and began, "Hi, my name is Abby Carlin and I am in charge of training the new employees to operate these machines. I was wondering if I could ask you a few questions." Big Jon stared and shrugged. Andrew signaled to Abby that he couldn't hear her. "My first lesson learned," Abby said to herself. "It's instinct to talk to the worker to get information, but I can see that's not going to work here." Abby decided to just observe what Jon was doing. "I'm going to have to come back and really watch him," she thought to herself, "but he's moving so fast I'm going to have a hard time writing down what he's doing." Andrew signaled it was time to move on.

An hour later they finished their tour of the plant floor. As Abby took off her safety gear, she commented, "Well, Andrew, that was an eye opener. This is going to be a bigger job than I first realized. I'd like to come back tomorrow to observe Jon and try to document the process." "That's not a problem," Andrew told her. "Keep your safety glasses, earplugs, and hardhat and, when you come in tomorrow, stop by my office and I will give you the proper identification to get on the floor."

As she was walking to her car, Abby recalled that one of the things Andrew had mentioned was that the only way the learners could really learn how to operate the equipment was on the equipment. "Where do I begin?" she thought on her way back to LT3 headquarters.

The following day, Abby was back at the plant, watching Jon as he operated one of the blanker stamping machines. She tried to write down the steps he was taking but had difficulty seeing the buttons he was pushing. In fact, she had problems seeing at all with the poor lighting and the safety glasses. Abby also felt frustrated, since she couldn't talk to Jon as he worked, and he showed no interest in slowing down or demonstrating the steps for her. "I can see now how the trainees need to learn on this equipment, but I can't even write down the steps they need to follow, let alone create classroom training here on the plant floor," she thought. "I can't believe I have to train everyone while keeping up production," she said to herself. "Boy, do I need to talk with Dr. Abbott." Abby left the plant after stopping by Andrew's office, where he reiterated the tight deadline. "Don't forget, Abby, we need three shifts of employees trained in 90 days," he reminded her. "You can count on us," she assured him. As she made her way to the parking lot, she didn't feel as confident as she sounded.

On her drive to LT3, Abby had a comforting thought, "I think the blanker operators hold the key to making this training a success. I must figure out a way to document the steps they take in operating the equipment and how to talk to them where they can hear me. Then, I have to figure out a way to train the new employees on the equipment. I'm sure I can do this. I just need to figure it out."

A short time later, while in conversation with Dr. Abbott, Abby began to feel more confident. "The most important thing for you to do, Abby, is to think outside of the box. I brought you in on this project because you didn't seem to be stuck in a certain design or delivery mode. Let's take a minute and list what we know and all of the needs and constraints we have to work with. Once you write down what you know, that will help you define our needs and constraints. Then we can develop our plan. Let's begin with our list." Dr. Abbott wrote the words "Our Needs" on one sheet of flip chart paper and used a second one to write "Our Constraints." "Let's begin here," said Dr. Abbott, pointing at the first flip chart.

PRELIMINARY ANALYSIS QUESTIONS

1. Looking at the lists Abby and Joyce are creating, what should be listed on each one?
2. How can Abby work with the current employees to document the steps of operating the blanker stamping equipment?
3. What did Abby observe while on the plant floor that can help her in creating the training?
4. Given the constraints in the case, what instructional strategies can be used to deliver the training?

IMPLICATIONS FOR ID PRACTICE

1. How can designers perform a task analysis in situations where it is difficult to capture and document task components?
2. What are some of the challenges and advantages to delivering training in a manufacturing environment?
3. How can instructional designers gather task information from subject matter experts who are unable or unwilling to provide all the required information?

Case Study 4

Ross Caslon

BY ANN KOVALCHICK

THE SUMMER INTERSESSION

Ross Caslon was baffled. As soon as possible, he needed to initiate a series of training sessions for 750 faculty members at Lane State West (LSW) on how to use WebPath, a course-management tool, to support web-based instruction. LSW was planning to roll out WebPath, university-wide, within the next year. Web-Path allowed faculty members with limited technology skills, or faculty members who had limited interest in learning technology skills, to gain familiarity with the Web as an instructional resource. Yet the System Administration (Sys Admin) group of the Office of Technology and Communications (OTC) seemed reluctant to set up and support a test environment and to provide demo course accounts to use in faculty training sessions. They preferred to build their own course management tool and didn't appreciate the high degree of customization WebPath offered, since it complicated their efforts to automate LSW's information and data integration systems.

The director of OTC had formed a WebPath implementation project team consisting of Zinny Welch, OTC's UNIX Group manager, and Sam Gilbert, its database administrator. Jamie Witkowski, a lead member of the Help Desk staff, had also been asked to participate. After working for five years in the local school district as a technology lab manager, Jamie had taken a position at LSW, so that she could complete her graduate degree. Due to her previous experience working in an educational environment, she had established herself as a leader among the Help Desk staff as she sought to better coordinate LSW's technical support services. Yet, as the only instructional designer on the project team, Ross worried that the others were unlikely to imagine the challenges most faculty members faced when using technology as a teaching resource. Zinny and Sam were entirely focused on engineering the production server environment and developing the data-processing models that would support WebPath's portal and course features. Zinny had made it clear that the UNIX Group didn't want to deal with the "end user needs," though to Ross it seemed that the group of programmers and server administrators had some very clear ideas about how the faculty should be allowed to *use* the technology tools.

As with most IT (instructional technology) technical staff charged with network and system administration, the UNIX Group was primarily concerned with data security, redundancy, integrity, and backup and preservation. Given the complexities of maintaining a university network, the Unix Group also sought to automate where possible, and this meant that a standardized set of user practices was desirable. OTC's director hadn't designated a project sponsor, and it was unclear exactly who was supposed to manage the project team, leaving the four of them to work out their conflicting priorities without clear leadership. Ross wasn't sure how successful he would be ensuring that the faculty did more than use WebPath simply to post their course syllabi.

At the moment, Ross felt bogged down by Zinny's concern about not setting too many precedents for providing services that couldn't be automated. Until they had figured out how to completely automate the process of creating course and user accounts in WebPath, they wanted to limit access to the system. The university had yet to tackle the challenge of upgrading and synchronizing a number of information systems. LSW's student data system (SDS)— the source of the faculty, student, and course data that populated WebPath course accounts— and LSW's directory service—the source of user-authenticated data—weren't linked in a logical fashion. Furthermore, no one from the SDS group was on the project team. As a result, the UNIX Group faced some thorny data-management issues. Zinny had also disabled the chat tool, claiming it presented a security risk, since it did not run under SSL (Secure Socket Layer) and, until the vendor could resolve that, he considered it a network and data security risk.

Ross had persistently stated at every meeting over the past six months that the features the faculty needed in order to use WebPath meaningfully ought to drive the management of the WebPath implementation. How could he reasonably expect the faculty to use WebPath when he couldn't provide an authentic learning environment for them to see how WebPath might be used? It was hard enough to assist the faculty in using new technologies on campus when critical support services were not developed or coordinated. While most classrooms were supposedly wired with Ethernet connections, the faculty constantly pointed out that they were unable to use computer technologies at the point of instruction. Consequently, Ross assumed that most students would be expected to use WebPath outside of their classroom experiences.

Across the university, interest in using online technologies to support distance and nonformal education was increasing. The staff in LSW's hugely successful print-based correspondence study program in the Office of Continuing Education (OCE) was anxious to use WebPath to jump-start LSW's entrance into the distance education market. Ross knew that the OCE staff planned to use WebPath to deliver the same content that the faculty had previously given them to edit into print-based modules. In addition, the faculty's skepticism regarding the level of support available worried Ross. If the faculty didn't feel that the IT unit was responsive, it wouldn't be possible to help them see the added value that instructional technologies could offer. He had to speak up: "Look, I can develop a series of faculty training sessions and include the technical support staff in the academic departments. They're our first line of support—they'll help relieve the load of calls directed to the Help

Desk." Ross looked over at Jamie Witkowski. Jamie's Help Desk was chronically under-staffed, and, with only one full-time staff member on hand who was familiar with Web-Path's features, Ross was also worried that the faculty wouldn't be able to rely on the Help Desk for user support. "We've got to provide training for the technical staff in the academic departments as well as for the faculty. We need some demo course accounts for people to use and to play with as part of a training and orientation process." Ross hoped that, by in-cluding the technical support staff, the Sys Admin group would see the value of moving ahead with account creation before all the kinks were worked out. Getting a training envi-ronment up and running as soon as possible was his first priority.

"It *would* help if the technical support staff had a few trial course accounts," Jamie added. That way we could start learning the product, too. None of the Help Desk staff are familiar with the product." Jamie passed around a sheet of paper with a Venn diagram. "Here's a model of how I think we should approach this roll-out" (see Figure 4–1).

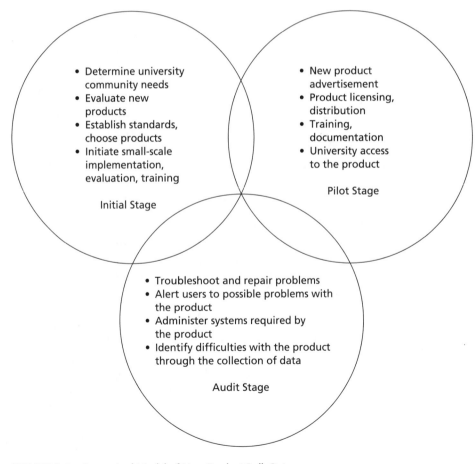

FIGURE 4–1   Conceptual Model of New Product Roll-Out

With a quick glance at Jamie's model, Zinny waved away the paper and reluctantly agreed to set up a dozen test courses for training the faculty and technical support staff. "That ought to be enough. We really can't burn the calories to support a training environment, too, not if we're going to have this roll-out ready by the end of the summer." Zinny was worried that his group had too much to do and not enough staff. He had initially thought that the WebPath implementation would be a simple process, but the complications were piling up fast, and he was annoyed that the product had some bugs that required constant tinkering by Sam. He wanted Sam working on other projects; adding test courses would mean that Sam would end up running a lot of manual processes until they could get the information systems functioning properly.

Ross winced. Twelve temporary accounts could hardly provide an optimal training environment for the faculty or for the departmental technical support staff. Ross consistently heard from the faculty that "OTC wasn't any help." Although Jamie had worked hard over the past year to staff a functioning support desk, the OTC had to undo years of negative perceptions among the faculty regarding its technical services in support of instruction. Ross had two years worth of survey results of the faculty's perceptions of the use of information technologies for instruction. Unfortunately, not much attention had been paid to these data. Although it was true that the response rate had been low, Ross wondered if little attention was paid because the results had reflected a degree of dissatisfaction with OTC's academic support, yet LSW was not an exception. Didn't everyone know by now that the major barriers to faculty use of information technologies were the lack of support and the lack of time to learn technology and redesign course materials? Maybe WebPath made it a little easier, but it alone would hardly make a dent in addressing these two problems.

"I like this model, Jamie," Ross said, studying it carefully. "I think we're in the initial stage right now." Reluctantly, he added, "With the 12 demo accounts, I guess we can do a small-scale implementation and training pilot project." He was the junior member of the team and doubted that his recently completed MA degree in education from LSW carried much weight. Even most of the faculty thought he was still a student, since he had been working on the degree for years. He had to take what he could get.

Zinny spoke slowly as if having to, again, point out the obvious. "This model also includes the evaluation of new products. WebPath is basically a lousy product. The company isn't mature enough. The technology isn't mature. Its software design model is faulty. Even its business model is bad—the company basically wants to build us a customized system that will make us wholly dependent on it for upgrades, and we'll pay out the nose on consulting fees. So we've got to simplify our level of technical support and aim for bare bones functionality." Zinny folded his arms across his chest. He had made his point.

THE FALL SEMESTER

"Very nice! What a high-end facility! It's perfectly designed for using any technology imaginable!" Professor Ruth Newton was clearly impressed. An enthusiastic and early adopter of technology, Ruth was one of LSW's champions. When the Web was in its infancy, she had painstakingly mastered HTML in order to build an interactive chemistry lab and, since then, had received a number of external and internal grants to develop materials for delivery in a web and CD-ROM format. Ross knew she considered WebPath with some disdain. She thought the interface too bland and had wanted to give it her own look and feel. Ross was secretly relieved that she couldn't. Her handcrafted interface for her own web materials was filled with things that blinked, dashed across the screen, and usually froze up any machine that didn't have sufficient memory or the very latest browser. In addition, her page took forever to download over a dial-up modem connection. Ross was fairly certain that students could reliably access her materials only from an on-campus location.

Ross handed her the list of participants (see Figure 4–2). "Seven faculty confirmed by late yesterday that they would attend the session today. And then there will also be three technical support staff from different departments."

Ross had followed up on Jamie's suggestion that Ruth lead the WebPath training session. Jamie and Ruth had worked together on a project, and she admired Ruth's technical skill. Though plenty worried that Ruth's "high-tech" experience might eclipse the instructional emphasis he had wanted to incorporate into the training session, Ross had to admit that she had effectively used animation to create a series of 3-D analyses of molecular change for use in her interactive chemistry lab. She had crafted a visual model of a DNA helix that students could rotate in order to see proteins linked to the helix under various conditions. She had been motivated to do this to address a recurring problem: Students were unable to visualize dynamic molecular change using the two-dimensional images typical of a textbook. She also claimed that her students' test scores had improved since she began us-

---

Introduction to WebPath: Using the Web-Based Instruction

Confirmed for attendance on 31/8/01

1. Joe Cabrini, Asst. Professor, Biology, College of Arts & Sciences: jsc7u@lswest.edu
2. Prasad Mehta, Professor, Aviation: pmf4r@lswest.edu
3. June Schoney, Asst. Professor, Marketing, College of Business: jjsOr@lswest.edu
4. Pat McGuffey, Instructor, Art Education, College of Fine Arts: pam2w@lswest.edu
5. Debbie Anderson, Asst. Professor, School of Nursing: dja6y@lswest.edu
6. Chen Yin-Zdong, Assoc. Professor, Political Science, College of Arts & Sciences: yzc5t@lswest.edu
7. Rini Frankel, Manager, Sports Recreation, School of Health: rrf5t@lswest.edy
8. Dave Barnouw, Tech Manager, Math, College of Arts & Sciences: djb6e@lswest.edu
9. Cherie Six, Webmaster, College of Fine Arts: cms4r@lswest.edu
10. Frank Huey, Lab Manager, Physics, College of Arts & Sciences: fwh8z@lswest.edu

FIGURE 4–2   Participants in WebPath Pilot Training

ing her materials as required homework exercises. The information Ross had gathered seven months ago indicated that both the faculty and technical support staff had limited knowledge of how WebPath might be used to support effective instructional strategies. Ross thought that Ruth might be able to share her experiences and that, along with the $300 stipend provided to the faculty attending the training, he would be able to build a group of willing WebPath users.

Ross pulled out the training session materials. "Maybe we could take a few minutes and review the training session agenda? I never heard back from you whether there were changes and how. . . ."

"Jamie! This is a fabulous room! I see you're equipped for wireless too!" Ruth fondly greeted Jamie.

"It's probably the smartest classroom on campus," Jamie answered. "Though, of course, it's not a classroom. Mostly we use it for our staff meetings and conferences."

"Ross! I have an idea." Ruth turned toward him. "Let's use the question-and-answer period to demonstrate some of the advanced technologies available here. Jamie, you're set up for Internet video conferencing aren't you? You wanted to show collaboration, right, Ross? I could go down the hall to Jamie's office and take questions and answers online. . . ."

THE SPRING SEMESTER

Ross had spent all of Friday afternoon looking at the WebPath courses offered in the fall by the seven faculty members who had attended the training session at the start of the semester. He could identify only three courses that appeared to have been in use over the whole semester. The other four courses had some content in them but mostly contained syllabi, bibliographies of course readings and recommended readings, lectures posted using SlideShow, lecture notes, and study guides. The three courses that seemed most active had used the discussion threads and two of those courses had extensive lists of URLs in the Cybrary. He looked carefully at all the course syllabi and then quickly added up the total number of different types of assignments and assessments listed within the syllabi of the seven courses:

1. Six courses required a final paper.
2. Four courses required a final individual project.
3. Two courses required a final group project.
4. One course required a final individual presentation.
5. Three courses listed multiple-choice midterm exams.
6. One course required students to keep a biweekly lab journal.
7. Three courses used weekly in-class quizzes to review reading assignments.
8. Two courses required students to submit a bibliography.

All courses except one listed weekly lecture topics and readings. The exception was Pat McGuffey's course, which she had organized around students' weekly presentations.

Ross looked again at the syllabi of the three courses that used the discussion threads. Two had used the discussion tool to encourage weekly postings, though the student postings

"I enjoyed the ability to post announcements in cyberspace."

"I use it to enhance my traditional course but not to replace traditional features, like books."

"The Discussion board is neat."

"Probably the two features that WebPath has that my existing on-line syllabus does not are the announcements and the e-mail."

"It was great! I could access it from the airport in Houston once when I needed to add an assignment."

"Good one-stop model for moving around documents!"

"I like that I didn't need to know how to make a web page to make a list of web links for my students to visit."

"The students really appreciated the online grade book."

"It was wonderful to be able to upload handouts rather than have to spend time in class passing them out."

"I was better able to organize my course."

"The students loved it. They really learned a lot!"

FIGURE 4–3   Faculty Comments Regarding Use of WebPath

struck Ross as weak and perfunctory. The other course had used the discussions to manage post-lecture topic reviews and looked to be the most heavily used, although he knew the particular course, June Schoney's Introduction to Marketing, was a large class of nearly 175 students.

It seemed to Ross that there was nothing more than information delivery going on here, yet the pilot faculty had all reported positive reviews of their experience using WebPath (see Figure 4–3). They thought it was easy to use, especially the e-mail feature, since it allowed them to send e-mail quickly to all class participants. They also liked the fact they could "easily post lecture notes," as well as "direct students to a list of online resources using the Cybrary." In spite of the positive reviews, however, no one was interested in redesigning his or her course to obtain the $500 stipend he could offer as an incentive. Debbie Anderson had expressed some interest, but, after talking with Ross, she decided it would take too much time, and she needed to spend the summer working on research that would count more toward tenure.

The report back from the technical support staff suggested that WebPath was a lot of trouble for them. After the training session, Ross had offered course accounts to the faculty in the departments where the technical staff worked, based on their recommendations. Although it looked to Ross that these faculty members had used their WebPath courses in much the same manner as the seven faculty members who had attended the training session, the technical staff had described numerous problems to him. One faculty member had to abandon the WebPath course altogether after trying to upload his 30-page syllabus and the account had inexplicably froze. "I couldn't fix it and there didn't seem to be any point in telling you," Cherie Six had said to Ross. "I just designed a separate web site for him."

All three of the technical staff had reported that none of the faculty in their departments had asked how to use the asynchronous discussion or e-mail tools. They had been excited to find a chat tool option in WebPath, but, when they attempted to use it and found it disabled, it really dampened enthusiasm. Frank Huey had gone ahead and found a chat tool, which he set up on their NT server, and it had been wildly popular.

Dave Barnouw concluded that the math faculty members weren't interested in using WebPath because there was no easy way to produce specialized math characters. Frank had also said that the physics faculty members weren't too impressed with WebPath, since it "didn't do anything." Cherie reported that the fine arts faculty liked the fact that they could scan artwork and easily post image files for students to review after class, although she had heard some students complain that now they had even more work to do.

Ross knew that the director of OTC would want the project team to offer suggestions for WebPath training and implementation when they met with him next week. He also knew that Zinny was recommending against its implementation. Jamie could go either way. Her analysis had shown that there had been a lot of user login problems, but that was a relatively simple training problem. Ross didn't have much to go on. There wasn't even one course he could point to that had used WebPath for more than information delivery. All he really had was a list of positive comments.

What WebPath training and implementation suggestions should he make?

PRELIMINARY ANALYSIS QUESTIONS

1. What are the primary factors in this case that might have implications for training?
2. Given the factors identified in question # 1, how would you design training to meet various stakeholders' needs?
3. Suggest strategies to increase the probability that faculty members will apply what they've learned during training to their own online teaching.
4. Describe the impact of unclear project leadership on Ross's effort to encourage the effective uses of WebPath.

IMPLICATIONS FOR ID PRACTICE

1. What information-gathering and analysis methods can instructional designers use to determine the effect of context on ID decisions?
2. How can an instructional designer meet the needs of learners who go to training with vastly different backgrounds and ways of thinking and who have widely different goals?
3. What are the ways that an instructional designer can affect an organizational context to ensure transfer?

Rebekka Chapman

BY SARA JANE COFFMAN

Monday morning I was sitting in my office at the Faculty Instructional Services Center, trying to catch up on some paperwork, when the phone rang. George Allen, a department head on campus, explained he'd just had a group of students in his office complaining about their instructor. Tami Linden was new to campus and rather "strong-willed." The class was *extremely* upset with her. George didn't think he'd have much luck getting this instructor to change her teaching style (even though it was midsemester and an ideal time to make changes), so he asked if I'd call her and offer my assistance.

It had never worked in the past for me to call an instructor and say, "Listen, you don't know me, but I hear you're having some trouble with your class," So I told the department head I'd be happy to work with her, but only if she initiated the request. I could tell he didn't relish going back to this "strong-willed" woman and suggesting she call an instructional developer for help with her course. I figured that was the last I'd hear about it.

Much to my surprise, within the next few minutes, the phone rang again. It was the alleged "strong-willed" instructor, asking for help with her teaching. She was surprisingly friendly. (Did this indicate a problem between her and her department head?) She said that she would love to talk to me; she was feeling frustrated and discouraged that students from her class had gone to the department head to complain. She thought her class was going fairly well. We scheduled a meeting in her office that afternoon.

Because it sounded like an interesting case, I asked a colleague, Lenny Russell to come along. Maybe there would be an advantage to getting two views on the situation. It sounded as if this class was on fire and that this instructor could use all the help she could get.

Tami Linden had an interesting office. Lenny and I sat on little futons that were inches off the ground, while Tami loomed way above us in a regulation-sized chair. She offered us soft drinks from a refrigerator she'd brought into the office. We finished our drinks way before Tami finished talking about her class.

Tami was short and had bright red hair. She had just graduated with her Ph.D. from a school on the East Coast two weeks before the semester began. At age 40, she'd also recently gotten married and moved to campus. Needless to say, her life had been stressful lately. But she explained that she had been thoroughly looking forward to teaching at the university—this is what she'd wanted to do for a long time. She was thrilled to be at such a prestigious university. Even though she'd had little time to put together her course syllabus, it looked clear and solid. It was a required consumer retailing course, with more than 100 juniors and seniors.

"Uh oh," I thought. I hated it when department heads put brand-new people in such large classes for their first teaching assignments.

After listening to her, I felt that the students and instructor had a lack of respect for each other. The students were very upset about their grades. They thought they were being graded too harshly. They also didn't understand why they had to do so many writing assignments—about one per week. The reason, according to Tami, was because they'd be writing on their jobs, which were just a year or two away. Their level of writing was appalling, as far as Tami was concerned. She was extremely committed to the writing assignments. Where else were they going to learn to write well before they graduated? It was impressive to see how much feedback she was giving her students on their papers. Their papers were due on Fridays, and she would spend the entire weekend grading them. "What a way to spend weekends—especially as a newlywed," I thought.

On the positive side, their writing *was* improving. Tami was very encouraged by the learning that was occurring. This is why she thought everything was going so well.

Lenny and I began by giving her suggestions to regain the students' respect. We encouraged her to dress more formally and to teach from behind the podium. Lenny especially encouraged her to share articles with her class from people in the field of consumer retailing, explaining the importance of being able to write. I also offered to sit in her class the next day.

I came away from our first meeting unsure of who owned this problem. Were the students—who'd been in classes with each other and who had a good relationship with the department head—ganging up on a new instructor so they could get higher grades with less work? Or was Tami, whose faster and more abrupt communication style (typical of the East Coast but uncommon in the Midwest), to blame?

When I sat in Tami's class the next day, I noticed that she was giving off all sorts of signals that she wanted her students to like her—she kept going out into the center aisle, leaning in toward them, and engaging them in questions. But, when students answered, they used it as an opportunity to overtly challenge her and/or talk about her under their breath. My impression was, if she were going to salvage things, she would need to assert more authority: Lecture more; stop asking questions.

The content of the lecture seemed fine to me, so I asked Tami if I could conduct a Small Group Instructional Diagnosis (SGID) to find out what the class was thinking. SGID is a course/instructor evaluation technique in which an outside facilitator elicits feedback (based on group consensus) about what students like about a course and what suggestions they have for improving it.

This was agreeable to Tami. I conducted the SGID the next class period. The results revealed the following suggestions:

1. Give fewer writing assignments.
2. Give more directions on assignments.
3. Clarify the point system.
4. Let us see the test average.
5. Provide reviews for exams.
6. Stop teaching straight from the book and use more discussion.
7. Provide better organization.
8. Treat us more like adults.
9. Get happy.
10. Get rid of this instructor.

After I had conducted the evaluation, several students came up to me and explained that they didn't see why they had to do writing assignments in this class. They'd already earned *As* in English 101 in their freshman year and felt Dr. Linden had no business grading them on their writing. So here was a good teaching goal—to improve their writing—certainly not being appreciated by the students. The students also mentioned that they didn't have to write in *any* of their other classes in this department.

This was probably a big part of the problem. It's always hard to introduce a new teaching technique into a department—especially if you're a newcomer.

PRELIMINARY ANALYSIS QUESTIONS

1. Identify the problem(s) Tami is currently facing in her class.
2. Discuss these problems from both the students' and the professor's point of view.
3. Suggest possible changes in course design and implementation in response to student evaluations.

IMPLICATIONS FOR ID PRACTICE

1. Consider the impact of a new instructor making changes to an established curriculum. What challenges does this pose for students? for the instructor? for the program area?
2. Discuss strategies for implementing new activities and requirements in an established course, including gaining support from stakeholders.
3. Suggest intervention strategies for salvaging a poor beginning to a course. Provide a rationale for recommended strategies.

Case Study 6

Denny Clifford

BY PEGGY A. ERTMER
AND KATHERINE S. CENNAMO

Denny Clifford, an independent instructional design (ID) consultant, had never felt so bewildered—Dr. Cynthia Oakes was one of the most complex clients he had ever worked for! Denny wasn't sure if this were due to the difference in their ages, gender, or educational experiences or simply due to the nature of the project, but he found himself completely incapable of carrying on a meaningful conversation with Cynthia. They just didn't seem to speak the same language.

Denny was an experienced design consultant—he had worked for a video production firm for the past five years and was an Air Force technical designer/trainer prior to that. He had created a wide variety of instructional materials, including computer-based lessons, multimedia simulations, and distance education courses. Although Cynthia had personally requested his help with the development of a set of innovative materials for middle school science teachers, this was the most difficult job he had ever accepted. Originally, he had thought that his basic understanding of science and technology would be a distinct advantage, compared with other projects he had worked on; now he wasn't so sure. Maybe if he understood a little bit more about Cynthia's teaching philosophy, he wouldn't be so confused.

Cynthia, a professor of science education at the local university, believed wholeheartedly in the constructivist approach to teaching and learning. Denny learned, early on, that this translated into an aversion to such words as *objectives, criterion-referenced test items, directed instruction,* and *right answers.* Still, Cynthia had requested Denny's assistance in creating some instructional materials to help local middle school teachers teach in a manner consistent with science reform initiatives.

As in most middle schools, students at the local schools change classes for instruction in various content areas; thus, certain teachers are responsible for teaching science to multiple groups of students each day. Although some of these teachers have an interest in science, most are simply assigned to teach science without much training or interest in the topic. Several years ago, Cynthia received a large grant to develop science materials for this group of teachers.

As a national leader in the area of science education, Cynthia developed an innovative curriculum based on a social constructivist view of learning. Quite simply, the curriculum consisted of a set of "problems" for students to solve. Cynthia introduced the curriculum in local workshops, where she explained her constructivist philosophy and provided an overview of the materials. The curriculum was wildly popular, leading to multiple requests from other school districts for Cynthia to present workshops and in-services at their locality.

Now, Cynthia has received a large grant to develop professional development materials for this audience. Money does not seem to be a concern; however, she has introduced a number of constraints to the project.

THE MIDDLE SCHOOL SCIENCE PROJECT

First, Cynthia indicated that the purpose of this project was to help middle school science teachers (1) generate multiple ideas from their students about how to solve a scientific problem, (2) listen to and make sense of the students' ideas about science, and (3) know what to do with these ideas (i.e., respond in ways that value the students' ideas and provide opportunities for them to explicate their problem-solving strategies). Cynthia didn't really care what specific content from the science curriculum Denny focused on; instead, she wanted the teachers to learn an alternative way of teaching science to middle school students—that was the content she was most interested in teaching. In fact, she wasn't interested in *teaching* her content at all. She simply wanted to provide opportunities for teachers to "explore issues related to reform-based science teaching" in a "socially supportive" environment.

Second, Cynthia believed deeply in the effectiveness of her approach to developing scientific reasoning. From earlier discussions, Denny learned that science lessons typically begin with pairs of students working on a problem from the curriculum and end with their sharing their problem-solving strategies and solutions with the whole class in a large-group discussion. It didn't matter to Oakes if the middle school students gave the right answers to the problems; her interest was in developing the problem-solving *process,* not achieving particular learning outcomes in terms of content. In fact, she mentioned that there *are* no absolute right answers, since "all knowledge is socially constructed." Thus, she wanted teachers to develop their pedagogical knowledge of science teaching in a similar manner.

Third, Cynthia was particularly sensitive to her participants' needs. She was well aware that classroom teachers were extremely busy people. She was hoping to provide instruction in a format that allowed teachers to work on their own time, possibly at school or home. Of course, she expected that teachers would start using innovative approaches to science instruction in their own classrooms.

Fourth, Cynthia didn't have the time, or the desire, to conduct a series of in-services or workshops for the local teachers. She had done this a number of times over the past few years and was no longer interested in continuing in this vein. Her main interest was research. She was deeply interested in the effects of the curriculum on students' scientific thinking. Typically, she provided extensive follow-up for each teacher who participated in her workshops. She observed their classes weekly and followed these with individual meetings in which she discussed her observations. In fact, she had published numerous articles in which she discussed children's learning in her problem-centered science curriculum.

It seemed to Denny that Cynthia was willing to find a way to meet the need for the workshops but wasn't interested in delivering them. In fact, it seemed that she had not really thought much about how to package the instruction. Denny wondered if much of her previous "instruction" on the curriculum had occurred during one-on-one meetings with the teachers. Although she did not want to spend her time conducting workshops, Cynthia indicated that she was willing to meet with teachers for an occasional half-day to "share experiences and stories." But, of course, that would be impossible if the program were eventually distributed nationally, as she envisioned. With the large number of requests for workshops, Cynthia just didn't have time to do it all. That's why she contacted Denny—to design another way to distribute the information.

WHAT TO DO?

At Denny's prior meeting with Cynthia, she had made it quite clear that she expected him to provide a list of suggestions regarding his proposed materials and delivery method at their next meeting, scheduled within a week's time. Yet, to date, Denny hasn't completed *any* of his normal ID tasks. For example, he hasn't been able to develop a list of objectives or assessment instruments. He has no specific content to work with; Cynthia seems to be the only subject matter expert available; in fact, he doesn't even have a list of learner characteristics. Despite having had four meetings with Cynthia, Denny hasn't been able to obtain the information that he normally gets from clients at the start of a project.

On reflection, however, Denny realized that the following possible resources, mentioned in conversations with Cynthia, may provide him with some direction, or at least a starting point:

- A list of 24 teachers who had completed the workshops in previous years; many of these people were teaching in local schools and, for the most part, were still practicing the techniques they had learned
- A box of videotapes, labeled by observation date, of these teachers in their classrooms as they were gaining experience with this approach
- A copy of the grant proposal that funded the development of the materials for teachers
- A list of local teachers who expressed interest in learning to teach science in a new way
- A couple of articles that had been written by both Cynthia and a former participant who was entering her fifth year of teaching science in a manner Cynthia advocated

Denny has his notes (see Figure 6–1) from these meetings and the resources provided by Cynthia, but the information still seems only remotely related to his assignment. How is he going to deliver effective instruction when he can't seem to begin designing it?

- Group discussions are important to allow opportunities for kids to create shared meaning of scientific ideas.
- Productive discussions allow kids to develop their scientific reasoning, to articulate their ideas, and to reflect on their reasoning and the reasoning of others.
- Teachers need assistance in becoming good discussion facilitators.
- Teachers need continual support while in the process of changing their practice.
- The teacher's role is critical in fostering students' ability to develop skills in scientific reasoning.
- Teaching in a manner consistent with reform initiatives requires a shift away from traditional teaching and a change in teacher practice.
- Change in practice is especially important in terms of conducting successful class discussions during science, which are critical to the success of this approach.
- Teachers lack the time and social support necessary to reflect on their practice.
- Materials are targeted for both new and experienced teachers, reinforcing teaching in a manner consistent with reform initiatives in science education.
- Participants should have already accepted the need for a learner-centered practice.
- Participants enroll voluntarily, so they usually have a positive attitude toward developing their practice. May have some anxiety about trying something new. Important to create trust and a nonjudgmental environment.
- Want participants to reflect on classroom practices of their own and others, and to develop action plans for continual development of practice.

FIGURE 6–1   Denny's Notes from Meetings with Cynthia

PRELIMINARY ANALYSIS QUESTIONS

1. Describe the communication barriers operating in this case. Suggest strategies for circumventing or eliminating those barriers.
2. Describe how the identified resources can be repurposed to address specific ID needs.
3. What type of media, delivery mode, and instructional techniques might be appropriate for this content, audience, and client? Justify your recommendations.

IMPLICATIONS FOR ID PRACTICE

1. Suggest strategies to facilitate a mutually beneficial relationship between people with different philosophical backgrounds.
2. Draft an instructional strategy for a sample lesson that introduces teachers to a constructivist approach to science teaching.
3. Describe the importance of matching delivery mode, media, and instructional techniques to client and learner needs.

Case Study 7

Iris Daniels

BY TIMOTHY W. SPANNAUS
AND TONI STOKES JONES

PROTOTYPE REVIEW MEETING

Finally, the project was coming together! Iris Daniels and her team had just agreed to create a prototype and present it to the seven-member consortium of software users. The prototype would show both instructional and technical approaches of the computer-based training software program that they wanted to see developed. Iris was hopeful that the prototype would be positively received by all of the consortium members and would enable development to proceed. Iris had worked for Jim Huggins on many projects with their client, Hill Industries, and knew the importance of prototyping to communicate design, instructional approach, or feasibility. But getting to this prototype had taken longer than anyone had expected. This was Iris's first time working with an international team and, in addition to having to reach consensus regarding the prototype, she had to learn the corporate cultures of the organizations who made up the consortium.

TWO YEARS AGO: INITIAL CBT DESIGN

Hill Industries depended on a complex suite of manufacturing management software products, used by thousands of engineers and product designers within Hill and its suppliers. The software was developed by French software developer Lapin. For years, all of the training on the software had been in the classroom, led by a trainer. Several years ago, Hill Industries joined a consortium of large companies from several countries. About two years ago, the consortium members began to push Lapin to offer computer-based training (CBT) for the software. That request fit with Lapin's business strategy, so they began developing the CBT.

The initial version Lapin produced had disappointed some members of the seven-member consortium, especially the U.S. Americans. The CBT was attractively designed and very well written, especially considering that the developers were all working in a second language. However, it was not very interactive. For example, a lesson about designing a piston consisted of descriptions for the learner to read, followed by step-by-step exercises to be completed using the software. Because the lessons were not written in an interactive authoring system but in a word processor, there was no feedback. In fact, the learner could do anything or nothing in the exercise and the lesson did not respond at all. Learners had little control; they could only access a menu or click "Next" or "Back."

CBT Review Meeting

The Lapin development team had demonstrated the CBT at a consortium meeting. The consortium members were happy to have something to work with. However, the U.S. Americans pushed for a more interactive design, with simulations, case studies, and feedback to help learners improve their performance. Still, Lapin believed that there were technical constraints, beginning with the requirement that the CBT run on a wide variety of operating systems and hardware, sharply limiting what development tools would work. The consortium members agreed that the technical issues would work themselves out over time, as training moved to a web environment and the development tools improved. Far more difficult, it seemed, were the expectations of which training approach made sense for the users. The design that Lapin had produced was one with which it was comfortable. The U.S. Americans, influenced by their instructional design training, were expecting something more task-oriented and interactive.

Iris began the discussion by raising questions about practice, feedback, and transfer. The blank stares from the French and German participants were a surprise to the U.S. Americans. Jonathan Naik, a U.S. American engineer from another large Lapin software customer, described some of the CBT with which he was familiar. "In the past, we have demonstrated the procedure, then had the learner practice it, decreasing the amount of help and reinforcement as he or she continued to practice."

"Are you sure that's what learners want or expect now?" was the polite but incredulous response from Jacqueline Colbert, the lead training developer from Lapin. She had never used such a design and wasn't quite sure what to think of it. "I think they might want a theory section, and then a problem to work on, don't you? Maybe we could run a screen capture video to demonstrate the task. That would take care of it." For the rest of the afternoon, the consortium talked through various design approaches, without coming to any agreement. Not only could they not agree, but it seemed that, though everyone was speaking English, they were not communicating.

Iris and Jacqueline left the meeting together, talking about the design of Lapin's CBT. Back in Jacqueline's office, Iris showed her some CBT and web-based training her company had developed for other large clients. "We have always tried to avoid any long sections where the learner is just reading. We've used a couple of case studies, walking the learner through the first one. The learner is always doing something, maybe clicking or filling in a field to respond to a question or problem, but it's always related to the task or procedure. That way, from the beginning, the learner is practicing," Iris explained. Jacqueline went through a portion of Iris's demo, then responded, "To me this seems as if it might work, though I think some users would think it's too simple. I'd still like to have a theory section to explain what it is we want the learner to do, and why."

When the user consortium met again the next morning, there were two agenda items—one on design, the other on technical standards. They decided to start with design. Dieter Hoffman, the engineering representative from a German aircraft company, asked if he could speak. Dieter spoke only rarely at the consortium meetings but was always well prepared and worth listening to whenever he did speak. He plugged his laptop computer into the projector and began what appeared to be a prepared presentation. Very thorough and nuanced, he restated everyone's positions on design, including both theoretical and practical viewpoints. He observed, as no one else had, that instructional design language and thinking pervaded U.S. American, but not French, training. Indeed, French universities generally do not have anything like instructional design in their programs. "So yesterday's discussion," Dieter observed, "did not move us forward, but only around each other."

As the meeting continued, Iris observed that some of the things she had said to Jacqueline in their private conversation yesterday were coming out in the meeting. Jacqueline shared with the group that, after some consideration of the U.S. American approach to having practice and feedback as part of the CBT, she felt it was appropriate. The consortium didn't come to any agreement on design, but at least they understood each other's positions a little better, thanks to Dieter.

The afternoon session dealt with technical standards, about which there was little disagreement. The only reasonable way to achieve the cross-platform compatibility necessary was to adopt Internet and web standards, avoid plug-ins, and use the two major web browsers. The decision not to use plug-ins took a while to sort through, but the objective was that the CBT should run the same on Windows NT or 2000 PCs and several varieties of Unix. Plug-ins might not exist for all those platforms, or they might not work identically. With a little better understanding on design and agreement on technology, the consortium members headed home from the meeting, agreeing to meet again in three months in the United States.

BACK IN THE OFFICE

Once back in the office, Iris debriefed with Jim Huggins about the plans for meeting with Hill Industries in a day or so. Jim thought the technical decisions made at the consortium meeting were good, but the design decision (or lack of it) baffled him. Then, when Iris talked about the way the meetings went, a thought struck him. "OK, let me see if I understand. During discussions in the meeting, you and Jacqueline didn't seem to connect. She basically used the meeting to report on what she had decided. Discussion seemed to go nowhere." "Right," Iris replied. "Then, when we talked outside the meeting, we had a good exchange of ideas. However, the next morning, she reported some of our discussion as her ideas."

"Got it. So maybe what you want to do is make sure you have more one-on-one discussions with Jacqueline. You might also want to meet individually with the other French people, hash out ideas, then use the meetings as a forum where people can bring decisions to be ratified," noted Jim. "I think we might find that different cultures view the purposes of meetings differently. As I recall from my business trip to France last year, the French are more comfortable making decisions outside of public meetings. The U.S. American idea of coming to a meeting for the purpose of discussing and deciding is quite literally foreign to them," continued Jim. "Meanwhile, why don't we prototype a short learning module that demonstrates our design ideas and that incorporates elements of the French approach? Let's talk it over with Hill and see if we can build something that will communicate our ideas better than the discussion did."

A Meeting at Hill Industries

The next day, Jim and Iris met with Kimberly Mooney, their client at Hill Industries. Kimberly was the project leader of the group that trained the prospective users of the Lapin software. Kimberly thought the prototype would help communicate the design approach the U.S. Americans had in mind and would show that the technical approach the consortium agreed on would work. Jim agreed that they could show feasibility with the prototype, but it would be a challenge. After all, they needed to simulate a complex system, with just a browser and no plug-ins. Jim, Iris, and Kimberly agreed to create a prototype to demonstrate the design they wanted and to demonstrate that it could actually be done, given the technical constraints.

The design would need the following segments and would need to allow the user to modify an existing part with and without assistance:

- A theory section, which they called "logic," that explained the procedure and showed which functions of the software were used
- A demonstration, which used a screen capture video to show the procedure, with a voice-over narration; they decided to call this one "show me"
- A guided simulation, in which the learner completed all the steps in the procedure, with step-by-step prompts; they called this one "try it with a little help"
- An unguided simulation, in which the learner completed all the steps but without the prompts; they called this one "on your own"
- An assessment, in which the learner used the Lapin software to complete the procedure and then compare his or her result to the result in the lesson, using a checklist to highlight important measures of accuracy; they called this one "putting it all together"

"This is a good start," said Jim. "Now the hard part begins. Let's get to work on developing our prototype."

PRELIMINARY ANALYSIS QUESTIONS

1. How was the design process from the initial design of the CBT to the proposed elements of the prototype influenced by the different backgrounds of the consortium members?
2. Evaluate Jim and Iris's approach to handling cultural differences among consortium members.

3. Critique the elements of the prototype proposed by Iris, Jim, and Kimberly. What would you add or eliminate, if anything?
4. What outcomes might Iris expect from the demonstration of the prototype?

IMPLICATIONS FOR ID PRACTICE

1. What steps can a designer take in preparation for working on a cross-cultural team?
2. Discuss the importance of bringing to the surface assumptions about teaching and learning among members of an instructional design team.
3. In what ways can the development of a prototype help or hinder further design and development work?

Lynn Dorman

BY MARIANNE L. SEBOK
AND WILLIAM J. DORIN

On a cold December morning in the Midwest, Lynn Dorman, newly graduated from a prestigious university with a master's degree in instructional design (ID), sipped a coffee in her four-wheel-drive truck while on her way to work. One month before, she had interviewed on campus with Roofing Industries; she was subsequently offered the position of instructional designer. This was her first day on the job, and she was both nervous and excited to meet the new challenges.

As Lynn continued her drive, she remembered the conversations she had with the production manager, Dave Okon, during her visit to the plant the previous week. Dave, a robust, bearded man in his fifties remarked how much "his people" need training; specifically, he cited the increase of employee accidents as cause for concern regarding plant training. Lynn began to think of potential reasons for the accident increase and discovered she was nearing the plant parking lot. She was amazed at the speed of her morning commute, partially due to her preoccupation with her first major job assignment.

After Lynn unpacked supplies and began to settle into her new office later that morning, she began to review some of the materials Dave had given her at their previous meeting. She studied two charts showing the amount and type of accidents over a six-month period a year apart (see Figures 8–1 and 8–2). She could certainly see why the company was concerned with the rate of accidents; there seemed to be many more than expected.

As she was about to call Human Resources to ask about access to accident reports, Dave called and asked to meet with her on the shop floor. Lynn agreed to meet and put on the steel-toed shoes and hardhat required in the plant area. Although this was her second time in the plant area, she was impressed by the large, noisy machines that created veritable canyons throughout. As she walked through the work areas, she noticed they were not well illuminated. She noticed the amount of dirt, dust, and grease that seemed to cover the floor and much of the machinery. A horn honk startled her as she moved out of the way of a forklift carrying a large skid of finished roofing shingles to the warehouse. She

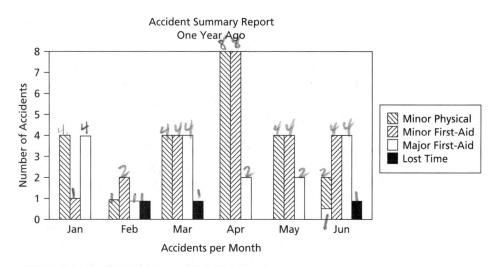

FIGURE 8–1   Roofing Industry Accidents One Year Ago

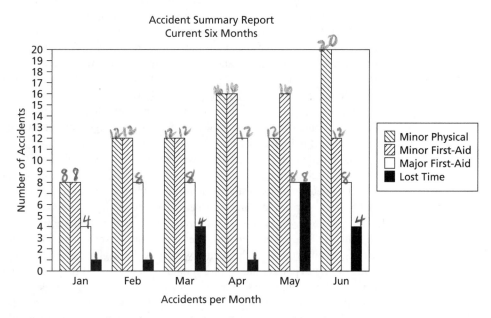

FIGURE 8–2   Roofing Industry Accidents in the Current Six Months

noticed the grease even more as she brushed her shop coat up against a packing machine. As she spotted Dave at the end of a long corridor, she took note of workers doing certain tasks with a routine rhythm. She was especially impressed with individuals placing the asphalt sheets on the press with such precise timing that it appeared effortless. In her short walk from her office to the meeting place with Dave, she felt that she was absorbing more information than she would be able to handle.

Dave's demeanor was cordial yet firm; he was concerned about his employees and would like them to take a required training course dealing with the fundamental aspects of plant/machine safety. "Even some of the old timers need training," he said with a slight grin. He further explained the new advances in computer technology recently undertaken by Roofing Industries. Primarily, the new computer programs focus on quality-control specifications and require employees to conduct random sampling of products. These samples are used to determine if quality specifications match customer orders. Such controls are innovations that had been installed within the previous several months.

In addition to mentioning the new computer controls, Dave stated that production speed had increased considerably during the previous six months. "Due to customer demand, we have had to increase our line speed; a lot of our people have been angry they have to work harder. Some of my people don't realize they are getting careless while they are working. Now that I think about it, it seems like a lot of the old-timers have trouble trying to keep up with the new pace. I'm sure some training would help all my employees."

Lynn mentioned that she had started to look at the data just before Dave called her. She asked him if he could give some specifics about the different types of accidents. As he looked down the rows of machines, he motioned for her to follow him. He stopped at one of the presses that was down and told her how one man was injured when he failed to use the rake to pull some roofing sheets forward. Dave described how the guy reached in to the press and did not notice the hot tar dripping down.

"Bad enough he reaches into a 2,000-pound press, but it was the hot tar that gave him third-degree burns on his arm. He wasn't wearing the long-sleeve elbow guards," said Dave. Lynn bent over to look under the press and saw the now-cooled dry tar and roofing material. Dave motioned to her again, and they walked to the raw materials area. Here Lynn saw workers pulling packing crates and boxes apart with knives, hammers, shears, and crowbars. She noticed immediately how a steel band recoiled when someone cut it off the box. She also noticed how the staples flew around when pulled out with the crowbars. She paid attention to how the workers were dressed and turned to Dave with a question. "What type of injuries happen here?" she asked. Dave told her it was mostly small abrasions, cuts, and material in the eyes. "Don't you make these guys wear gloves and goggles doing this job?" Lynn asked. Dave said it was policy, and workers could get written up if they were injured, but many of them complained they could not work quickly while wearing gloves. He added that most of the workers did wear their goggles on windy days when dust was really flying around. Just then, Dave's pager sounded, and he abruptly left Lynn as he answered his call. She stood, watching for a few more minutes, and then headed back to her office.

Later in the privacy of her office, she jotted down the mental notes she had compiled during her discussion with Dave. Subsequently, she made other notations about the facts surrounding this situation:

- Approximately 500 employees work in the roofing plant; 60% of the employees have been on the job for more than 10 years; 95% have high school diplomas and are able to read and speak English
- Categories of employees include production manager (1); shift supervisors (14); production employees (460); cleaning crew staff (20); and office staff, including clerical workers, instructional designer, office manager, accounting manager, and human resources personnel (9)
- Production operates on two shifts: 7:00 A.M.–3:30 P.M. and 4:00 P.M.–12:30 A.M.; cleaning crew: 12:00 A.M.–8:30 A.M. (all employees receive two 15-minute breaks and a 30-minute lunch/dinner break)
- Most accidents originate from the production employees, although cleaning crew staff do have accidents from time to time
- The budget for a potential needs assessment has been designated at $1,000 (including materials and possible downtime associated with production)
- Should a needs assessment occur, the production manager stated it must be completed within 30–45 days. The production manager believes in and supports training initiatives; however, downtime and scheduling should be kept to a minimum.

Given these facts, Lynn must decide how to best proceed. What data should she collect? How can she collect the data that she needs? Can she manage to collect all the information she needs within the time frame imposed by management? Will she have sufficient access to factory personnel and activities to assess the situation? Lynn pondered all these questions as she reflected on her first morning on the job. She had heard and seen a lot, and now she wondered if she could make sense of it all.

PRELIMINARY ANALYSIS QUESTIONS

1. Describe information Lynn currently has. What further information does she need to obtain?
2. Suggest appropriate needs assessment strategies for this situation.
3. Propose appropriate information-gathering instruments and develop the principal elements of each recommended instrument.
4. Develop a timeline for the entire needs assessment process.

IMPLICATIONS FOR ID PRACTICE

1. Cite the advantages and disadvantages of various data-collection strategies.
2. How do different types of data compare in terms of resources needed for collection and analysis?
3. Specify the factors that need to be taken into account when developing a timeline for a needs assessment.

Carla Fox

BY KARA DAWSON, ROSE PRINGLE, AND SKIP MARSHALL

Carla's mind is racing a mile a minute as she sits in the first faculty meeting of the third nine weeks. Now that she is halfway through her first year at Thompson Run Elementary School and is pleased with her fifth-grade students' progress, her thoughts have turned to what the principal, Shannon Ensman, said when she was hired: "Carla, I am delighted to offer you a position at Thompson Run. Obviously, your first and foremost responsibility is to your students and your teaching. However, with your background in instructional design and strong record of innovative teaching, I also expect you to help our school move toward more innovative teaching practices." At the time, Carla saw this as a dream come true—an administrator who recognized her expertise in both teaching and instructional design. Now, as she sits and listens to her colleagues discuss potential schoolwide changes, she wonders if this dual role is possible.

According to Shannon, not only is this possible but it is the reason she hired Carla Fox. Shannon has been principal of Thompson Run Elementary School for one year; she had come with visions of modeling her new school after the school where she had served as an assistant principal for five years. She had visions of promoting and facilitating constructivist teaching and learning strategies and interdisciplinary approaches that could take advantage of the many hands-on materials and technology-based resources the district has invested in so heavily over the past few years. While many faculty members have expressed an interest in exploring and implementing interdisciplinary teaching, technology integration, and alternative assessment measures, there are others who continue to focus on promoting rote memorization and teaching to statewide, standardized tests. As a teacher, Carla is expected to model new teaching approaches and become a model for other teachers. As an instructional designer, Carla is expected to lead efforts to identify, plan for, and implement the necessary changes embodied in Shannon's visions for the school.

Shannon is an administrator who is knowledgeable about how to help teachers change their practices, and she recognizes the costs that the process incurs.

Shannon hopes that she will be able to provide funds to facilitate the process and has been working on ways to adjust the school's budget. Her plan is to use monies to provide faculty in-service sessions; to hire substitute teachers, so that her teachers can attend professional conferences and participate in peer observations; and to offer incentive money for teachers interested in curriculum development. Likewise, she is committed to hiring innovative teachers, such as Carla, who embrace constructivist philosophies and who can model for, and work with, current faculty members to promote change.

Carla is a master teacher who has received recognition for her teaching and involvement in schoolwide reform efforts, including "County Teacher of the Year" and "Innovative Instructor for Region 10." She is noted for her creativity, intelligence, and motivational strategies, and her students have consistently topped the state's average in academic achievement. This led to a feature in the local press, documenting her achievements as well as describing how she conducts her classes. Of interest were her ease in interacting with the students, her knowledge in the areas of interdisciplinary teaching and learning, her use of alternative assessment measures, her ability to work with students with special needs, and her passion for technology integration.

Six years ago, Carla graduated from a reputable state teacher education program known for its innovative five-year program that includes two semesters of integrated courses—one in math, science, and technology and the other in social studies, language arts, and English as a second language. Carla also has received a graduate specialization in educational technology. Recently, Carla earned a master's degree in instructional design. When the position at Thompson Run opened, Carla believed that it provided her with a good opportunity to integrate many of these skills into her work.

As the meeting continued, Carla's thoughts are interrupted by the familiar yet unpleasant voice of Mrs. Hodge, a veteran teacher: "I don't see why we're having this discussion. I've been here for 25 years, through six principals, and we've always been comfortable with our achievements. Our students always meet the mean scores on state standardized tests, so what else really matters? All this talk of reform is an unnecessary waste of our valuable time." Mrs. Hodge continues to stress that Thompson Run is not the worst school in the district: "I know that we are not perfect, but much of what I am hearing will not change what happens here." Carla notices that five or six other teachers are nodding as Mrs. Hodge speaks.

Mr. Schlegelmilch responds, "I, for one, agree with Mrs. Hodge. I don't know about the rest of you, but I already give enough time to this school. I would expect compensation for any additional work we are asked to complete, and even then I don't think I'd be happy about the additional demands on my time." Carla definitely agrees with the issue of compensation and often feels anxious about the demands placed on her time as well. But she finds it hard to understand why teachers would not want to work toward continual improvement, particularly in a supportive environment. After all, the goal of schooling is meaningful learning, and there is always room for improvement.

Mr. Puskorious, a relatively new teacher, says with a touch of hesitation, "I really want my students to do well. I am all for reform, but right now I am directing all my energies into classroom-management issues. This is where I really need support."

After an uncomfortable pause, Mr. Zurovachak, a respected veteran teacher says with an air of confidence, "I don't think as educators we can allow ourselves to be comfortable with the status quo or to take solace in the fact that we're not the worst school in the district. If I remember, many of us willingly welcomed our new principal because of her ideas, and now we must welcome and support the changes that she is leading. Yes, we've had successes, but I also think we can take our students so much further. This is an opportunity to do so under supportive leadership and collaboration between veteran and new teachers."

As if on cue, Mr. Fitzgerald, a first-year teacher with an outgoing personality chimes in, "As you know, I have recently graduated, and I am really interested in collaborating with my colleagues to implement many of the strategies and techniques I learned in college. Mrs. Ensman's goals and vision convinced me to take this job because I wanted to grow and develop in a collaborative and innovative school environment."

Mrs. Hodge responds, "One of the hallmarks of Thompson Run has been the collegiality, particularly in the teacher's lounge and at school functions. I don't see how these university innovations, such as alternative assessment measures, technology integration, interdisciplinary teaching, and the like, will improve our students' test scores. We've done some of those things in the past and there was no change in the scores. However, the classrooms were chaotic and the planning took so much more effort and time."

As Mrs. Hodge speaks, Carla notices Mrs. Lynn wince slightly in discomfort. Carla knows from her collaboration with Mrs. Lynn that, although she is a quiet and reserved colleague, she is a dynamic teacher who integrates innovative teaching strategies into her classroom. Carla also knows, through conversations with Mrs. Lynn, that teachers such as Mrs. Hodge were the reason that other reform efforts were dropped in the past. Mrs. Lynn specifically told Carla about teachers' responses to workshops initiated by a past principal related to interdisciplinary teaching, a strategy that integrates subjects in meaningful ways rather than teaching individual subjects in isolated blocks of time. Although the initiative failed on a schoolwide level because of a lack of teacher support, Mrs. Lynn applied the initiatives in her own classroom. Mrs. Lynn also told Carla that she hoped the principal and other new teachers could generate enough interest to bring about schoolwide change. As Carla makes a mental note to talk to Mrs. Lynn about the faculty meeting, Shannon thanks the teachers for their input and suggests that the conversation be continued at the next faculty meeting. The buses are beginning to arrive, signaling the start of a new day. As the meeting adjourns, Shannon asks Carla to stop by her office after school.

As Carla's fifth-grade students file into her room, they immediately begin to work on their insect projects in preparation for their collaboration with Mrs. Lynn's primary students. Whereas some students are creating a presentation based on digital pictures captured during a nature hike, others are using chart paper to plot the variety and number of insects observed. At about 10:00, Carla gives some final reminders to the students about the collaborative work they will be doing with Mrs. Lynn's students, and they depart hurriedly and excitedly to her room. As Carla is walking her students across the school, she notes what is going on in other classrooms. Some classrooms are absolutely silent, with desks in rows and students doing seatwork. In others, students are arranged around large tables but are still involved in individual work while others are communicating and collaborating. As she walks by Mr. Puskorious's class, she notices the chaos, coupled with his loud and directing voice attempting to get control. As he sees Carla, he peeks his head out and says, "Do you see what I am talking about? These kids are impossible to control!" Carla also notices that Mrs. Hodge's room is completely silent. She is seated at her desk at the front of the room, grading papers, while her students are working on the numerous worksheets she has listed on the chalkboard. As her class arrives in Mrs. Lynn's room, Carla feels excitement about the teaching approach she is implementing and the level of collaboration being achieved with Mrs. Lynn. Carla and Mrs. Lynn envision that the collaboration will lead to a jointly sponsored science fair or community action project. As Carla watches her students with satisfaction and pride, she cannot help but think about all the things she wants to do, both in her classroom and for the school.

After the students leave for the day, Carla walks down to Shannon's office. Shannon's first words are, "I just finished talking to the mother of one of your students. Your insect unit was a topic of discussion during many family dinners and she couldn't be more pleased. Nice work." Carla smiles. The principal continues, "I hope you weren't discouraged by the discussions this morning. I saw it as very positive, since last year at this time there were no discussions. I have even received a few e-mails from teachers who didn't speak in the meeting, saying that they are interested and willing to try new things in their classrooms." As the principal speaks, Carla thinks back to her trip to Mrs. Lynn's room this afternoon and the types of learning environments she briefly observed along the hallway. The principal continues, "I received approval for our long-term budget from central office today. We have discretionary funds to apply toward the types of changes we've been discussing." Carla's posture immediately becomes more alert and she leans forward as she asks, "Do you think such funds will be able to make a difference?"

Shannon responded, "Well, some of the teachers' concerns about time, incentives, and compensation could be addressed. Plus, we'll be able to provide more equipment and resources. But I still think the big issue is having a teacher-led plan for reform. That is why I'd like to compile an ad hoc committee to explore these issues. I'd like you to chair this committee. Are there any teachers you think should be included?"

"Yes, definitely Mrs. Lynn and Mr. Zurovachak." The principal smiles as she jots down these names because both teachers had written e-mails to her, expressing support for reform after the faculty meeting. "Excellent, now that we've got the committee, let's meet as soon as possible."

PRELIMINARY ANALYSIS QUESTIONS

1. Identify the characteristics of Thompson Run Elementary that might impact efforts to initiate and sustain change.
2. What is your reaction to Carla's thoughts as she observes her colleagues and their teaching methods? What is your reaction to Carla's teaching methods as described in the case?
3. Evaluate the tentative makeup of the ad hoc committee. Would you recommend changes? Why or why not?
4. Outline a plan for what Carla should do at the first meeting of the committee. Include a rationale for each component of the outline.

5. What factors must Carla and the committee members take into account when outlining a plan of action?
6. What are some indicators of progress that the committee should look for?

IMPLICATIONS FOR ID PRACTICE

1. Describe how culture and context influence the implementation of instructional design processes.
2. Outline the issues that change agents face when they are members of the system in which change is implemented.
3. How can knowledge of the stages of adoption help designers implement plans for change?

Case Study 10

Suzanne Garner

BY TERESA FRANKLIN

Suzanne Garner, technology coordinator for Spring Wells High School, had secured a grant for $20,000 from the Teacher Professional Development Grant Fund (TPDG) through the State Education Agency. TPDG funds were to be used to improve teacher skills and knowledge in providing new environments for learning. When she wrote the grant, Suzanne envisioned using the funds for technology training to encourage the integration of technology into the high school classrooms and to meet state professional development requirements for technology funding. Suzanne believed that the use of technology would help promote new and different ways of learning through a technology-enriched and -supported curriculum. She was very excited about the possibility of using electronic portfolios, project-based learning, and problem solving with technology.

After receiving the funds, however, the principal, Terrence Oren, and the curriculum coordinator, Alicia Graham, suggested that the funds might have more impact if they were spent in the content areas to improve the proficiency scores on the state-mandated proficiency tests. Terrence and Alicia suggested providing seminars for teachers that focus on assessment and the implementation of curriculum standards.

The Professional Development Team (PDT), consisting of the principal, curriculum coordinator, technology coordinator, and content area leaders was meeting to decide on the use of funds for professional development. As Suzanne glanced over at Terrence, she reminded herself of the need to impress upon him the success that many schools have had by using technology to enhance teaching and learning in the classroom. Having recently visited several school districts, Suzanne had observed examples of teachers using technology as a way of motivating students to excel in various areas of the required proficiency testing. Suzanne reached into her briefcase and pulled out research she had gathered on the use of technology to improve academic achievement. She passed a copy to all of the members of the team. As the team thumbed through the materials, Suzanne reflected, "How can we work together to meet both the technology and testing needs of this school and keep everyone happy?"

SPRING WELLS HIGH TODAY

Spring Wells High is a low socioeconomic urban high school in the Midwest, serving approximately 1,800 students with 120 teachers and staff. Presently, Spring Wells High has two labs of 30 computers each for Business Education, Introduction to the Internet, and Computer Science courses. The machines in the lab are less than three years old, and all are connected to the Internet. Additionally, each classroom has one computer for the teacher's use and two computers for use by students. The library maintains several new computers, which access the city library and the local university library. The high school building was wired three years ago for Internet access in each classroom, the lab, the library, and school offices. Computers have also been placed in the administrative offices of the high school and in the offices of the coaching staff.

Over the past three years, all of the technology purchases in the school have been the result of SchoolTech Equity funding from the state. The amount of technology equity funds sent to each building was determined by the socioeconomic status of the district and has been under the control of the principal. As part of this funding, schools were required to provide professional development for their teachers in order for them to obtain novice, practitioner, and expert certification. Novice certification signifies that teachers have developed proficiency in the use of the computer as a tool. Practitioner certification signifies proficiency in the application of the tools by students and teachers in the classroom. Expert certification indicates that the teacher has developed proficiency in the use of authoring software and online course development.

Schools are required to have 100% of their teachers with novice certification and 75% of their teachers with practitioner certification by the end of three years after receiving their SchoolTech Equity funds. Spring Wells High School is in its third year of SchoolTech Equity funding. If these standards are not met this year, Spring Wells will lose its funding for technology equipment purchases. Of the 120 teachers in the school, 30 of them still do not meet the novice certification requirements. Forty percent of the teachers have earned the practitioner certification as the result of the last year's training.

Furthermore, Spring Wells High has been designated "in emergency" by the State Education Agency due to its low proficiency test scores. This year, the school's principal and curriculum coordinator have been provided with detailed information concerning the student scores in the areas of the state proficiency tests: reading, writing, mathematics, science, and social studies.

The school has two years to increase its proficiency scores from the "in emergency" level to the "continuous improvement" designation. Otherwise, the State Education Agency will take control of the school and implement the budget and educational changes it thinks are necessary to meet the proficiency standards. Everyone involved is well aware of the high stakes issues affecting Spring Wells High.

Worried about the pressure on Terrence and Alicia to meet the testing needs and still maintain the technology funding, Suzanne wonders how this will influence the professional development she plans to offer the teachers. Suzanne has been the technology coordinator at Spring Wells for two years and taught Computer Science 101 for six years prior to that.

Suzanne's recent work on her master's degree provided her with many opportunities to examine the instructional design techniques used to improve teaching and learning. Suzanne had planned to use the professional development funds to help teachers gain a better understanding of how instructional design can support not only the improvement of proficiency scores but also the implementation of technology.

Last year, Suzanne provided after-school and summer workshops to help teachers earn their novice and practitioner certifications. Teachers had complained that the training was not provided at a time they could attend, that the training did not meet their needs in the classroom, and that coaching and classroom duties did not require computer use. Suzanne had planned to use the grant to complete the novice certification for the remaining 30 teachers and complete the practitioner certification for 75% of the teachers.

CONFLICTING ROLES AND VIEWS

As Terrence called the PDT meeting to order, he passed out copies of the results of the state proficiency tests for each content area to the members of the committee.

"Welcome back from a summer of rest and relaxation," he said with a smile. "I'm sure that everyone is ready for another year of great achievement by our students and teachers. We have good news on the proficiency scores; we increased our scores by 6%!"

Team members looked pleased until Terrence continued. "However, this still fell below the 'continuous improvement' benchmark. I thought that we would meet the benchmarks this time, but apparently not. We will just have to work harder and think of new ways to motivate the students to learn," he added. "Our goal for today is to plan the workshops for the year that will do just that—help us help our students learn."

Peggy Goodwin, the lead teacher for the English department, and Bill Ellis from the social studies department gave each other a pained look. Bill whispered, "Here we go again, more 'innovative' workshops that will not do anyone any good!"

Peggy frowned. Although she was not sure exactly what could be done to improve the proficiency scores, last year's workshops had been a waste. Peggy had hoped to hear that the workshops were already planned and ready to implement. She needed concrete answers as to why the low reading and writing scores were occurring and how they might be improved.

Terrence continued, "We have received $20,000 in additional funds for professional development this year. Suzanne was instrumental in securing those funds for us and has suggested that the funds be used for technology training. She has visited several schools in the state and has seen how using technology in the classroom can be a great motivator for our students. I am somewhat concerned that we have lots of equipment in the classrooms and, except for the science department and courses that use the computers everyday, such as business education, very few teachers are using them in their individual classrooms. I have noticed that, as I walk through the halls, most of the computers are turned off and many have never been used."

Terrence paused to see the effect of his statement on the group. After a moment, he continued, "I would like to ask Suzanne to talk for a few moments about the state requirements and the SchoolTech Equity funds."

Suzanne began, "As you all remember, last year we had hoped to meet the state goal of 100% novice certification for our teachers and then to concentrate on the practitioner certification this year. We reached 75% on the novice and 40% on practitioner certification last year. We only have this year to meet the state goal or we will forfeit our technology equipment funds. I am really worried. We can't afford to lose this funding source. But I also know that there is a need to meet the proficiency test requirements."

Sandy Green listened attentively. She had been using technology for more than 15 years. The loss of technology funds would be devastating to her program. Sandy slowly lifted her hand as Suzanne paused. Suzanne nodded to Sandy to speak. "This is very worrisome to hear. The science department uses computers constantly. We need these funds to maintain the equipment we have and to purchase new equipment, so that the students have computers to use with the scientific probes, digital cameras, and software. The science scores are meeting the state requirements. I don't understand why the teachers are not attending the technology training and why they are not using the proficiency template to see how the curriculum aligns with the proficiency standards. It would be crazy for us to neglect this and lose these funds!"

The group around the table began to comment. Phil Nelson, from the math department, spoke up. "I did not get the certification last year. I don't really see any need for it; I will retire in two years and it is too much time spent on technology. I'll admit our math scores are low, but these students need to do computations, not play games on the computers."

Jim Wilkins from physical education asked, "What am I going to do with the technology in my course? I don't mind doing the training, but I coach after school, like a lot of other teachers. If we want to keep the funding, there has to be a better way to work out a training schedule during the day when we are all here, rather than after school."

Peggy Goodwin added, "My new teachers want to use the technology, but we're concerned about having students working on the Internet. I really don't even know where to begin in making technology work in my classroom."

"Where to begin would be to make the computers work more than half of the time," commented Bill Ellis. "The network or computers never work on the days I have something planned that uses the computer. I can't constantly change my lessons depending on whether the equipment is working or not."

Terrence responded after the group commented, "I hear what everyone is saying about the technology, but we must get the proficiency scores in line with state requirements, or we are going to be in more trouble than just losing technology funds."

Alicia added, "I believe that some of the teachers do not know how to align their curriculum with the state proficiency requirements and therefore are not using the proficiency template. This prevents them from determining the instructional needs of their courses as they relate to the proficiencies. Teachers also need new and more innovative ways to assess if the proficiency standards have been met. They need to do these assessments on a daily and weekly basis, not wait until we get the proficiency scores back each year. The use of drill and practice and lecture has replaced some of the active learning that used to occur in our classrooms. This concerns me greatly."

Terrence stated, "Now that we have the state proficiency results in everyone's hands, I would like each of you to meet with your content teachers to discuss possible uses of the professional development funds. We must meet the proficiency standards as well as the novice and practitioner certifications for technology. Each is critical to the success of our students. We will meet again in a week to finalize our decision on the use of the teacher professional development funds."

As the meeting ended, Suzanne leaned over to Alicia and confided in her, "The teachers keep hearing about the need to use technology. However, several have commented that, if Terrence doesn't use the technology, why should they? How do you think we can convince Terrence that he can't just use his computer as a paperweight?"

Alicia chuckled softly, "Yes, it is hard to motivate the teachers to use technology when the principal doesn't. I'm having trouble getting them to use the proficiency template as well."

Suzanne knew she had Alicia's support for using computers in the classroom. Alicia has been an avid computer user and had developed the proficiency template. This template allowed each teacher to match his or her curricular objectives with the state proficiency standards. Once the curricular objectives were entered, the template created a printout of the proficiencies that were not covered. By entering the school proficiency scores from the state for corresponding sections of the proficiency, the teacher could compare the curriculum to the scores. Each teacher could be provided with a complete assessment of strengths and weaknesses of a course in relationship to the standards. In developing the Proficiency Template, Alicia had hoped to save the teachers time by using the software to locate the proficiency standards that were not covered in each content area.

"I can't figure it out," Suzanne replied. "You would think that the teachers would use the template to see what is going on in their courses. It tells them exactly the areas where they need to improve their teaching of the material or add more content."

"You would think so, but it isn't happening and, with the few that have put in their numbers, I am seeing more lectures and drill and practice. The fun poster sessions, student-written plays, and social studies field trips are becoming fewer and fewer. The teachers are obsessed with this proficiency testing. I have heard more than just a few teachers say they are not going to lose their jobs to proficiency testing, so they teach what is on the test," Alicia stated with a sigh.

Suzanne added, "It's too bad that this strong testing focus is seeming to cause teachers to eliminate some of the more active learning strategies in their classrooms. We seem to be taking a step backwards. I've got to get the teachers to use the technology to help them do these things, but I am having trouble just getting them to the training."

PRELIMINARY ANALYSIS QUESTIONS

1. Describe the range of critical needs facing Spring Wells High School at this time.
2. Identify the available resources and existing constraints that apply in this case.
3. Describe a plan for meeting the needs identified in question 1.
4. Specify the steps required for implementing the plan you developed in question 3, keeping in mind the resources and constraints present in the case.
5. What are the ethical issues related to the use of funding for assessment and curriculum alignment when the grant was originally written for technology professional development?

IMPLICATIONS FOR ID PRACTICE

1. Develop a set of questions to guide an instructional designer who is attempting to meet multiple needs with limited resources.
2. Recommend appropriate strategies for meeting the technology professional development needs of a variety of teachers, keeping in mind the constraints of a K–12 environment.
3. How does an instructional designer address the ethical issues involved in maintaining grant expenditures in alignment with the stated goals of a grant?

Malcolm Gibson

BY JOANNA C. DUNLAP

DEAN'S CONFERENCE ROOM, BENTLEY HALL, CRAIGER UNIVERSITY—9:05 A.M.

"OK, let's go ahead and get started," directed Dr. Teresa Tsagas. "Does everyone have an agenda? As you know, the purpose of our work session today is to pull together all of the sections of the PTTP proposal, including the work that Malcolm has done. In fact, assuming all of you have already had a chance to look at the attachments Malcolm sent a couple of days ago, I'd like to go ahead and start with Malcolm, since his work is the core of the proposal. Malcolm, would you mind getting us started by walking us through your proposed certificate program structure, and then the online module?"

BACKGROUND

Craiger University is located in one of the top five technology states, ranking number three in terms of the number of high-technology companies. However, the information technology industry in the state is in crisis because there are not enough resident skilled employees to meet demand. Instead of continuing the practice of hiring people from out of state, a number of the state's information technology (IT) organizations have formed the Information Technology Consortium (ITC) with support from the state government. The mission of the consortium is to increase substantially the number of IT graduates over the next five years by funding programs that will increase the availability of highly qualified IT professionals. The ITC has released a *Preparing Tomorrow's Technology Professionals (PTTP)* Request for Proposals (RFP; see Appendix 11.A) that offers financial support to educational institutions that propose innovative methods for preparing an increased number of technology professionals for the workplace. The ITC will award up to $2 million to educational institutions during a first round of funding.

The School of Engineering at Craiger University has a computer science (CS) undergraduate program that the department chair, Dr. Teresa Tsagas, and the faculty believe could be easily repurposed for the PTTP initiative. According to the RFP, one of the possible program formats deemed appropriate for preparing IT professionals was online certificate and degree programs. The CS faculty had been thinking about making the computer science major available online for the past year and a half but hadn't moved forward because of a perceived lack of resources. The PTTP money could be the shot in the arm that the department needed to leap into online delivery.

Initial Plan of Action

Dr. Tsagas and the CS faculty decided to propose a program that would make use of the existing face-to-face courses required for the CS major to offer four online certificate programs. Given this structure, people could take all four online certificates and apply them to the Bachelor of Science degree in computer science, or people not interested in a degree and just needing to update their knowledge and skills could take one certificate or a subset of certificates.

To create the certificates, the faculty divided the existing courses into the four categories depicted in Figure 11–1. In general, the faculty proposed that the CS curriculum be evenly distributed across the four certificates. Since each certificate would build on information gained in the previous certificate, they would be taken in sequence, from beginning to advanced. Each certificate program would be completed in 40 weeks (each course would be 8 weeks long). If a student applied the certificates to the BS in computer science, the major could be completed in two years.

One requirement of the RFP was to provide an example of the proposed approach to an online instructional module or course. To help the CS faculty address this requirement, Dr. Tsagas contacted Malcolm Gibson, a local instructional technologist with expertise in online/web-based course development. Because he is also an information technology professional, Dr. Tsagas asked Malcolm to review and provide feedback on their proposed certificate program structure in light of the RFP.

After reviewing the RFP and Dr. Tsagas's proposal, Malcolm accepted the contract, hoping it would lead to more instructional design and online course development work, not only with the CS department but with Craiger University overall.

Project Challenges

During Malcolm's first information-gathering meeting with Dr. Tsagas and the CS faculty, he realized that it was going to be a challenge for him to work on this project. For one thing, he didn't become involved in the project until late in the process. The CS faculty had already been putting together information for various sections of the proposal, and the structure and content of the proposed program and curriculum were already determined. In addition, the proposal was due in six weeks. That didn't leave him a lot of time to develop the sample online module.

Certificate I: Fundamentals of Information Technology

CS 145	Calculus
CS 115	Computing Fundamentals
CS 160	Data Structures
CS 165	Discrete Structures
CS 180	Assembly Language

Certificate II: Algorithms and Basic Languages

CS 150	Advanced Calculus
CS 210	Applied Linear Algebra
CS 225	Algorithms
CS 215	Differential Equations
CS 250	Fundamentals of Programming Languages

Certificate III: Operating Systems and Software Engineering

CS 245	Operating Systems
CS 315	Principles of Software Engineering
CS 260	Theoretical Foundations of Computer Science
CS 265	Numerical Analysis
CS 280	Graph Theory

Certificate IV: Advanced Computer Science

CS 390	Applied Probability
CS 410	Computer Architecture
CS 360	Advanced Software Engineering
CS 482	Ethical Decision Making in Computer Science
CS 475	Software Development Project

FIGURE 11–1   Preliminary Certificate Structure

Malcolm was also very concerned about the faculty's proposed certificate structure because he didn't believe it would meet the goals of the PTTP initiative. Unlike other certificate programs, Craiger's proposed certificates were unable to stand on their own. The certificates relied on repurposing the same courses, in the same sequence, currently being delivered in the face-to-face program. The existing program appeared to Malcolm to be a sequence of isolated, decontextualized concepts and problems leading to a simplified capstone project completed in the final semester. If the current program were already "preparing tomorrow's technology professionals," there would be no need for the PTTP initiative.

Finally, Malcolm's expertise related to designing instruction that incorporates authentic learning activities. A lot of the content for this project (e.g., computer programming) was procedural. Malcolm hadn't really designed instruction for rule-based content before and wasn't quite sure how to do it in a meaningful and relevant way for students, which was a core requirement of the RFP. He was also concerned about his ability to develop a course that would be delivered in an accelerated, eight-week format. With as much diplomacy as he could muster, Malcolm expressed his concerns to Dr. Tsagas.

"Malcolm, I understand your concerns, and the fact that you have them reinforces my decision to hire you. If I'm hearing you correctly, your primary concerns are the structure of the certificate programs and the timeline?"

"Yes," responded Malcolm, "I guess that's accurate." "But," Malcolm thought, "I really am worried about everything!"

"Well, I can't do anything about the timeline, but I would like to give you some leeway to explore—and present back to us—different ways to structure the curriculum into certificate programs. We need all the help we can get if we want to present a competitive proposal to the ITC, so if you want to take a stab at it. . . .Would you like to propose a different structure to the faculty at the next work-session meeting?"

Malcolm agreed to develop a web-based module (one week of a proposed eight-week course) for inclusion in the proposal (and for stimulating further faculty buy-in for converting the CS courses to an online delivery format) and to propose a different structure for the certificate programs. Unfortunately, Malcolm had even less time to accomplish both tasks than he thought. Since the proposal was due in six weeks, he really had only four weeks to complete his task in order to be prepared to work with the CS faculty during their final session.

MALCOLM'S WORK

Based on Dr. Tsagas's request, the first thing Malcolm did was to reexamine the certificate plans of study that the faculty had constructed (review Figure 11–1). Based on his understanding of the marketplace and the requirements of the RFP, Malcolm generated an alternative certificate structure for the faculty to review (see Figure 11–2). Using the new structure, Malcolm decided to develop a module for the Programming with PHP and JavaScript course (a course he added to the Web Engineer Certificate). As a web developer, he was very familiar with the content and skills that students needed to learn in that course and, with only four weeks to develop an example good enough to help win the funding and future work at Craiger, he knew he wouldn't have time to work on any unfamiliar content.

For the next four weeks, Malcolm worked continuously in order to meet the deadline. Three days prior to the scheduled work session at Craiger, Malcolm sent his version of the certificate program curricular structure and the web-based module as attachments to Dr. Tsagas and the CS faculty for their review prior to the work session (review Figure 11–2 and see Appendix 11.B).

TO: Dr. Teresa Tsagas

FR: Malcolm Gibson

RE: DRAFT—CS Certificates

Per your request, below is an alternative mapping of computer science curriculum to four certificate programs, organized by in-demand information technology positions. Each certificate stands alone—it's a vertical orientation as opposed to the original horizontal orientation. For example, in the Systems Engineer Certificate, the courses are sequenced from beginning to advanced—as opposed to the original structure of the certificates where the certificates themselves are structured from beginning to advanced. This structure, based on positions in the information technology field, better addresses the PTTP initiative because it is focused on preparing students for specific jobs in the workplace.

The challenge is that the current courses will not directly map to this alternative structure. As you see, the Data Structures course is now split out across all four certificates, but the content of each Data Structures course will be specific to the position students are being prepared for—i.e., network engineer or web engineer. Sorry, I didn't include course numbers because I am not that familiar with what is covered in each of your existing courses. But I am assuming that content from existing courses can be repurposed for use in these courses. I look forward to discussing this at our next meeting.

Systems Engineer Certificate
Fundamentals of Systems
Systems Algorithms and Data Structures
Programming Language: C/C++
Systems Architecture
Applied Systems Engineering

Network Engineer Certificate
Fundamentals of Networking
Network Algorithms and Data Structures
Programming Language: C/C++
Network Architecture
Applied Network Engineering

Database Engineer Certificate
Fundamentals of Databases
Database Algorithms and Data Structures
Programming Language: SQL
Database Architecture
Applied Database Engineering

Web Engineer Certificate
Fundamentals of the Web
Web Algorithms and Data Structures
Programming with PHP and JavaScript
Web Architecture
Applied Web Engineering

FIGURE 11–2 Malcolm's Proposed Certificate Program

BACK IN THE DEAN'S CONFERENCE ROOM—9:06 A.M.

Malcolm stood up and walked over to the table in the front of the conference room, put a transparency copy of his curriculum-restructuring memo on the overhead projector, and turned the projector on.

"Hello again, everyone. Since you've already had a chance to review this, I don't want to spend too much time on it, if we don't need to. Maybe we could start with your comments and concerns."

It was obvious that the faculty had read the materials and had looked at the online lesson. Over the next 15–20 minutes, Malcolm fielded a quick succession of questions. The faculty began by expressing their concerns about facilitating online instruction.

Dr. Will Jacobs started the discussion. "When I'm explaining programming concepts, I like to look at my students' faces to see if they're getting it. I can tell by looking at them if they don't understand what I'm presenting, and then I can try to say it in a different way. How will I know if the students get it in an online environment?"

"Can I jump in?" asked Dr. Judy Ruzic. "You know, some of the content in our courses is really challenging. I often see students before and after class, working together on different problems. Sometimes they form study groups. I just don't see how they can do this on the Web."

"That reminds me. I don't know about the rest of you, but I am mostly worried about controlling and managing student activities in an online course. If I don't see them, how will I know they are doing their *own* work? Or doing any work at all?" asked Dr. Eli Anton.

"I'm less worried about that, Eli," considered Dr. Angela Wang. "I'm worried mostly about keeping students engaged in the learning. I've seen some online courses that are just the syllabus and calendar online, with assigned readings and questions to answer in an online discussion area. Or the course is just an online textbook—either way, boring. There has got to be a better way of doing online courses, or I'm not particularly interested in participating."

Dr. Chris Newman took up where Dr. Wang left off. "Angela's right. Besides being concerned about keeping students engaged, I really like 16-week-long courses because they give students time to reflect. If a course is condensed to 8 weeks *and* is online, how will students have time to reflect on what they are doing in class and on what they are learning?"

After Malcolm addressed the faculty's questions about online facilitation, Dr. Tsagas called for a 10-minute break before discussing Malcolm's proposed certificate structure. As the faculty filed out of the conference room, Malcolm reviewed his notes about the new structure. He knew from the quality of the faculty's questions about the online module that he would need to be sharp during the rest of the work session.

PRELIMINARY ANALYSIS QUESTIONS

1. Why did Malcolm structure the certificates the way he did?
2. How do you think the faculty reacted to Malcolm's curricular restructuring for the proposed certificate programs?

3. Why did Malcolm design the module the way he did? How well do you think he did with his instructional strategy selection, given

   - The goals of the PTTP initiative?
   - The nature of the content?
   - The accelerated delivery format?
   - The web-based delivery medium?

4. How do you think the CS faculty reacted to Malcolm's web-based module?
5. How would you conduct a formative evaluation on Malcolm's online module?

IMPLICATIONS FOR ID PRACTICE

1. Discuss the differences in design when incorporating authentic learning activities, time for reflection, and collaborative activities into online instruction versus face-to-face instruction.
2. Discuss the challenges and constraints involved when using the strategies outlined in question 1, in a course that will be delivered in an accelerated format.
3. Discuss the advantages and disadvantages of repurposing existing courses, as opposed to developing new courses.

Appendix 11-A

Preparing Tomorrow's Technology Professionals Request for Proposals (RFP)

Preparing Tomorrow's Technology Professionals

Request for Proposals

In June of this year, the Association of Information Technology Professionals (AITP) released a study–*Building Our Information Technology Infrastructure.* This study stated that, although the number of information technology (IT) professionals in the United States has stayed the same over the past two years (at approximately 10 million), industry is attempting to fill about 1 million new positions. To address the shortage of IT professionals in our state, the Information Technology Consortium (ITC) is working to ensure the availability of qualified IT professionals in our state by providing financial support for educational institutions that will work with us to increase the number of IT graduates that enter the workplace.

Program Description

During this initial round of funding ($2 million is available), the ITC will consider awarding funds to educational institutions that propose projects that address one of the following needs:

- Programs that increase the number of students graduating from existing two- and four-year undergraduate programs

- Online certificate or degree programs
- Certification programs for professionals who need to update their technology knowledge and skills

To be competitive, the project must provide clear evidence that the new curriculum responds to changes in industry standards. New curriculum must prepare students for the IT industry, and learning activities must be relevant to the IT workplace.

Proposal Contents

All proposals must include

- Cover sheet—title and type of project, contact information, date submitted
- Project summary (one page)
- Description of the program, curriculum, objectives, outcomes, audience, and delivery format
- Timeline showing when students involved in the proposed program will be ready to enter the workplace
- Data supporting the proposed curriculum's ability to address the needs of the information technology industry in the state
- Letters of support from the educational institution, the faculty, and industry partners
- Budget and project timeline
- Example of curriculum (e.g., if proposing an online program, provide an example of an online module or course)

Appendix 11-B

Module for the Programming with PHP and JavaScript course

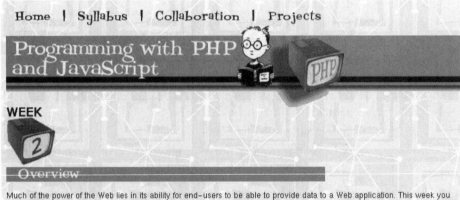

Home | Syllabus | Collaboration | Projects

Programming with PHP and JavaScript

WEEK

2

Overview

Much of the power of the Web lies in its ability for end–users to be able to provide data to a Web application. This week you will start working with variables and forms in PHP. Forms allow users to enter data. Variables allow you to manipulate that data in your PHP scripts.

Study Guide

Variables

The PHP book describes variables as containers for data. Variables are foundational to Web programming (or any programming for that matter). When we think of data we normally think of lists of numbers coming from a database. Although this does correctly characterize data in the traditional sense, it is a very narrow definition. In the context of HTML, every word you type into a form, every checkbox you check (or don't check), every drop–down menu that you select an item from is data that can be stored in a variable. In fact, deciding to click one anchor (aka link) as opposed to another can be valuable data to a PHP application.

In PHP, variables can be identified by the dollar sign in front of them. Create this script and run it on the Web server. Name it **vars.php**:

```
<html>
<head><title>Vars</title></head>
<body>
<?php
// Assign values to variables
$pi=3.14;
$pie="Apple";
$py="Pythagoras loves to eat $pie";
$two="The countdown finished...\"two\", \"one\", \"liftoff!\"";

// Print out the variables
print("1. PI is $pi<br>");
print("2. $pie is a fruit<br>");
print("3. $py<br>");
print("4. {$py}s<br>");
print("5. $two<br>");
print("6. \$two<br>");
?>
</body>
</html>
```

HTML Forms and PHP

There are two things to keep in mind when using HTML forms with PHP:

1. The form tag must have an action attribute whose value is a PHP script that will process the form data:
   `<form action="process_form.php">`
   ("process_form.php" would be replaced with the name of your own PHP script)
2. Each field on the form should have a name. This name becomes a variable in the script that processes the form data:
   `<input type="text" name="age">`
   The name *age* can be accessed as the variable `$age` in the script that processes the data.

PHP `print()` made easier

HTML forms (and HTML in general) has a lot of quotes. Since quotes in print statements must be preceded by a backslash, it can make for a pretty miserable time. Take this print statement:

To print out this simple table tag, there are a total of six quotes that have to be preceded by a backslash (As an aside, one nice thing about print statements is that they can span multiple lines as shown above. This can make your PHP much more readable). Here is a variant on the print statement that eliminates the quoting problem:

In short, after the word **print** type in three less–than symbols and a word. I chose a goofy word to emphasize that you can use any word you like. On the following lines you put in all of the text, variables, quotes, etc. that you want to print out. To end the print statement you repeat the word and end it with a semi-colon. If you have a lot of HTML to print out and you want to avoid placing a backslash before each quote, this is a good alternative.

There are some guidelines to follow if you use this type of print statement:

1. The first **print** line and the last line with the word should appear on their own lines.
2. The last line with the word must not be indented.
3. No spaces should follow either the first or last line.
4. Although it is not required by the language, convention says that the word that you choose should be entirely in upper-case.

Readings/Surfings

PHP for the World Wide Web
    Chapter 2
    Chapter 3

Online Elaboration
    Hidden form fields

1. Add to the PHP script you created in Week 1. Tell the user what kind of browser they are using (hint, see the last page of Chapter 2).
2. Create a quiz form. The quiz should have at least one of each of the following:
   - Multiple choice question (using radio buttons)
   - Short answer question (using an input field of type *text*).
   - An essay question (using a *textarea*).

   Even though this quiz can be built entirely as HTML, name the file **quiz.php**. We will be adding PHP code to it later in the course.
3. Add a link to **index.html** that goes to your quiz.
4. When users press the submit button on the quiz, it should go to a php script that prints the answers that the user selected on the form.
5. A simple red "bar" can be done this way in HTML:

   ```
   <table bgcolor="red" width="100"><tr><td> </td></tr></table>
   ```

   A. Create a script **bar.php** that simply prints a red bar exactly as shown above.
   B. Create a file **barform.html** that has a form that takes two values: A number for the width of the bar, and a name for the color of the bar. The action of the form should call **bar.php**. Change **bar.php** so that it uses the form fields (variables) for the color and width.
6. Add a link to **index.html** that goes to **barform.html**.

Hacker's Challenge (aka, Optional Question)

1. Combine the contents of **barform.html** and **bar.php** into **bar.php**. That is, **bar.php** should contain the form followed by the code that prints the bar. Try entering several values for colors and widths to confirm that you can do it repetedly.

Super Hacker's Challenge (aka, Boy, this is really optional)

1. Add another type of question to your quiz: a multiple choice question with more than one correct answer (e.g. Which of the following numbers are prime numbers: 1, 2, 3, 4, 5, 6, 7, 8). You will need to use an input field of type "select" with the *multiple* attribute. Creating the quiestion is not the hard part. The hard part is printing the user's answers.

1. Now that you've completed two weeks' worth of PHP, how confident are you feeling? Does PHP feel like an "in-town" horse and buggy or does it feel like a barely controlled stagecoach flung along by galloping clydesdales?
2. What would you like to do with forms in *your* work that isn't obvious based on what you've done this week?
3. **Macro View:** Talk a little about your problem-solving process. How are you getting your questions answered? What resources do you use? Have you tried using any Web resources?
4. **Micro View:** What about debugging? What is your routine when you seem to have most (or all) of the code in place and you are trying to get rid of a "parse" error?

In PHP's early days, large shipping containers were used for variables. These two programmers are preparing to assign a number to the variable they've pulled out of the rack in the background.
The archives don't explain why there is a lawnmower behind their chairs.

Sam Gonzales

BY BRENDA SUGRUE

Atlantic Airlines was expanding and was about to hire 200 new flight attendants. The existing corps of flight attendants had been working with the airline for an average of five years and, based on current evaluations (customer satisfaction and supervisor ratings), was doing a very good job. The director of Human Performance Technology, Sam Gonzales, wanted to increase the consistency between the criteria used to evaluate performance at the end of training and the criteria for judging on-the-job performance.

He decided that asking trainees to answer questions about videotaped situations would increase the authenticity of end-of-training assessments. He planned to try out his idea with one group of 20 trainees for 2 of the 18 performance goals included in the basic training. He selected the goals of "performing preflight checks" and "dealing with difficult passengers" from the job map of level 1 flight attendants (see Figure 12–1). For each goal, he asked his instructional designer, Linda McMillan, to do the following:

1. Write a performance goal to represent each task in the job map
2. For each goal, make eight short video clips. Two should show a flight attendant performing the task correctly in frequently occurring situations. Two should show a flight attendant performing the task with errors in frequently occurring situations. Two should show a flight attendant performing the task correctly in unusual situations. Two should show a flight attendant performing the task with errors in unusual situations.

Thus, sixteen video clips, each lasting about two minutes, were produced. Half of the clips were to be used as practice activities during the training, and half were to be used as end-of-training assessments. The end-of-training clips were embedded in a computer program that asked students related questions.

Sam thought that the ability to identify errors in the performance of the attendants in the video clips would predict the ability to perform well in situations similar to those portrayed in the videos. He was convinced that this type of assessment would be more valid than the previous end-of-training assessments,

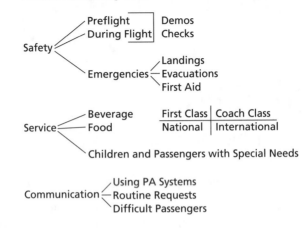

FIGURE 12–1   Simplified Job Map for Level 1 Flight Attendants

which were paper-and-pencil tests. The paper-and-pencil tests had a variety of types of questions, including multiple-choice questions asking trainees to select the correct sequence of steps for performing various tasks and questions that depicted situations and asked students to write short answers describing what should be done in the situation.

Sam also thought that short-answer items were too time-consuming to score and that the new multimedia assessments should have only multiple-choice questions, administered by computers to permit automatic scoring and immediate generation of data. The items related to a video clip would typically ask students to (1) identify what job task was being performed in the video, from a list of choices; (2) decide if the attendant in the video made any errors in performing the task; and (3) if there were errors, identify what they were, from a list of choices; or (4) if there were no errors, identify the most critical aspect of the attendant's performance in the video, from a list of choices. Scores for any one video scenario could range from 0 to 8. An example of the questions that accompanied one "difficult passenger" video is provided in Figure 12–2.

Once selected, the trainees completed their training in groups of 20, each with a different instructor, with one group of 20 using the new assessments (instead of pencil-and-paper tests) on the two selected performance goals (preflight checks and dealing with difficult passengers). This group received the same assessments as every other group on all other performance goals. Some of the trainees in this group were concerned about how the new assessments would affect their overall end-of-training scores, but they were not allowed to switch to another group. When the end-of-training results came out, the overall results of this group were slightly lower than the other groups. Two students (students 1 and 17 in Table 12–1), who got particularly low scores, were upset and blamed their low scores on the new assessments. They wrote a letter to Sam, stating that the new assessments were unfair and that they should be allowed to complete the old set of questions for the two performance goals that had brought down their overall scores. The instructor who taught the special group

1. Which of the following job tasks is illustrated in the video?
   a. Serving dinner on an international flight
   b. Responding to a common passenger request
   c. Dealing with a difficult passenger
   d. Dealing with a passenger with special needs
2. Did the attendant in the video make any errors?
   a. Yes
   b. No
   c. I'm not sure.
      If yes, question 3 would be displayed.
      If no, question 4 would be displayed.
      If not sure, question 5 would be displayed.
3. Which of the following errors did the attendant make?
   a. She did not ask the passenger to go to the back of the cabin so that she could discuss the problem.
   b. She did not smile.
   c. She did not promise the passenger that she would mention the problem to the supervisor.
   d. She did not repeat the passenger's concern in her own words.
   e. a and b
   f. b and d
4. Which of the following actions was the most critical aspect of the attendant's behavior in this situation?
   a. She isolated the passenger from other passengers.
   b. She talked to her supervisor.
   c. She repeated the passenger's concern back to him.
   d. She did not appear annoyed.
   e. a and c
   f. b and c
5. Which of the following makes you unsure?
   a. The situation appeared to be resolved.
   b. You did not spend enough time studying this aspect of the course.
   c. The attendant in the video did not follow the procedure you learned exactly and that confused you.
   d. The situation did not appear to be resolved.

FIGURE 12–2   Sample Multiple-Choice Questions to Accompany a Video Clip

TABLE 12–1 *Scores on End-of-Training Video Assessments for Two Performance Goals*

	Performance Goal 1: Preflight Checks				Performance Goal 2: Dealing with Difficult Passengers			
	Frequent Situations		Unusual Situations		Frequent Situations		Unusual Situations	
Trainee	Clip 1	Clip 2	Clip 3	Clip 4	Clip 5	Clip 6	Clip 7	Clip 8
1	4	4	6	2	2	4	6	4
2	8	8	6	4	6	8	6	6
3	8	8	2	0	8	6	4	2
4	8	4	4	4	8	8	4	4
5	2	4	4	2	4	6	6	6
6	8	8	2	0	8	6	4	2
7	6	6	6	2	8	6	6	4
8	8	8	8	4	8	8	6	6
9	6	8	4	0	8	4	4	2
10	6	6	6	4	8	6	6	0
11	6	6	8	2	6	6	6	4
12	8	8	2	0	8	6	4	2
13	4	4	6	2	4	6	6	6
14	8	8	6	6	6	8	6	6
15	8	8	4	0	8	8	6	2
16	6	6	8	4	8	8	4	4
17	2	4	4	2	2	6	3	2
18	8	2	6	0	8	6	4	2
19	8	6	6	6	8	6	8	8
20	8	8	8	4	6	8	8	2
Mean	6.5	6.2	5.3	2.4	6.6	6.5	5.35	3.7

also complained that the new assessments were more difficult than the paper-and-pencil tests for those performance goals and that the new assessments made it look as if he were not a good instructor. He suggested to Sam that the multimedia assessments be abandoned.

To make an informed decision, Sam asked for a complete breakdown of the data for the 20 students on the multimedia assessments. He also asked for the on-the-job evaluation data for this group of students on tasks related to the performance goals measured by the new assessments. During the first two months after training, the performances of trainees were evaluated on the job. Scores on each on-the-job task evaluation could range from 0 to 6. The checklist used to evaluate performance in dealing with difficult passengers is shown in Figure 12–3.

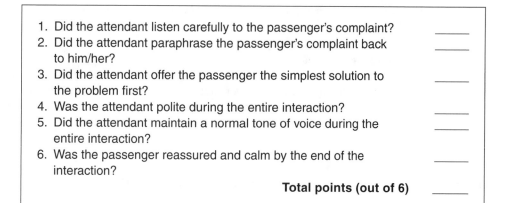

1. Did the attendant listen carefully to the passenger's complaint? _____
2. Did the attendant paraphrase the passenger's complaint back to him/her? _____
3. Did the attendant offer the passenger the simplest solution to the problem first? _____
4. Was the attendant polite during the entire interaction? _____
5. Did the attendant maintain a normal tone of voice during the entire interaction? _____
6. Was the passenger reassured and calm by the end of the interaction? _____

Total points (out of 6) _____

FIGURE 12–3 Checklist for Evaluating Performance When Dealing with a Difficult Passenger

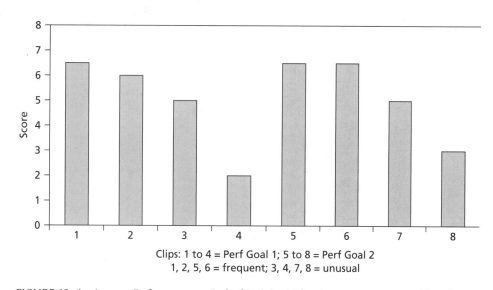

Clips: 1 to 4 = Perf Goal 1; 5 to 8 = Perf Goal 2
1, 2, 5, 6 = frequent; 3, 4, 7, 8 = unusual

FIGURE 12–4 Average Performance on End-of-Training Video Assessments Across Video Clips

Table 12–1 shows the scores for all 20 students on end-of-training assessments for the two performance goals. Figure 12–4 shows average performance across the eight end-of-training video assessments. The traditional measure of reliability (Cronbach's alpha) was .49 if one considered the four end-of-training scores as a single measure of mastery of performance goal 1. If one considered the four video clips as measuring two different aspects of performance—ability to handle routine tasks and ability to deal with unusual situations related to that goal—the reliability coefficients increased to .72 and .75 for frequent and unusual situations, respectively. Cronbach's alpha for performance goal 2 (considering the four clips as measuring the same goal) was .32; when frequent and unusual situations are treated as separate subgoals, coefficients increased to .40 and .61, indicating that the two frequently occurring clips for performance goal 2 were not yielding comparable estimates for some students.

Figure 12–5 shows the performance of the two students (students 1 and 17) who complained that the assessments were unfair. Table 12–2 shows total end-of-training scores for the two performance goals and average performance in a situation on the job that corresponded to each goal. The correlation between end-of-training and on-the-job performance

TABLE 12–2 *Total Scores on End-of-Training and on-the-Job Performance for Two Performance Goals*

| Trainee | Performance Goal 1: Preflight Safety Checks | | Performance Goal 2: Dealing with Difficult Passengers | |
	End of Training (max = 32)	On the Job (max = 6)	End of Training (max = 32)	On the Job (max = 6)
1	16	3	16	3
2	26	6	26	6
3	18	4	20	4
4	20	4	24	5
5	12	2	22	5
6	18	4	20	4
7	20	4	24	5
8	28	6	28	6
9	18	4	18	4
10	22	5	20	4
11	22	5	22	5
12	18	4	20	4
13	16	3	22	5
14	28	6	26	6
15	20	4	24	5
16	24	5	24	5
17	12	2	13	2
18	16	3	20	4
19	26	6	30	6
20	28	6	24	6
Mean	20.4	4.3	22.15	4.7

Correlation between end-of-training and on-the-job performance = .95

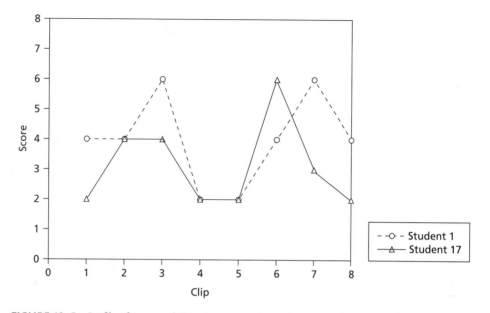

FIGURE 12–5 Profile of Scores of Low–Scoring Students 1 and 17 on End–of–Training Assessments

scores was .95. Typically, correlation between end-of-training pencil-and-paper assessments and on-the-job evaluations was .80.

PRELIMINARY ANALYSIS QUESTIONS

1. Determine the reliability and validity of the assessment instruments in this case.
2. What modifications (if any) to the new assessments would you suggest if Sam is to continue to use them as an end-of-training tool?
3. What weaknesses in the training program do the data suggest?
4. What weaknesses in individual students and groups of students do the data suggest?
5. How should Sam respond to the trainees and instructor who complained that the assessments were not fair?

IMPLICATIONS FOR ID PRACTICE

1. Discuss the advantages and disadvantages of different types of instruments (paper-and-pencil, multiple-choice, multimedia multiple-choice, open-ended responses) in assessing performance.
2. Distinguish between using assessment information for the purpose of learner certification versus using assessment information for program evaluation.
3. Compare the usefulness of data collected at the end of training to data collected on the job to determine training effectiveness.

Craig Gregersen

BY STEPHEN DUNDIS

Craig Gregersen kept trying to think of how he could see his way through what no longer seemed to be such a golden opportunity for his budding consulting practice. Five weeks previously, he had been hired by a large international corporation to design an important training program that would be delivered to its employees around the world. The assignment had seemed to be a perfect fit when the Electron Corporation asked him to be the lead designer for a course on product liability. He did, after all, have a law degree and had just received his Ph.D. in instructional design a year earlier. However, now it seemed that his name was going to be associated with a course with which no one would be satisfied and that would almost certainly not accomplish its intended goals.

BACKGROUND

When Craig had originally spoken with the training project manager and the chair of the Safety Steering Committee at Electron, he had been invigorated by the prospect of using both his degrees to educate people about an important issue and to increase the company's bottom line. The Electron Corporation was a leader in the design and manufacture of two-way radio systems, cellular telephones, pagers, and other communication devices, including accompanying software. Stan Neuhaus, one of the senior design engineers for the company and chair of the Safety Steering Committee, described how Electron took the quality and safety of its products seriously. Although product liability suits were not a large problem for the company, Electron was becoming aware of a number of situations that might produce liability—transmission systems interfering with the operation of other electronic equipment in hospitals, defective software causing shutdowns in police communication systems, battery disposal problems, and so on. And, as Electron became more and more involved in the production of consumer-oriented products, it was becoming increasingly concerned about appropriate designs and warnings for consumers.

Both Stan and the training project manager, Louise Masoff, told Craig that the course was intended to provide a proactive approach to product safety—one that would prevent lawsuits from happening. Other than that, however, the content of the course was up to Craig—whatever he thought was needed to make employees more conscious of product liability in their daily behavior. Both Stan and Louise stressed that they wanted a course that would address concerns at every level of the company. In this regard, they presented Craig with a list of initial telephone contacts with line engineers and management at several installations across the country. He was also given free rein to make any other contacts that might prove useful.

Then, of course, the other shoe dropped. Craig was asked to start immediately because there was a lot of pressure to get a course up and running very quickly. Louise believed that two weeks of telephone interviews would be enough time to determine what content needed to be included in the course, then another three weeks to develop the course. The course itself could be only a day long, maximum. According to Louise, even though this was considered an important topic, there were just too many other demands on employees' time. And, of course, the legal department ("legal") would need to be consulted on everything. Louise was sure that legal would have plenty of ideas for him but that sometimes "they could be pretty unapproachable." Stan added that legal felt rather strongly that it should be carrying out the training in this area but that a prior course it had put together had not gone over especially well.

However, Craig was not discouraged. He was already used to quick turnarounds. Legal might be a problem, but, looking on the bright side, it could be very helpful providing content for the course, including pending cases that might be used as examples. After all, Craig was a lawyer, too. That should eliminate a lot of communication problems. After some initial research, he was ready to start contacting the names he had been given.

GATHERING THE DATA

It didn't take Craig long to realize that there were more aspects to product liability at Electron than had been discussed in the original meeting. The basic law dealing with product liability was difficult for a layperson to understand, but, with Electron having plants in 16 countries and doing business in almost every other country, just understanding the international differences in liability would be a challenge. In addition, engineering issues were not limited to design considerations. There were also process engineers, who dealt with the manufacturing process and attendant safety concerns, and field engineers, who dealt with the construction and maintenance of large systems, such as transmission antennas and radio relay stations. There was also a multitude of concerns ranging from appropriate procedures for product recalls and risk evaluations to attempts at keeping up with the constant regulatory changes issued by various standards organizations.

The first person Craig interviewed was Richard Mull, the legal contact he had been given. However, if Craig had expected a willing ear for what he saw as the challenges in designing the course, he was mistaken. Although cordial, Richard didn't waste time making it clear that he believed legal should be handling the education on these issues, rather than an outside consultant. When Craig started talking about the various content issues, Richard interjected that, rather than worrying about all the details, engineers needed to develop a general sensitivity to the "legal realities" and that just designing a product to the best of their ability might not be enough. In response to Craig's request for relevant examples, Richard stated that he couldn't discuss ongoing cases and that using any of these as an example in a class would be out of the question. Statements made about these cases could possibly be used against the company. He ended the conversation by suggesting to Craig that he review the four-hour course that Richard and his colleagues had developed several years back—a course that he still considered would be perfectly acceptable with just a few modifications.

Somewhat chastened, Craig started interviewing other people in Electron. He found that his list of suggested contacts blossomed (or maybe "*exploded*" was a better term) as he spoke with more and more people. Engineering not only broke down into process, product, and field concerns but also included management concerns that often tended to differ considerably from the concerns of engineers on the line. Line engineers wanted to know how to fix specific problems, whereas their managers wanted to know how to make the correct decisions about protecting their areas of responsibility along a number of fronts, often international in scope. Marketing and sales were also making themselves heard. For instance, how far could they go in making claims about various products without these claims coming back to haunt them later? There were also the installation, servicing, and maintenance sectors. What effects on liability could occur from improper repair or installation? Who took customer complaints, and how should they be processed and documented? How should products be disposed of safely? And there seemed to be no one entity responsible for keeping employees current on all of the manufacturing and design standards that were being promulgated.

COMPLICATIONS

In a follow-up discussion with Stan Neuhaus, Craig became aware of an even bigger problem. Stan confided that many in engineering had believed for some time that product liability at Electron was much more a communication than a knowledge issue. He argued that, in spite of what legal thought, most engineers were already sensitive to product liability issues. What was lacking, according to these engineers, was a company-wide, systematic approach to these issues that addressed specific questions, such as the following: What was the chain of command for handling product liability issues throughout the company? Should there be a monitoring system for actively searching out potential product defects, and what should be included within it? What was the procedure for taking corrective action, such as a product recall, in a particular instance? How did one document the decision to warn rather than initiate a redesign, or should one do nothing at all? And what were the acceptable time frames?

Stan produced the draft of a company-wide product safety program that established a comprehensive organizational structure and detailed procedures for a number of the issues he had mentioned. He believed that a course that centered on building an understanding of these procedures would go a long way toward educating people about what they needed to *do,* instead of discussing these issues in a general way. Stan added that the prior course that legal had presented was too mired in such generalities. They had provided few, if any, concrete answers as to what to do in particular situations. Besides, it had been almost all lecture and, after the first hour of hearing about common law principles, "people had found it pretty hard to stay awake."

Although Craig recognized that many engineers had a propensity to see product liability in terms of black and white (which he knew, as a lawyer, was not always possible), he also agreed that providing them with a structured way of dealing with a variety of day-to-day problems made sense. The draft of the company-wide product safety program was extensive. It provided an excellent start for a content outline for what he now considered to be a major part of the training. However, when Craig ran his idea by legal, Richard Mull curtly informed him that the draft had never been approved and that it should never have been passed around, particularly to an outside consultant. Richard argued that the problem with internal standards and procedures, especially when they were more stringent than general regulations and the common law, was that they, in effect, became a new standard to which the company could be held in a court of law, regardless of their intent as only general guidelines. Providing training on specific procedures and policies could be regarded as being legally equivalent to a written standard because it evidenced the company's intentions as to those procedures and policies. When Craig countered that the alternative might be even less palatable, Richard replied that this was why Electron had legal to advise it. He reiterated that the course needed to stay away from details, although he did not object to "jazzing it up somewhat" to keep everyone interested.

Craig left the meeting with the growing realization that the project was expanding and moving in several directions. He arranged a meeting with Louise Masoff to brainstorm ways of coping with the scope of the project. But he soon discovered that Louise did not feel in a position to press for any changes to the course's one-day, all-in-one structure. She certainly did not want to get involved in a political tug of war with legal about the direction of the course. As he listened to Louise, Craig began to believe that he had been handed what many in Electron had probably already known was an instructional design minefield, with no readily acceptable solutions. In the end, he suspected, the prevailing wisdom had been to let someone from the outside take the fall.

WHAT TO DO NOW?

Craig sat in his hotel room, contemplating a project that seemed to be unraveling in front of his eyes. He had more content than he knew what to do with and a rapidly expanding group of target learners with varying interests, all squeezed into a course "box" that seemed way too small. Worse yet, he was being told to go in a design direction that would probably result in little performance change in the company. There would be almost no difference between Craig's course and the older and instructionally ineffective one, except that now the course would have his name on it. His sense of pride, as well as his ethics, would not let him accept this without a struggle. Craig truly wanted to design a course that would make a difference for Electron and its employees, but, with all the conflicting demands that he faced, how could he do this?

PRELIMINARY ANALYSIS QUESTIONS

1. Identify the key issues Craig must consider as he decides what to do next. It might be useful to think in terms of types of issues—needs assessment, organizational development, instructional content analysis, and so on.
2. For each issue that you identify, what solution(s) would you suggest? Then consider the *interaction* of these issues. What effect will these interactions have on your proposed solutions?
3. How would you go about dealing with the impasse between the desire for specifics (engineering) and the desire for generalities (legal)?
4. Do you believe it is possible to accommodate the varying content interests in a day-long course? If so, how would you design the course? If not, what changes would you advise?
5. If you could get no agreement from the various interests and it was decided that you would present essentially a "regurgitated" version of the previous course, how would you react? Provide a rationale for your reaction.

IMPLICATIONS FOR ID PRACTICE

1. What organizational issues within a corporate setting can affect the success of an instructional design project?
2. Describe strategies for achieving agreement and buy-in for a training project, when stakeholder groups have differing and opposing needs. How might an outside consultant go about making his or her voice heard within a large corporation when decision makers are unable or unwilling to break through an impasse?
3. Describe strategies for dealing with resource and time limitations that interfere with the adequate completion of an instructional design project. How does one make an objective determination of what is "adequate" under a particular set of circumstances?
4. What issues need to be discussed and made part of the consultant/client contract at the beginning of an instructional design project?
5. What are the ethical issues involved for an instructional designer when the client insists on something that the consultant does not believe is in the best interests of the overall project?

Sandra Hernandez and Jake Spaulding

BY JOHN P. CAMPBELL

Sandra Hernandez was a new faculty member in the College of Engineering who arrived at the college touted as a "super teacher." She won numerous teaching awards as a graduate student and had just started her first position as an assistant professor. Previously, she was an aerospace engineer for nearly 10 years. Her first teaching assignment was the Engineering Methods and Graphical Communications course required for all freshmen. Sandra soon discovered that this assignment was not a "prize" assignment but, rather, one that other faculty members did not want.

The Engineering Methods and Graphical Communications course is an introduction to engineering design, data collection, and visual representation. The goal of the course is to develop a strong conceptual understanding of basic engineering principles, including fluid dynamics, electricity, and force. Students practice developing hypotheses, setting up experiments, collecting data, and presenting results. Sandra was frustrated with the lack of laboratory equipment, which was further complicated by the large number of students. During an average semester, there are eight sections of 30 students. To help with the teaching load, Sandra was assigned three graduate engineering students. Last semester, the first semester she coordinated, the class was a disaster. She felt she had not adequately covered the content and felt frustrated that the students did not have enough hands-on and real-world experiences.

During a typical class, students are given basic engineering problems. For example, a problem may look like this:

> If water from a bathroom sink (capacity 4 gallons, 18-inch diameter) is drained into a basin 2 feet below the sink using a standard 1-inch PVC pipe, what will the flow rate be? What happens if the sink basin is increased in diameter? What type of relationship exists? What happens to the flow rate if the drainpipe diameter is changed? What type of relationship exists?

The students are then required to set up the experiment and collect data. Often, they are rushing to complete the experiment, forcing the next section to be late starting. Sandra was convinced that the general goal of getting students to make informed predictions on basic engineering concepts was valid, but she needed to find new ways of approaching the class.

She decided to visit the Instructional Development Center (IDC) on campus, even though she was worried about the time involved. The center was established to help the faculty with a variety of instructional problems and consists of a staff of 14 professionals serving nearly 2,000 faculty members. The staff members have a variety of backgrounds, including instructional designers, programmers, graphic artists, evaluation specialists, and publication designers. Sandra's case was assigned to Jake Spaulding, an instructional designer hired six months previously. Although new to the center, he had spent the two previous years as a designer for a major consulting company. He came to the university to complete his doctoral degree and found it difficult learning to deal with this new type of client. He often found that faculty priorities were more focused on research than on teaching. He mentioned that working with the faculty was as difficult as "herding cats."

Jake met Sandra in her office on the other side of campus. "So, Professor Hernandez, how can the Instructional Development Center help you?" Sandra responded, "First, please call me Sandra. I have never adjusted to being called Professor. I don't have much time, so let me give you a quick synopsis. I am currently in charge of the Engineering Methods and Graphical Communications course. The course is designed to provide students with hands-on experiences revolving around various engineering principles. Few incoming college students have a strong conceptual understanding of the basic principles, such as fluid dynamics, electricity, and force. Their lack of conceptual understanding, whether attributed to poor academic preparation or few hands-on experiences, has a profound impact on future engineering courses. Students have difficulty in the laboratory distinguishing correct answers from those answers that are 'unlikely' or 'way off.' Additionally, they have trouble applying what is learned in the classroom to producing engineering design solutions."

"So where do problems occur?" Jake asked. Sandra explained the difficulty in providing students with realistic examples. She continued by describing how students often spend two or more hours of a three-hour lab just setting up one portion of the lab. Students often waste time during the setup and fail to collect enough data. "I like using a hands-on approach, but there has to be a more effective use of class time. The problems get even more complicated when you consider a topic such as fluid dynamics. Students are conducting experiments with plastic tubing and PVC pipe but are unable to envision other factors of fluid dynamics."

She continued, "Students need to develop hypotheses concerning the physical relationships among various elements of a fluid system, construct a simulated system, collect data, and evaluate their results. The ultimate pedagogical goal is to help students develop a better conceptual understanding of these relationships within fluid systems. I believe that, if they are going to achieve this goal, they need to be able to experiment with more elements of fluid systems. It would be especially valuable if they could use different types and sizes of pipes and fluids. But I'm getting carried away; the time and budget do not even begin to allow them to reach that goal."

"Is the fluid dynamics portion of the course one of the most difficult parts to teach?" Jake asked. Sandra thought the fluid dynamics portion was a good place to start, so they agreed to meet again. In that meeting, Jake asked Sandra to describe the ideal fluid dynamics lab. The following is his summary of key elements:

- Provide students with a variety of real-world lab experiments
- Allow the use of a variety of pipe components, including 90° elbows, 45° elbows, and different-sized tanks
- Allow the addition of flow valves and meters at any point in the system to collect data
- Allow the placement of a pressure gauge at any point in the system
- Allow the use of a variety of pipe materials and sizes, particularly concrete, copper, PVC, and steel
- Provide the use of a variety of fluids, including crude oil, kerosene, molasses, and water

At the end of the conversation, Sandra was frustrated. She did not see how describing her view of an ideal fluid lab would help her when resources and time were limited. Before leaving the meeting, however, she provided Jake with three additional problems she would like students to solve:

1. Show that, if a typical bathroom sink (capacity 4 gallons, 18-inch diameter) is drained into a basin 2 feet below the sink using a standard 1-inch PVC pipe, the flow rate will be from 7.2 to 6.7 feet per second. How long does it take for a full sink to empty?
2. A pump is required to move water from a large reservoir to a point 120 feet above the base of the reservoir. The pump head is 155 feet. If the volumetric flow rate is to be approximately 125 gallons per minute, when there are 3 feet of water in the reservoir, select the pipe from those available: (a) 150 feet of 3-inch PVC, (b) 130 feet of 2-inch PVC, (c) 125 feet of 3-inch steel, or (d) 130 feet of 2-inch copper.
3. A small pump is to be used to pump water from the reservoir tank to the filter holder in a new design of a coffee maker. Assume you have 0.25 gallon of water to transport. Knowing that the system (tubing, pump, and reservoir) must fit within a 4-inch-wide, 8-inch-high, and 4-inch-deep volume, lay out the design so that you can achieve a "quick" pot of coffee. Note: The 4-inch by 4-inch by 8-inch space does not include space for filter or pot. Justify your design by describing (1) relative cost, (2) feasibility, and (3) practicality.

Jake was becoming more and more puzzled. Not understanding fluid dynamics, he attempted to gather more information from Sandra via e-mail. During their exchange, he was able to collect information about her ideal instructional capabilities. His summary of the information is shown in Table 14–1.

PRELIMINARY ANALYSIS QUESTIONS

1. What problems did Sandra present in this case?
2. What additional data are needed to get a better picture of the problems? How would you collect the necessary data?

TABLE 14–1   *Ideal Lab Capabilities*

Element	Options
Pipe	Materials: steel, concrete, PVC, and copper Length: inches to 10,000 feet Diameter: 0.125 to 84 inches
Fluid types	Water, oil, molasses, kerosene
Connections	45° and 90° elbows
Valves	Ability to set valve at 0%, 25%, 50%, 75%, and 100% open
Pump	Pump head specified by user in feet or pounds per square inch (psi)
Tanks	Inlet and outlets on top and bottom of tanks; capacity ranging from cubic inches to infinite reservoirs
Data collection	Pressure gauge Flow meters Temperature gauge Time clock

3. Suggest possible solutions to the presenting problems, taking into account the resource requirements and potential constraints for various solutions.
4. Suggest implementation strategies for the solutions described in question 3.

IMPLICATIONS FOR ID PRACTICE

1. Suggest consulting strategies that an instructional designer might use when working with college faculty. How might consulting with college faculty differ from consulting with corporate clients?
2. What data-collection methods can be used by an instructional designer when evaluating a course or program? How might the amount of time available affect the choice of data-collection methods?
3. Discuss issues related to designing instruction when the designer is unfamiliar with the subject matter.

Jim Huggins

BY TIMOTHY W. SPANNAUS

Jim Huggins sat and stared at the report just delivered to him on the use of a large-scale computer-based training (CBT) innovation on which he had worked for most of the past two years. His client, Hill Industries, a leading, high-tech manufacturing organization, had spent several million dollars developing a large-scale CBT system for training employees on a new product development (PD) process. He could not believe the information he was reading. Repeatedly, he read through the executive summary:

- Relatively few members of the target population were actually using the CBT, probably less than 15%. The total target population was more than 15,000, and, based on survey data, fewer than 3,000 used the CBT on a regular basis.
- Engineers in the target population were more inclined to ask a local expert for technical information than to consult the CBT, even though the CBT information was generally more current and more accurate than the local expert.
- Process development leaders reported that, in their meetings with program teams, people didn't have information that was available from the CBT.
- Process development leaders relied heavily on the CBT to distribute current information about the PD process. They were disappointed to find that their information was not getting out to the whole company as they thought it was. They had become so dependent on the CBT that they no longer used any other mass communication tool.
- Many members of the target population did not get an opportunity to practice using the CBT to solve process design problems.

"Probably less than 15% used the CBT on a regular basis"—over and over again, Jim stared at this finding. Any one of the findings by itself was extremely unfavorable, but together they constituted a major failure of the project. What, if anything, could be done to salvage the project at this stage? As the reality of the survey results began to settle in his mind, Jim looked back over the course of the project, searching for clues as to why the CBT innovation might have so clearly failed to achieve its objectives.

BACKGROUND

Hill Industries was a large, high-tech producer of manufacturing plant machinery. The machinery was complex, with a lot of variety in what customers wanted as accessories or configuration (power, custom tooling, capacity). Although basically mechanical, the machinery had an increasingly electronic dimension (controls, communications, instruments). In earlier decades—when the range of products wasn't as great, the products were not as complicated, and there were fewer government regulations—the company could design and produce a totally new product in about two years, with a small team. However, over the years, the process and the product became more complex and more expensive. Everyone in the domestic and European segments of the industry was experiencing the same problem of increasing costs and longer product cycles.

In addition, in the past 10 years, new companies, both domestic and foreign, had entered the business. Their agility and speed took market share from the old-line companies. The new companies seemed to have new products every year or so. The products were very good and less expensive. These new products were selling well and, indeed, some old-line manufacturers went out of business, merged, or were in bankruptcy. At the same time, the market seemed to demand a greater variety of machines. The new competitors, with their fast time to market, could launch new products much faster than the older companies could.

Hill Industries responded to the competitive threat by revamping the PD process, trying to reduce time and cost while improving quality. Typically, this process took years to complete, from creating the initial idea to delivering a new product to the first customer. An idea for a new product might have involved improvements to an existing product (known as a *freshening,* or a *midlife kicker*) or a totally new line of products, perhaps a line of small presses for use by job shops. If it were a freshening, the PD process could require a couple of years. A totally new product might have required six or seven years, especially if a new manufacturing plant was required.

The PD process was the responsibility of the product development organization (PDO). Under the old process, PDO had coordinated work by various functional organizations in Hill, such as design, engineering, marketing, and so on. Now PDO was to form teams for each new product and assign a project manager, who was to be in charge of schedule, budget, quality, staffing, facilities, and all the things that are the responsibility of any project manager. There were milestones to be met, defined by deliverables, quality criteria, dates, and responsibilities. Such milestones included concept approval, tooling, prototype approvals, pilot assembly, mass production, and so on. Teams consisted of people from engineering, testing, design, manufacturing, marketing, finance, purchasing, and all the other affected functions of the company. There were also suppliers on the team, since the company purchased about 40% of the content of the product, including most of the electronics, plastic parts, cabinets, and so on. Most people in PDO went from team to team, spending from two to seven years on a team.

The new PD process at Hill Industries had a flatter organization (fewer middle managers), fewer approval steps by executive management, fewer prototypes, early involvement of manufacturing and marketing, more reliance on design and engineering, and a wide variety of other changes. The process included more than 10,000 people at major company locations in North America and Europe, as well as smaller groups with affiliated companies in Pacific Rim countries and South America.

Such major changes in the PD process created a need for a variety of training interventions, and a steering committee was convened to take on the responsibility for PD training. The steering committee included representatives of the process owners (high-level executives with responsibility for defining and maintaining the PD process); members of the training department; and representatives of senior management, who were under pressure to accelerate the PD process while cutting costs. The chair of the committee was Bob Werner, a recent retiree who had returned to take charge of implementing the new PD process. He had gained a lot of respect in his years as the program director of some very successful product launches. The committee also hired Jim Huggins as an instructional design (ID) consultant because of his long experience in designing technical training and using technology to deliver training.

The steering committee quickly decided that time was a critical factor: Whatever training was needed had to be done quickly. Competitive pressure, particularly from foreign manufacturers, required improved quality, faster product development, and reduced costs. The steering committee concluded that the time factor alone ruled out classroom training, since the organization could not deliver it to everyone who needed training (15,000 salaried people) in a reasonable time frame. This decision was confirmed by the fact that the PD process continued to change quickly enough that Hill Industries could not get its personnel through before it changed again.

The first training initiative was a one-day overview class. So much of the new PD process depended on cross-functional teams that the steering committee asked for a class to address that issue specifically. Product development teams were new to Hill, so people did not really know how they would work.

Jim's company responded with a highly interactive class based on case studies. For each case study, the class broke into small teams, with each team including people from design, engineering, manufacturing, and finance. Each team then worked through real PD problems, using the new PD process. The class design emphasized working together in cross-disciplinary teams. The faculty team for each class session included an experienced PD engineer and a team facilitator, to make sure both the PD process and the team function objectives were met. The overview class was immediately implemented throughout the organization as part of the PD training process.

Making the Case for CBT

In the meantime, Jim had been given primary responsibility for determining training delivery methods for the remainder of the content and was asked to present a report detailing preferred delivery methods to the steering committee. After several weeks of analysis of current and projected resources, he presented his report to a regular meeting of the steering committee: "I suggest that our response to the PD process training problem is to design and develop a hypermedia, computer-based training program. Since all members of the target population have PCs on their desktops, most of which are soon to be on networks connected by a backbone wide-area network (WAN), we already have the technical infrastructure to implement such a program.

"The CBT will provide information on the PD process, including design, engineering, testing, finance, product management, and product planning. The hypermedia will provide text and graphics, with extensive links among processes, organizations, and product subsystems. The typical screen for the hypertext CBT will include text and graphics. Terms in the text will be linked to glossary definitions of the term. The graphic area will include links to additional details, usually provided as pop-up boxes on the current page. Users will have ready access to a lot of information, with ready access to additional levels of detail if they choose to use it. Additional changes to the PD process could be quickly included in the CBT and distributed over the network.

"The user will also be able to follow links between processes, so, for example, when he or she is learning the prototyping process, relevant financial or manufacturing information will be available by taking links from the prototyping pages. Those links might detail the financial requirements for prototype approval or manufacturing's involvement in prototyping."

The committee listened politely to the recommendation, then sat silently. The members then started asking questions, indicating they didn't understand what this recommendation had to do with training. "Do people go to the classes first and then use this CBT? I don't understand how it works," said one committee member. "Do you have a class for each process, as we had before?" asked another.

Jim had thought the case for CBT was obvious, so he wasn't expecting much opposition. He took a deep breath and explained there were no classes, other than the "overview" that had been running for several weeks now. He referred them back to the audience and context analyses he had conducted to show that the size of the audience, its diversity, and the amount of time required for training all meant that sit-down classes would not work well. He reminded them of all their complaints about the previous classes, how long they'd taken, how they never seemed to be available when people needed them, how much money the instructors cost, and what it cost to update the class materials.

Some committee members nodded in agreement, but not many. John Eggleston, a training supervisor in PDO, understood exactly what Jim was saying. Over the years, John had worked in this very traditional training environment ("butts in seats") and had noted widespread unhappiness with previous PD training. But knowing what was wrong with classroom training was a long way from jumping to CBT. "Can people actually learn from CBT? I mean, we've had some here and it was pretty bad. People just had to read text from the screen. No one liked it. I don't think that's what we want to do here. I've seen some CBT for computer skills, but that's not what this is about. Has anyone used CBT for this kind of training?"

In an attempt to respond to some of these questions and objections, Jim offered to put together a paper describing some history of CBT, how various companies used it, and how it could be done effectively. The committee readily accepted the offer and agreed to meet one week later. In a week, Jim took his paper in and presented it to the committee. He cited academic studies showing that people learn from CBT and that CBT takes less time. Then he summarized case studies from other large companies demonstrating that what he was proposing was not new or leading edge but fairly common practice. He also cited other groups in Hill Industries that had some experience with CBT, to defuse the concern that PDO was breaking new ground.

The committee members liked what they read but still needed more. The idea of adopting CBT for such important training made them nervous. They didn't really know how it would work or how people in PDO would react to it. Bob Werner, the steering committee chair, suggested they benchmark the companies Jim cited, plus any others they could find that used CBT for engineering training. Although he had little training experience and almost no experience with computers (which he often called "confusers"), his daughter worked for a software company. In the week between meetings, he had called her to ask her if CBT made any sense. She listed some potential problems but basically gave her approval to the idea. With her approval and Jim's paper, Bob was ready to press the case for CBT. As a program director, he had always pushed for the inclusion of new technology. CBT seemed like just another technology they should adopt. Bob led the benchmarking effort, gaining confidence with each conference call to training managers, project managers, and engineers in several other companies.

With Bob on board, Jim felt more confident the proposal would work, but they still had many committee members to convince. Several of the companies mentioned a concern associated with the cost of developing CBT. Several members of the steering committee, including John Eggleston, seized on that issue, calling it a show stopper. Bob arranged for Jim to meet with a manager in finance, who helped put together a cost-benefit analysis for the project. Jim knew the importance of using trusted numbers and stating any assumptions, so that the analysis would be solid. However, he also knew that, although he often had to do cost-benefit analyses to get CBT projects going, they never really convinced anyone to go ahead. In any event, the cost-benefit was better than expected. The project would pay for itself within six months, before all the CBT was even developed.

Jim and Bob reviewed their progress. They had shown that CBT would work by getting case studies from other companies. They had shown that it would pay for itself, though there was a high front-end cost for design and development. But there were still important and vocal members of the committee who weren't on board.

Bob decided to push the committee really hard at the next meeting to try to get its approval to go ahead. As an engineer and successful manager, he was used to making decisions even when full information was not available, confident that they would be able to make the CBT work. He felt frustrated that the training community didn't seem to work the same way. At the next meeting, Bob laid out the case while Jim listened to the objections. Finally, he realized that the problem was that the committee members could not visualize the CBT. Their idea of CBT was based on some pretty awful mainframe CBT they had seen years ago. Jim offered to build a prototype they could try out with their own engineers—they could use their new process as the content. If it worked, the cost would be reasonable and the risk for both the company and the consultant would be low.

While Jim huddled with a senior instructional designer and operations manager to figure out what to prototype and how much to charge, Bob presented the proposal to the committee. Quick agreement came when the price for the prototype was less than the committee had agreed it would be willing to spend. Bob was pretty sure most of the committee members didn't know what they had just bought, but agreeing to the prototype served the purpose of moving the decision process along.

IMPLEMENTING THE CBT

Within Jim's company, the work now shifted from a consulting and change effort to CBT design and development. Working with subject matter experts from the committee, he led the effort to put together a demo module for the committee to review. The attractive, easy-to-use program worked. The committee now understood what Jim and Bob were trying to do but questioned the start-up of the CBT. Jim proposed that, as employees complete the overview class, they be given access to the CBT. The committee agreed to this and to go ahead with the development of the CBT.

Jim worked with Leslie Santulli, the operations manager, to put together his design and development team, including subject matter experts from the steering committee. The team prioritized modules, built schedules, allocated resources, and established review schedules. Development was finally underway.

In the meantime, John Eggleston and Bob worked on implementation issues. Hill Industries, rather than Jim's consulting firm, had taken responsibility for implementation. Its approach was to use the training coordinators already in place throughout the company to lead the way. Its implementation plan consisted of meetings of the training coordinators, in which they demonstrated the new CBT and directed the coordinators to ensure that employees had access to the CBT from their desktop computers.

This top-down approach was not very participative but was consistent with the corporate culture. Many of the coordinators saw their value to the company as advising employees, monitoring training plans, and scheduling classes efficiently for their organization. They did a terrific job of making sure people registered for and completed the PD overview class.

One year later, many thousands of engineers, analysts, managers, and planners had completed this class, yet only a few thousand had used the CBT at all, even though by now there were 10 modules, about 15 hours of instruction.

To try to get a handle on why implementation was so slow, the steering committee commissioned a formal study by a third-party evaluator. The evaluator's first task was to determine how much the CBT was being used. A month later, she was back with her report. Jim sat down to read his copy.

PRELIMINARY ANALYSIS QUESTIONS

1. Evaluate Jim's performance in convincing the steering committee to adopt CBT.
2. What obstacles in Hill Industries may have caused such a low level of adoption of CBT?
3. What factors supported the adoption of CBT within Hill Industries?
4. What could be done at this stage to increase the use of CBT within the organization?

IMPLICATIONS FOR ID PRACTICE

1. Identify the factors that can inhibit the implementation of CBT in an organization.
2. Identify the factors that can support the implementation of CBT in an organization.
3. Suggest strategies to reduce inhibiting factors and reinforce supporting factors.

David Jimenez

by Marti F. Julian, Valerie A. Larsen,
and Mable B. Kinzie

Carillon Productions is an instructional design firm that grew from a small team of instructional designers in the late 1990s to well over 50 employees in only a few years. Carillon became well known, among its clients of educational publishers, for its development of multimedia-based supplemental textbook materials. David Jimenez was an instructional designer at Carillon who had been specializing in the design of science and mathematics instruction for the past four years. His innovative and award-winning designs covered a wide range of applications from interactive problem-solving physics modules to 3-D calculus tutorials. David credited the successful design of his products to his skills as an instructional designer, to his programming skills, and to his 10 years as a secondary science teacher. His teaching experience provided him with insight into learners' needs and enabled him to serve as both content expert and instructional developer. In this way, he was able to work on his own as he designed and developed products for Carillon's clients. David had to modify his formula for success, however, when he was promoted to project manager and assigned to head up a project for Dragone Drilling Technologies, a leading manufacturer of petroleum analysis tools and extraction equipment. Due for market release in 90 days, Dragone Drilling's Odysseus System was being promoted as a cost-effective technology that had the potential to revolutionize natural gas hydrate exploration. The firm wanted a training module that would encourage the use of this new analysis, archiving, and forecasting system.

The Odysseus System project would be David's first experience as a manager and his first as a designer dependent on others for their content expertise. However, David was enthusiastic about these new challenges and saw this as an opportunity to expand his leadership and instructional design (ID) skills. Dragone had conducted a field test with the beta version of the Odysseus System, and it cited results that it thought pointed to a need for training among its users. According to executives at Dragone, this need was demonstrated by the engineers' resistance to using the product, a problem they thought was generally common to organizations introducing new technologies. In their report, they noted specifically that 17 engineers had been asked to use the technology for a period of two months in the field. By the end of the second month, the engineers had abandoned the new technology and had returned to their standard data-collection tools.

DAVID'S TEAM

Once Carillon had won the Dragone contract, its Department of Human Resources allocated one graphic designer, three software/interface programmers, and two entry-level instructional designers for the Odysseus System project, all working under David's direction. David thought it important to introduce the client to his "stellar" team and arranged for the graphics designer and lead interface programmer to participate in their first face-to-face meeting with the client. David had each of them describe the variety of products they had produced as he pointed to the numerous awards their educational materials had received. A manager from Human Resources at Dragone Drilling and the marketing director for the Odysseus System represented the client.

After introductions, the marketing director for Dragone presented the promotions packet for the Odysseus System and described its functionality. He explained that standard methods for data collection were laborious, necessitating hours of manual gauge calibration, along with the manual recording of each data probe in the field, followed by lengthy analysis in an off-site lab. The Odysseus System streamlined this process, with automated calibration and on-site analysis: The system involved a three-stage, on-site digital system that collected data on compositional gradients and hydrate gases from potential drill sites. Multivariate analyses of the reservoir fluid properties were automated and integrated with satellite-networked databases, equipped with algorithms for forecasting site productivity.

According to the marketing director, the petroleum industry was facing a combination of finite, diminishing petroleum resources and increased competition. Those firms with access to new technologies for natural gas hydrate exploration, such as the Odysseus System, had the potential to maintain or increase their market share.

Representatives from Dragone Drilling explained what they were looking for from Carillon Productions: an interactive, self-study training module that would be ready for distribution with the final release of Odysseus in three months. Dragone wanted the engineers to experience the benefits of the Odysseus technology and recognize its ease of use. The goal was to ease the learning curve for the use of the Odysseus System in the field. Their thinking was that an effective training solution would lead to widespread adoption of the Odysseus System.

David shifted into high gear at this point in the meeting and segued into a discussion on the design process. He believed it was important to secure approval for a needs assessment, and, using examples from prior projects, he enthusiastically described how the process could pinpoint the needs of the field engineers and help match the training module to those needs. The Dragone Drilling representatives agreed that a needs assessment seemed a practical way to ensure that the training module resolved the problem of technology adoption. They emphasized that time was critical, however, and were reluctant to postpone development of the training module until the needs assessment was completed. As an alternative, Dragone Drilling suggested that David obtain any information he needed from the project manager of the programming team that was contracted to design and develop the Odysseus System.

After some discussion, David and his client agreed to a compromise: They brainstormed some initial ideas for the interface design and for the structure of the instructional module, including options for software or web-based materials. After the latter option was selected, David's team agreed to start development right away. To ensure that appropriate content was included in the module, however, David convinced his clients to approve an initial two-week time period for the collection and analysis of needs data from the Odysseus developers and potential users of the product.

Under David's supervision, then, his team members began to storyboard the instructional sequence, and he was pleased with his team's progress. He was impressed with the competence of his lead developers. Recognizing that he himself worked best when given wide latitude within general guidelines, he instructed them to proceed with the development of the interface components they'd discussed, designing the best interface they could for the anticipated content.

THE LOMPOC TECHNOLOGY TEAM

David made arrangements to begin the needs assessment with a visit to the software development company, Lompoc Technology Group (LTG), located in a southern California beach community. There he met Bill Peters, the project manager of the Odysseus development team, who would serve as his content expert for the instructional module.

Bill greeted David with a coffee mug and a company tour, where he met everyone from the chief information officer (CIO) to the company's interns. The LTG facility provided a friendly work environment, with music playing throughout the "house," a large, open workspace for the programmers and a conference/game room stocked with food and crash pads for those all too frequent times when programmers worked through the night. The programmers appeared absorbed in their work as they hammered away at their keyboards and stared intently at their monitors. David observed a small group of programmers congregated around a wipe-erase board as they engaged in an active discussion about a glitch with the logon form for the Odysseus intranet.

The tour of LTG concluded in the company's conference room with an overview of the intranet communications system that drove the Odysseus System and a striking visual display of the project's milestones. The first item on the display was a description of the guidelines that Dragone Drilling had presented to the Lompoc team in the form of a flowchart, which listed each of the required functions that the Odysseus System would perform. The last item was a chart displaying the final stage of revisions that began during the beta test of the product. Bill then led a discussion with David and the Odysseus software team about the product and its projected implementation. They walked David through the product demo on a laptop computer similar to those distributed with the Odysseus System. The software team, mostly young men and women averaging two to five years of experience in the software design industry, believed that Odysseus was vastly superior to the current manually driven analysis tools because it handled all of the data-collection and analysis tasks within a single product.

The programmers explained that Odysseus was a simple application to use once the user understood each of the screens and its functions. Also, given a built-in user's guide that was accessible from within the program and a smart tool that defined functions when pointed to, they believed that a separate training module for the engineers would be superfluous. One of the lead programmers noted, "The field engineers who don't 'get' Odysseus are the ones too set in their ways to adopt new technologies at this point in their careers." Another programmer suggested that it might take a new generation of engineers to break a tool such as this into the market.

David left LTG with an Odysseus System laptop and a copy of the beta software. The project manager provided contact information for the engineers who had participated in the Odysseus System beta test and phone numbers for overseas field engineers whom they thought were representative of the potential Odysseus System user population.

RESERVOIR FLUID PROPERTY ANALYSIS

Over the next four days, David was able to contact seven potential users of the Odysseus System. Six of the seven engineers whom David interviewed spoke English as a second language and practiced their profession in their home countries. They had earned their degrees from prominent U.S. schools of engineering, such as Texas A&M and Purdue University. They described their practice as 60% technical and 40% "a feeling of the gut." They had developed their skills under the guidance of experienced field engineers, and, although the standard equipment they used was old, they were comfortable with the process and found it to perform reliably under a variety of conditions. They claimed that they would embrace a tool that expedited the analysis and forecasting of hydrocarbon reserves, but it would have to perform the reservoir fluid property analysis efficiently and accurately. Four of the engineers were wary of using new technologies promoted by their superiors. They described previous tools that were supposed to "deliver the world," according to management. However, when the equipment failed, it was the engineers' performance that came into question, rather than the tools that management had adopted.

David spent his second week meeting with eight of the beta test engineers for the Odysseus System at various sites around the Houston area, four of whom were recent university graduates who planned to return to their native countries in the near future. David was able to observe the new data-collection methods and discuss the engineers' beta test experiences with them. According to the engineers, the first month of the beta test had focused on programming glitches. The intent was to resolve minor bugs and ensure functionality. The majority of the bugs identified involved intranet access (login problems) and problems with user input that caused the system to crash because it was not supported by the analysis algorithms. The engineers were then left to use the new technology in the field for a period of four weeks.

After taking Odysseus through its paces, the engineers reported that they had experienced some drawbacks, which one engineer described as "shining a new light on our old equipment, making the old methods seem like a model of modern perfection." They had found the Odysseus software difficult to navigate and described the multitude of screens that had to be set up for each drill site, with parameters specific to that site. The engineers explained that they often became lost in the system, which required them to start over with their data entry. Consequently, they did not feel confident using Odysseus and had elected to return to their standard tools to ensure accuracy. The beta test engineers remained reluctant to use the final release of the tool, explaining concerns about the functionality and the accuracy of their data entry.

ATTITUDES, PERFORMANCE, AND BETA TEST DATA

David returned to the Carillon office and spent the next few days compiling data from the interviews and his explorations of the Odysseus System. After several hours interacting with the software, its embedded user's guide, and job aid cards, he began to understand Odysseus's basic functions, as well as its drawbacks.

Meanwhile, David supervised his designers as they moved forward with a highly sophisticated and attractive interface for the learning module. When the needs assessment data were ready for a final analysis, David asked his instructional designers to take a break and help him review the findings. They found a complex series of problems (see Tables 16–1 and 16–2), which seemed unlikely to be solved by attempts at "attitude adjustment" (suggested by the software company) or "performance training" (requested by Dragone Drilling).

NEXT STEPS

As he reviewed these data, David wondered how he could move forward with a training module when it seemed the product itself needed to be revised. David needed his colleagues' input and a resolution for this dilemma. He had known all along that he could be compromising the effectiveness of the instructional design process when he had the team move directly into interface design before the needs were articulated. And, although he was aware of the potential problems that could result from beginning product development prior to the completion of a needs analysis, he was surprised to uncover problems that were not instructional.

TABLE 16–1 *Hardware Concerns Highlighted During Field Beta Tests of the Odysseus System*

Contrast/lighting

■ Laptop LCD screen presents significant lighting and contrast problems in direct sunlight. The earth-tone colors are attractive but are too similar to differentiate between objects on the screen, especially in varying lighting conditions.

Pulley system

■ Data probes must drop up to 20,000 feet underground. A pulley controls the probe cables and organizes the different probes for each type of sample. The device also reduces the tension placed on the laptop connections. The pulley occasionally crimps the wires, resulting in a negative reading.

Setup of the data probes

■ Setup takes approximately three hours (the same as the standard system). The engineers are accustomed to calibrating their tools prior to each data-collection session and are not comfortable with the "self-correcting" calibration in the new system.

TABLE 16–2   *Software Concerns Highlighted During Field Beta Tests of the Odysseus System*

Navigation

- There are between 8 and 14 windows among which a user must navigate for data entry and analysis.
- The only way to determine if data are missing is to run the analysis, which takes several minutes. After the analysis, a screen prompts the user for missing information.

Online Help

- The three engineers who spoke English as a second language found the help screens inadequate. The screens did not define the steps needed to complete the task in question, and the engineers didn't know what terms to input when searching for navigation tips.
- The two engineers for whom English was the primary language thought the help screens were too simplistic and were cumbersome to access.
- The search engine did not cover all of the system terminology and provided simplified definitions of functions.
- The user guidelines often referred to links or buttons without directing the user to their location.

Functionality

- Several of the software functions were assigned names unique to the software, rather than names reflecting their physical counterparts.

In less than 24 hours, David and his team would present their findings and their progress on the development of the instructional module interface. David and his team members needed to determine how they should address the discrepancies between the needs analysis data and the module that was now under development. As he leafed through the data tables, he thought, "If only Dragone Drilling would allow me to close myself in a room for the next year, I could redesign the Odysseus software and make it the innovative solution that they envision."

PRELIMINARY ANALYSIS QUESTIONS

1. What information led the client to conclude that there was an instructional need? How might David have explored this topic in greater depth at the initial meeting?
2. How can David diplomatically encourage the client's consideration of problems in its own product, instead of just problems with the users' knowledge, skills, and attitudes?
3. Considering the time constraints placed on this project, what other options might David have pursued concerning the immediate development of a training module?
4. Given the situation at the end of the case, how might David proceed with Dragone Drilling?

IMPLICATIONS FOR ID PRACTICE

1. How do you direct a client to consider all stakeholder perspectives when the client has predetermined an instructional need?
2. What project management skills does an instructional designer need to have to lead a design and development team?

Case Study | 17

Davey Jones

BY GARY ELSBERND AND DONALD A. STEPICH

Davey Jones had worked for WidgetMart for 10 years. He had begun as a technical writer, documenting procedures for the company's point-of-sale system, but had taken on a number of other responsibilities over the years. Because of his increasing knowledge of store operations and personnel, and the lack of formally trained instructional designers, Davey had been thrust into the roles of both instructional designer and stand-up trainer, responsible for teaching everything from new procedures to interpersonal skills.

WidgetMart was making a transition to an integrated electronic performance support system (EPSS) to replace its existing training and performance support materials. Existing materials were being repurposed and new information developed for online presentation. Davey's expertise in computer interface design made him a natural for the project, and he had been given the task of heading up the project team. It was a high-profile project, the kind of assignment that could be a real feather in Davey's cap. But it wasn't going to be easy.

BACKGROUND

WidgetMart had grown steadily, from 1 store in 1956, to 800 stores in 1979, to 4,000 stores in 1991. At the time of this project, it was the nation's largest discount widget retailer, with 5,000 stores throughout the United States, Puerto Rico, the U.S. Virgin Islands, and Canada. Each year, the company sold more than 250 million widgets to nearly 150 million customers, with sales of approximately $3 billion. The company was actually made up of three related stores:

- WidgetMart—selling high-quality widgets at affordable prices in self-service stores
- Universal Widgets—catering to the upscale widget market
- BuyMore—a leased sales operation with department space in large retail stores

Throughout the company's history, an effort had been made to teach the associates and managers working in the stores the best practices of day-to-day operations. During the old days (prior to 1979), most of this took the form of "sit with Fred" training, in which new trainee managers spent 6 to 18 months with experienced managers and district supervisors, who carried best practices from store to store.

However, there were several problems with this kind of training. One was that the procedures varied from region to region and sometimes from store to store. The six regional management offices could rarely agree on the most efficient procedure for anything from processing an incoming shipment to handling customer returns to setting displays. This resulted in six different sets of best practices and difficulties transferring associates from region to region. Another problem was that the information degenerated as it passed from person to person, much like a photocopy of a photocopy. The first trainer might understand the procedures and the rationale behind the procedures, but the next trainer might understand only the mechanics of the procedures. By the time the information had passed to the associates in the stores, the compelling business reasons were often lost and the procedures themselves were often changed, similar to the telephone game played by kids at camp. It's fine for the message to degrade in a game, but in business it leads to inefficient and ineffective performance.

These problems became more noticeable during the company's explosive growth in the 1980s. As a result, management had decided to make the information more formal and consistent. Company-wide standards were adopted, and a team of technical writers collected best practices throughout the stores and compiled them into an operations manual ("ops manual"). As an example, prior to 1979, merchandise displays were left to the individual store. Some managers displayed the best selling widgets, hoping to extend the sales of those units. Others displayed the widgets with the biggest inventory to increase product turnover and free up shelf space. Still others chose seasonal widgets to match their concepts of fashion. To make displays more consistent, the ops manual included a standard for product displays, based on projected sales throughout the company and designed to present a consistent image to customers. Similar standards were developed for other store operations.

The ops manual became the foundation for a set of structured workshops and paper-based, self-paced training materials, which were made available to all store managers and associates. However, the ops manual and the training materials were organized differently. The ops manual was organized by functional area within the corporate office: leadership, human resources, store administration, merchandise administration, marketing, loss prevention, and store maintenance. The training materials were organized by position responsibilities for store associates: orientation, merchandise, customer satisfaction, sales transactions, store administration, supervisory skills, and management skills. Over the years, the ops manual and the training materials were updated, but more effort went into adding new information than into deleting old, obsolete information.

In 1994, a text-based online reference tool was added, consisting of more than 1,100 topics presented as ASCII text files in an indexed and searchable browser. This opened up the possibility of reusable, hyperlinked information. But the technology available at the time limited the online reference to one megabyte of information within a DOS environment, and the system was, at best, rudimentary. Beginning in 1995, the company began to replace its outmoded computers with more sophisticated equipment. This opened up the prospect of overhauling the training and performance support of the associates.

THE EPSS DESIGN PLAN

The plan was to use the new, more sophisticated computer technology to update and replace the existing materials with a system that was entirely online. The online materials needed to be accessed easily and just as easily revised. They also had to include best practices related to all aspects of store operations—loss prevention, retail operations, merchandising, human resources, and so on. The goal was to embed the knowledge in the software as field edits, prompts, and error messages that provided the necessary knowledge or tools to perform the task on demand or in the background. This would radically redefine the work in the stores and would allow managers and associates to focus on tasks that required human intervention, rather than tasks that were more easily completed by the computer, such as looking up information or calculating numbers. One example was the scheduling system. Previously, the manager created work schedules manually, based on his or her knowledge of the workload, labor laws, and associates' requests. Under the new system, an EPSS scheduling function would take the current best knowledge of these factors and create a draft schedule for the manager to review and edit or approve, optimizing the scheduled work to the projected workload. As the manager made changes to the schedule, the software reviewed the change against workload, labor laws, and associates' requests and preferences, providing warnings or recommendations as necessary.

In tasks completed away from the computer, such as rack allocation, the EPSS software would present the necessary data (number of racks, inventory, etc.), the decision criteria (current and projected sales, seasonal promotions, etc.), and the recommended process (each rack charted by size and style) in an easy-to-use worksheet. The challenge was to create a system in which knowledge and best practices of every process were embedded in the EPSS software and support systems.

Some steps had already been taken. A thorough analysis of the performance environment had been performed to determine where and how information was used in the stores. Because WidgetMart was a self-service store, associates were rarely on or near the computer. They spent most of their time processing shipments in the backroom or stocking displays on the sales floor. Store managers spent only about 15% of their time on the computer, completing tasks such as scheduling and inventory tracking. Still, all managers and associates had access to the computer and used it for timing in and out. Based on this analysis, the EPSS would be made up of four functions:

■ Applications with embedded knowledge—software applications for computer-mediated tasks in which data, best practices, and business rules would be embedded, negating the need to learn or even review the knowledge. For example, an inventory finder with embedded suggestions for cross-selling would support customer satisfaction.

- A reference function—a repository of knowledge, which could be accessed whenever needed. For example, if a manager needed to determine how many days off were provided to an associate whose uncle had died, he or she could access this information.
- A job aid function—a collection of printable worksheets and reminders, which would be used away from the computer to support performance. For example, the rack allocation guidelines would dynamically generate the optimal display guidelines and outline the process for changing the racks for new associates.
- A computer-based instruction function—structured information and guidelines designed to help associates internalize the information. For example, when an irate customer walks in the door, the associate needs to be able to react properly in the absence of any external support. Therefore, associates must learn how to deal with difficult customers.

With these functions in mind, the project team decided to meet to work on the design of the EPSS. The first meeting was arranged for a Monday morning.

THE PROJECT TEAM MEETING

After coffee and rolls, everyone settled down so that Davey could explain the next stage of the project. Looking around the table, Davey thought about the knowledge represented by the team. No one had formal training in instructional design, but each member of the team was an expert in different aspects of store operations. Ellen understood merchandising processes and had designed many of the business applications that would be incorporated into the EPSS. She would also take on some of the project's administrative responsibilities, allowing Davey to continue to build sponsor support and advocacy and to determine a long-range strategy for the system. Josie worked on the acquisition team for Universal Widget and was instrumental in defining the training system for BuyMore. She understood better than anyone else the variations in the information required for WidgetMart, Universal Widgets, and BuyMore. Tim was the translation expert. He understood the variations needed in the information from country to country to account for customs, language, and governmental requirements. Barry, the newest member of the team, had been brought in for his experience in management development and interpersonal skills. His focus would be on the internal marketing and change management aspects of the system, rather than the technical implementation. The team had a wide range of talents and the knowledge necessary to complete the project.

"You know the background," Davey began. "We're creating an online performance support system with four functions—applications with embedded knowledge, a reference function, a job aid function, and a computer-based instruction function. The problem is that there is a massive amount of information. Information has been accumulating in the ops manual and training programs over the years, and not much has been done to combine or weed out the outdated information. The information sometimes overlaps. Sometimes it's downright contradictory. And, sometimes, different employees get different information at different times in their careers, which confuses things even more. To make matters worse, there is a whole collection of new information that comes with the change we're making to a new system and new processes.

"In order to create the new online system, this information will have to be collected, sifted, and assigned to one of the four functions. The goal is to have a completely integrated system that presents accurate information in the most concise, reusable form possible. In other words, we have a big pile of information and four buckets—five, if you count the trash bucket. Our job is to figure out how to break down the information into the smallest usable bit, catalog it, and sort it. We'll have to come up with a way to decide what information to keep and a way to decide where each piece of information goes. We'll also have to figure out how to make sure that the functions support one another, without any inconsistencies.

"The challenge is to create a single, seamless package that includes everyone from entry-level shipment processors to district managers with responsibility for 20 to 30 stores, and it has to include variations of the information for our 3 stores—WidgetMart, Universal Widgets, and BuyMore—and the unique requirements for the various countries we're in.

"How should we start?"

PRELIMINARY ANALYSIS QUESTIONS

1. Outline a method (or methods) that can be used to gather all of the information. Describe how this information can be broken down into the smallest chunks that would be appropriate for the knowledge inventory.
2. Suggest a method that can be used to catalog the information into the five buckets mentioned in the project team meeting. That is, how can the team make consistent decisions about what information should be converted (vs. discarded) and about what information should be placed into each of the four established functions of the EPSS—maintaining the consistency of the information without making it unnecessarily redundant?
3. Describe a method that can be used to make sure the inventory is complete—that it includes all of the relevant information. Suggest a method or methods that can be used to maintain the inventory once it has been completed.
4. Describe a method that can be used to make sure the inventory is accurate.
5. Outline a plan for adapting the inventory for all the variations within WidgetMart (stores, countries, and languages).

IMPLICATIONS FOR ID PRACTICE

1. Electronic performance support systems are not appropriate for every situation. When can (and should) an EPSS be used, either in conjunction with or in place of traditional training?
2. What can be done to help ensure the successful adoption of an EPSS throughout an organization?
3. What criteria and methods might be used to assess the effectiveness of an EPSS and its value to an organization? How might such an evaluation be built into the design and delivery of the EPSS?

Jacci Joya

BY JULIE MUEHLHAUSEN AND PEGGY A. ERTMER

CURRENT STATUS—MAY (YEAR 1)

Jacci Joya walked out of the administration office with a sense of uneasiness. She and one of her co-teachers, Brandon Stohl, had just been asked to serve as technology coaches for the 43 teachers at Cunningham High School (CHS). The high school had recently installed a new grade book program, *QuickGrader,* as well as a new administrative package, *School Manager,* on the school intranet, and the administration was hoping to increase teachers' use (and satisfaction) by providing access to some one-on-one training. Although coaching sounded like a good idea, Jacci's thoughts about what had transpired since February prevented her from getting too excited. On the positive side, she liked the idea of possibly being able to use some of her recently learned instructional design skills, acquired during her master's program at a nearby university. On the negative side, however, recent history indicated little likelihood of even moderate success. She definitely felt skeptical.

CUNNINGHAM HIGH SCHOOL

It wasn't that CHS was hurting for resources. Even though Cunningham was located in a small rural community of just over 16,000 people, a new high school facility had been built just seven years ago, on an 80-acre stretch of land, at a cost of $31 million. Because of the new facility, the administration had made a strong commitment to the use of technology in the school. At the time the building opened, there were approximately 575 computers in various locations, including at least 8 labs, all networked to one of 9 servers throughout the building. In addition, there was a Macintosh™ writing lab operating independently. Every teacher, administrator, and secretary had been given a desktop computer with a printer. Within the past two years, all computers in the building, except for the Macintoshes™ in the writing lab, were upgraded. In addition, labs for math, industrial technology, science, social studies, and foreign language were replaced with 2 laptop carts (28 machines total), which were shared among the classes. The business department retained 3 labs, 2 with laptops and 1 with desk units. Teachers now used laptops instead of desktop computers; one printer was located in each department office. The superintendent, who was hired two years after the new school opened, was committed to converting the middle and high schools into laptop schools.

THINKING BACK: FEBRUARY–APRIL (YEAR 1)

Jacci remembered how upset everyone had been when the information technology (IT) staff sent out a memo last February, announcing that two new programs had been installed on the network and indicating that teachers should begin using them immediately. That is, teachers were asked to take attendance using the *School Manager* program and to record their grades using the *QuickGrader* program. Of course, the teachers were not familiar with either of these programs; they had been using another integrated program for the previous year and a half.

Needless to say, because of the timing of the installation, training had been difficult to accomplish. The IT staff had put together an "each-one-teach-one" method of instruction for teachers, which, unfortunately, resulted in almost no instruction whatsoever. Neither the IT staff nor the one teacher who had been drafted to train teachers knew how to use the program effectively. No one could teach the program to anyone.

To further complicate the situation, the *QuickGrader 4.0* interface was not Windows-based, which made it very difficult for anyone not used to working in a DOS environment to even begin to figure out how the software worked. Moreover, the 144-page user's guide was not well written. Only one copy of the guide had been purchased, and that was kept on file in the technology office. Consequently, only the most adventurous teachers even attempted to use *QuickGrader.*

Within a short time, it became apparent that if teachers were actually going to use *Quick-Grader* and *School Manager,* a new training plan had to be developed, yet it looked as though no one was available (or knowledgeable enough) to accomplish this formidable task. The IT staff was overwhelmed with responsibilities related to the proliferation of laptop computers at the middle school, as well as new technology being installed at the four elementary schools. There were not enough individuals who were capable of dealing with the myriad of problems related to computer use at the high school. Furthermore, the communication among the IT staff, administration, clerical staff, and teachers was less than efficient. Vital information could not be relayed clearly to the entire staff. Tension surrounding the use of technology increased.

MEET THE COACHES

Still, if anyone could be successful in this situation, Jacci and Brandon certainly could. They were both long-time members of the technology committee and were well respected by the administrators, teachers, and IT staff. In addition, they were flexible in their approaches to problem solving and eager to help their colleagues. An officer in the Army Reserve and a high school science teacher, Brandon was particularly adept at performing "techie" duties and could troubleshoot minor hardware, software, and network problems. Brandon had taught C++ and liked to tinker with computers. Unfortunately, he had a tendency to take over when solving problems, thus keeping others in the dark about the magic he performed.

A veteran teacher of 25 years, Jacci taught English/language arts in grades 9–12, as well as composition and English education methods courses at the college level. Her specific skills were related to language and instruction. Jacci had a strong knack for being able to interpret technology language, either written or oral, for the specific needs of the high school staff. Furthermore, her coursework at the university had resulted in a number of exceptional instructional products. She had a good understanding of how to reach an audience with diverse technology needs and was eager to work as a liaison.

Both Jacci and Bill had previously worked one-on-one with teachers and other staff members to solve problems and provide training, as well as to facilitate group instruction and communication. Brandon was prepared to put out fires, whereas Jacci looked for ways to prevent problems and, through good communication and instruction, help others learn to use the programs.

DEVELOPING TRAINING: JUNE–AUGUST (YEAR 1)

In order to prepare herself to coach others, Jacci needed to learn as much as possible about the *QuickGrader* software package. The expectation was that the staff would be able to use *QuickGrader* for both attendance and exporting grades to *School Manager*. To date (from February through the end of the school year), teachers had been taking attendance with *School Manager* (although they complained that it was incredibly slow) and had been using *QuickGrader* for their own recordkeeping, but without exporting grades to *School Manager*. Jacci studied the user's guide but could not make much sense of it. Moreover, she could not access the program because it had not been set up properly for the network. The customer representative who had sold the two software packages to the school had not been on-site to help the staff during the school year. When she finally arrived on-site in June, after school had been dismissed for summer vacation, she was not very familiar with the *QuickGrader* program herself. Thus, Jacci's training amounted to one day in June, at the convenience of the sales representative, looking over the shoulder of a technology staff member, whose main interest was the *School Manager* administrative package. Brandon was also present to observe the training but would not be available for the upcoming teacher training because of army responsibilities scheduled for that time.

The administration expected all the teachers to begin using both software programs on the first day of school (Year 2). Thus, they had to be trained during the one-day in-service scheduled for the day before school started in August. To facilitate staff training, Jacci asked six teachers to come to the high school one day in late July to learn at least as much as Jacci herself had learned about *QuickGrader*. This had to be done on the day when the sales representative was going to be in the building to work with the administrative and IT staff, so that she *might* be available to help with any problems with instruction. On that day, the six teachers (without compensation) learned the basics about setting up the grade book and taking attendance, as well as using the grade scale and grade symbols. The plan was that they would assist Jacci while she conducted both morning and afternoon training sessions for the teaching staff during the August in-service. The participating teachers brainstormed potential problems their colleagues might have learning the program, as well as the kinds of handouts that would be helpful.

INSERVICE TRAINING: AUGUST–DECEMBER (YEAR 2)

Although Jacci felt reasonably well prepared when she began the first training session on the morning of August 28, things still began somewhat rocky because the IT staff had not attached some network cables in the lab that the teachers were using. As a result, some teachers were unable to connect until an IT person solved the problem, about 45 minutes into the instruction. Some of the teachers commented to Jacci that this was just one more example of an ongoing lack of communication between the IT staff and teaching personnel. One frustrated teacher, Vera Moreno, expressed her anger, noting, "IT staff always seem to be doing *something* with the network yet never seem to remember to tell those of us who may be affected by their actions. Then, when we try to work with a program that the school has mandated, we can't; the IT person is completely unavailable or deeply involved in another job and cannot or will not respond. I don't know about the rest of you, but this certainly doesn't increase my confidence for trying to use these new programs on an ongoing basis."

Nevertheless, Jacci was pleased with the turnout. All but two CHS teachers attended the training sessions. Once the network cable problem was solved, the morning teachers breezed through the training. All six teachers, who had been trained in late July, were on hand to help their colleagues. The afternoon session, however, which included many teachers who were less adept with technology, proceeded more slowly. Only two of the teacher helpers participated because the others had their own class preparations to complete. Still, at the end of the day, all but two teachers had been trained, the participants had a set of handouts to get them started, and they all knew that Jacci would be available to help them. In addition, even though Brandon had not been able to make this initial training session, he would also be available to help them during the school year.

In order to support the high school faculty as they began to use the programs in the fall, Brandon and Jacci frequently talked with administrative staff about the types of data they were expecting to receive. The principals, guidance counselors, and secretaries outlined the specific data they needed and described the specific reports, such as grade sheets and midterm reports, that they expected the teachers to generate. Throughout the first grading period, Jacci created instructions for the teachers, based on the administrators' and secretaries' specific needs, as well as the teachers' specific requests for help. These directions were sent by e-mail to the teachers just prior to their need to implement the instructions. Jacci used the *QuickGrader* user's guide, the help portion of the software, and her own exploration of the various options within the program to develop these instructions.

Brandon and Jacci continually tried to assess their own performance and to anticipate future problems and needs. For example, reactions to the e-mailed directions were mixed.

One teacher complained that she thought that Jacci was treating the staff like "village idiots"; one said that she loved the directions because she could follow everything step by step; others requested that Brandon and Jacci meet with them one-on-one because they "just couldn't figure out the directions"; most of the teachers, however, thanked Jacci for the instructions. A few teachers explained that they were able to do their own exploration of additional features of *QuickGrader* because the basics were explained through e-mail.

Probably the most revealing reaction Jacci received was quite unintentional. A teacher came to her with two grade sheets for the end of the first six weeks. She asked why they did not look identical, since she "had done the same thing with both classes." Jacci replied that she did not know why they looked different but that they did not look like the grade sheet that would have been created using the directions that she had e-mailed them the week before. The teacher replied that she had not looked at the e-mail (which actually contained several sets of instructions vital to the end of the six weeks) because she did not like to follow numbered directions but preferred to "figure things out herself." The next morning, when Jacci went to the main office, a secretary showed her the grade sheets that 12 other teachers had submitted; only 3 had followed the directions. No one, other than the teacher who had wanted to know why her sheets did not look the same, had asked for help.

Unanticipated Problems: August–December (Year 2)

It was at about the same time that it became apparent that the *QuickGrader* software was inadequate in one key area. The high school had an attendance policy that reduced students' grades for unexcused absences. Students' grades were dropped 3% for every unexcused absence; this roughly translated into one-third of a letter grade per unexcused absence. The teachers received notification of how much to reduce the students' grades at the end of a grading period. In the past, the teachers merely changed the students' letter grades without considering the mathematics involved; for example, if a student had two unexcused absences, an earned $B+$ would become a $B-$. When the teacher averaged the students' grade at the end of the semester, the teacher used the value of the $B-$, not the numerical score earned with the $B+$ grade.

Realizing that *QuickGrader* kept the numerical score and would not allow the teachers to use the overwritten grade for averaging purposes, Brandon and Jacci tried to figure out the best way for teachers to determine semester grades when all grading periods would have to be averaged. Brandon wanted to put in a constant that could be used for each unexcused absence, so that the numerical score could be altered, thus resulting in the reduced grade. Such a system would have been fine if all the high school teachers had used the same grading scale, such as 90–100: *A*, 80–89: *B*, 70–79: *C*, 60–69: *D*, and 0–59: *F*. However, the teachers had the flexibility to use their own grading scales. Any change to a uniform grading scale for the school would have led to a dramatic confrontation with the faculty. The software just wouldn't allow the kind of freedom the teachers had enjoyed throughout the history of the school.

In response, the IT staff developed an elaborate floppy disk system for transferring grades from the grade book program to the administrative program. A member of the IT staff created a spreadsheet using the *School Manager* program and then copied it to individual disks for each teacher. The teachers then were responsible for transferring students' letter grades to the spreadsheet on the floppy and returning them to the department secretary. The secretaries then copied each spreadsheet to the administrative software to record the grades and generate report cards.

LOOKING FOR ALTERNATIVES: JANUARY–MARCH (YEAR 2)

By January, calls for help had become much less frequent. Minor problems occurred related to faulty floppy disks and disk drives, as well as to teachers' putting the wrong grades into the spreadsheet on the disks, but, in general, the disk solution to importing grades seemed to be fairly successful; at least it would carry them through to the end of the year.

Jacci began looking for other grade book software that might meet the needs of the school better but was limited to software that would interface with *School Manager*, even though the only feature that *School Manager* was using directly was attendance. At one point, Jacci thought she found a potential solution when she discovered that there was a newer version of *QuickGrader*. After further investigation, however, Jacci realized that, even though version 5.0 looked better on the surface (the interface looked more like a page from a grade book, and there were a few icons and buttons for frequent commands), behind the scenes, where the real work was done, it was almost identical to version 4.0. Apparently, upgrading to 5.0 would not solve the current computer grading and attendance problem at the high school. Logic indicated that *any* grade book software that was more user-friendly would be better than *QuickGrader*, at least on the grading side. However, Jacci couldn't help but think that logic and local needs just did not seem to carry much weight in this case.

TEACHER FEEDBACK: APRIL–JUNE (YEAR 2)

As the school year was drawing to an end, Jacci decided to gather some data from teachers about the grading program. She created and e-mailed a questionnaire to all of the teachers. About a dozen replied. Nine respondents checked "Although I have little difficulty with *QuickGrader*, I check myself according to e-mailed simplified directions to make sure I can handle required operations." Eight teachers noted that the "double bookkeeping" in order to send data to the administrative package was a serious flaw in the grading system; they wanted to be able to send grades through the network rather than by disk and spreadsheet. Other comments related to the choice of grade book software in general, saying, "The grade book seems to be the last thing considered when selecting school software. Let's not use it if it is not quicker and easier *for all involved*. The company support staff for this program is awful. She knew how to do little more than read the manual. I would think that a worthwhile company would provide training for all (a day would be enough)." Another was "We have gone backwards here." And "Thanks for asking our opinion." Respondents appreciated the work that Jacci and Brandon had done.

Jacci and Brandon did not want this problem to continue during the upcoming school year. The high school teaching staff needed a simple grade package that they could use easily, with minimal training and assistance, yet the administration was committed to using the *School Manager* program. How could Jacci and Brandon help their colleagues work with these two programs?

PRELIMINARY ANALYSIS QUESTIONS

1. Given the resources and constraints available, evaluate Jacci's and Brandon's technology training efforts.
2. How might the administrators and/or the IT staff have increased teacher buy-in for the new software products?
3. What are some of the ways that the administrators or IT staff might have prepared the school personnel for effective implementation of these new programs?
4. What can Jacci and Brandon do now to assist the teachers? Be specific.

IMPLICATIONS FOR ID PRACTICE

1. Describe the roles and responsibilities of technical support personnel in a K–12 environment.
2. Discuss the advantages and limitations of having K–12 technical support staff make decisions about software purchases for teacher use. Describe the ideal composition of a software evaluation and purchasing committee in the K–12 environment.
3. Outline an evaluation strategy related to the selection and purchase of new software.
4. Discuss the importance of timing as it relates to the introduction of new software in a work environment. How can users be brought up to speed when implementation is expected immediately?
5. Outline strategies for training a large number of people, with a wide range of skills, in a short amount of time.

Pat Kelsoe and Jean Fallon

BY CAROL S. KAMIN AND BRENT G. WILSON

BACKGROUND

State Medical University trains physicians, nurses, and health professionals in a variety of specialties. The training of physicians is fairly traditional, with two years of basic science instruction followed by third- and fourth-year clinical experiences. The primary teaching strategy for clinical experiences has been apprenticeships in hospital settings. However, due to a changing health care environment, fewer than 5% of all pediatric interactions result in hospitalization, and hospital stays have been greatly shortened. Therefore, increasing numbers of medical students do their required rotations in pediatrics offices around the state.

The pediatrics department is considered to be among the top 10 in the country, with a strong history of pediatric research. There are many older faculty members known to be excellent teachers and mentors. The chair of the department noted, "The faculty on this campus wrote the textbook on pediatrics." All medical students are required to take the pediatric clerkship in their third year. Thus, year-round the pediatrics department gets between 15 and 18 new third-year students every six weeks.

Dr. Jean Fallon is eager to begin a new project that will use technology to change how the pediatric clerkship is taught. She has called a planning meeting to brainstorm ideas, so that she can apply for a pilot grant through a recently released request for proposals (RFP) from the Office of the President.

MEET THE CHARACTERS

Jean Fallon—clerkship director and primary subject matter expert (SME): A physician in academic medicine, Dr. Jean Fallon recently switched her focus from laboratory research to educational research when she became the director of medical student education in pediatrics. After working for a year on a National Institutes of Health grant, she returned the award, at some risk to her tenure prospects, in order to assume these new responsibilities. The promotion and tenure guidelines recently changed to allow faculty to be promoted based on educational scholarship, and Jean wanted to take advantage of this opportunity. Colleagues have told her that she has given up a "sure thing" and has switched to an unproven track for promotion. Her mentors and section head have advised her to work on her interest in educational research *after she is tenured.* Nevertheless, she is enthusiastic and interested in initiating and evaluating innovative teaching methods. She is also ambitious and wants to make a difference in pediatric medical education nationally, as well as locally.

The pediatrics course in the third year of medical school is the only direct experience all medical students are sure to have caring for children. Physical examination courses and other generic skills are taught with an adult emphasis. As clerkship director, Jean is interested in adopting the recently created national pediatrics curriculum that stresses field experience, but she wants some standardization of this learning experience. She believes that, as practicing physicians, students will need the lifelong skills inherent in independent learning, problem-based learning, and electronic information retrieval. She is open to innovative instructional solutions.

When asked to name the one thing she wants medical students to know when they complete the clerkship, Jean's reply was, "To look at an infant or a child and know if his or her condition is urgent."

Pat Kelsoe—medical educator: A doctoral-level instructional designer, Dr. Pat Kelsoe is a brand new assistant professor in pediatrics accustomed to collaborating on development teams. She has been an instructional designer for the past six years, with all of her experience in academic medicine. She helped two other medical schools transition to problem-based learning. She worked full-time while she completed her doctoral degree in instructional technology a year ago. "I dragged my family across the country to accept this position; there's no way I'm going to take this job lightly," emphasized Pat.

There was no job description for Pat's position when she interviewed, so she asked the chair what success would look like in five years. His response was, "I want the department to have a national reputation as a center for scholarly work (educational research) in pediatric medical education." After she accepted the position, the chair confided, "The medical educator position is a new one for our department; some of the old guard were opposed to it."

To prepare for the planning meeting, Pat asked for past course materials and evaluations for the pediatric clerkship. She received 45 pages of qualitative comments from an open-ended student survey. After conducting a content analysis, she found that the strengths of the course appeared to be the teaching that was conducted primarily by pediatric residents. The primary weakness appeared to be the lack of course organization. The students who were dispersed to clinical sites seemed to enjoy the experience but felt somewhat isolated from their peers and unsure of the intended learning outcomes. They were not sure they were getting what they needed from the course or how it compared with what their peers at other sites were getting.

Sam McConnell—senior colleague: Dr. Sam McConnell, a senior faculty leader, was also asked to attend the planning meeting to discuss potential changes to the pediatric clerkship. Sam thought the new clerkship director had the potential to be a star, given the research she was doing, and was upset that she did not wait until after she was tenured to take this educational position. He has heard some of the grumbling from other faculty members about the medical educator position, and he, too, wonders why she was hired and what she will do to help the department's already excellent teachers.

Sam gets outstanding evaluations of his teaching, but he thinks one is either born a good teacher or not. He gives lectures on Wednesday afternoons and has students and residents in his clinics. As far as Sam is concerned, seeing patients is the only way to learn medicine. After all, that's the way he learned pediatrics. Most pediatrics faculty members prefer to teach residents who are going to be pediatricians. He's one of the few senior faculty members who teaches medical students, but he does it because he is committed to recruiting the best students possible for pediatrics. Sam is always disappointed when he gets a student who shows absolutely no interest in specializing in pediatrics.

Sam wonders why this group is meeting, anyway. He is convinced that students just need to work harder and see as many patients as possible. The clerkship gets good reviews, and the department has highly qualified applicants for its residency program. He believes that "if it's not broken, don't fix it." After all, there is constant pressure to produce revenue by getting large grants and seeing more patients. Sam believes that this is the only way to keep a medical school department afloat in a volatile health care environment. Even though pediatricians love to teach, as far as Sam is concerned, everyone knows that teaching does not generate revenue for the department.

Harry Lipsitz—department chair: Though he has received a lot of heat from some senior faculty members for creating a medical educator position and appointing a junior faculty member as clerkship director, Harry is excited about the potential of these young professors. He sees that there are many research questions to be asked in pediatric education and is anxious for his department to be a leader in this area. He believes that he has two very talented and hard-working faculty members who share his vision for the clerkship. Harry is concerned, however, about their overriding interest in technology. He recalls a colleague who took a sabbatical to create an educational software program. This colleague worked very hard on the project, but nothing ever came of it. Harry is afraid that ventures into educational technology could take a lot of time and money and end up being unproductive.

Harry considers that his most important job is to get these two junior faculty members promoted under the new evaluation system. They will be two of the first faculty members to attempt to secure tenure under these new guidelines. Although it's true that educational innovations are a risky venture for untenured professors, he believes that these two could perform some interesting studies and develop some interesting research findings.

THE PLANNING MEETING

Faculty members begin arriving in the department conference room. After several minutes of friendly banter, Jean begins the discussion:

Jean: Thank you all for making the meeting. I know it's a busy time of year, but I want to get this project off the ground. There are a lot of great things already in place with the clerkship, but there seems to be some room for trying out new ideas. The President's Office just came out with a grants program, and I thought we could compete for some of that money.

Sam: Always happy to take someone else's money!

Jean: That's right, and I think this project could be worth the investment. I've been thinking—our clerkship students often have great experiences out in the field, but they sometimes don't see any critical cases. It's a bit risky out there. Our students can get a great education, but we leave a lot to chance. So, I've been playing around with a possible solution. What if we developed a set of cases, such as computer-based case studies, covering some cases we think everyone should see—say, an urgent case of abuse? Then we'd be giving students something that's very close to real life, and we'd be able to guarantee they will actually encounter it during their clerkships.

Harry: You mean, show some video on the computer?

Jean: Yeah, show some video, either actors or real patients, depending on what we're thinking of. Give students a look at some symptoms and a situation, and let them ask questions, order tests, somehow leading to a diagnosis. Then we could give some feedback.

Harry: Wouldn't that be kind of expensive—putting all that into the computer?

Pat: Yes, a project like this could easily run up a budget. But I see the grant from the President's Office as a way to get it started. It could lead to some new ways to think about the clerkship.

Sam   [shifting in his seat]: Hold on a second. After having directed the clerkship for 12 years prior to your arrival here, Jean, I have to say that it's one of the most respected in the country. Our students come out very well versed in pediatrics. We get a good number of them deciding to specialize in pediatrics after their rotations.

Jean: That's important; we want students to be attracted to our department. I'm just thinking—maybe some video cases could even increase the attraction.

Harry: I'm still worried about the scope and cost of this kind of project.

Pat: Video production is getting cheaper and easier, but it's still a lot of work. We don't have a production facility here within the university; we would have to hire some of this work out. And we'd need to develop some expertise among ourselves.

Sam: That's just what I need, some fancy new technology to learn. I remember taking a *HyperCard* class once—never again!

Pat: I don't think faculty members should have to do all the authoring. We could get a couple of interns or part-time help to do most of the production. Your expertise, though, would be very helpful in determining how to approach a case, Sam.

Sam: I don't want to do *any* of the authoring. It will take far too much of my time and time is money.

Pat: Maybe I should clarify. We would have a team working on the case. The design and technical aspects would be handled by me and the interns. But we need experts to review the cases to ensure that they are realistic. This is what I mean when I say authoring.

Sam: Oh, well I could do that. Of course, you'd need some expert advice, since you're not a physician or pediatrician.

Harry: Tell me more about your ideas for the video case. Would it be like a tape that you watch?

Jean: Pat, why don't you share the ideas you were telling me about PBL, or problem-based learning?

Pat: As you know, PBL is heavily used in medical schools, but I'm not aware of very many problems or cases being presented electronically. Here is what Jean and I were talking about. We present a video case, with some footage and some background information—make it interactive, so that students can explore some information, order tests, and ask questions. That part is kind of standard, like an interactive case or a problem online. The part that I'm excited about is somehow connecting the students online—getting students and a faculty member on the Internet, talking to each other about the case. Students won't be so isolated in their different field sites; they will be able to learn from each other. Research suggests that case discussion is what makes this type of learning so powerful.

Harry: Wow, that sounds exciting. You're trying to get the best of both worlds—video on the computer, but then having people connect and talk about it from different locations.

Jean: That's right. You get the benefit of field experience but also some assurances that key learning experiences will be encountered and shared. That increases our confidence that they're all learning similar content. Not only would students have the lectures on-campus but they would stay connected throughout their field experiences.

Harry: It can get kind of isolated out there. Having some way to work together would be good.

PRELIMINARY ANALYSIS QUESTIONS

1. In small groups, complete a role-play exercise and finish the meeting. Delineate specific design ideas that would address the concerns of all parties, and satisfy the needs of the clerkship and the department.
2. Identify Sam's biases regarding this proposed new approach to pediatric education. Suggest strategies for dealing with these biases.
3. How should Jean deal with the chair's concerns as expressed in the meeting?
4. Develop a two-page outline responding to the grant proposal. Include in your proposed design five or more of the following concerns and how you will address them:
   - Dealing with file size, download time, video format, and integration of media
   - Getting access to the Web and technology throughout the state
   - Managing development cost, time, and resources
   - Encouraging high-quality reasoning, reflection, and defense of decisions
   - Encouraging collaboration, modeling, and exchange of ideas
   - Getting high resolution and realistic presentation of symptoms and problems
   - Enculturating students to fieldlike situations
   - Overcoming resistance from faculty members and students
   - Using the project as a springboard or basis for research

IMPLICATIONS FOR ID PRACTICE

1. Organizations, like people, have habits. These are the comfortable, established ways of doing things. Innovators and change agents often create tension within their working units by pushing for new goals, new methods, or both. What mistakes could innovators make if they were unaware of the political tensions arising from these different purposes and habits within the organization? What steps can innovators take to ease these tensions?
2. Innovations typically happen within the normal constraints of an organization—limited time, money, and expertise. Add to that list desire or will. In the face of these serious constraints, what "magic" has to happen for innovations to succeed? Draw on your own experience in addressing this question.
3. Think about cases in your experience of technology introduction, whether for learning or other objectives. Based on your experience and your reading, respond to the following questions:
   a. Organizations regularly go through significant changes—using new practices, adjusting to new requirements or competitive conditions, adopting new technologies. What can a work unit do to prepare itself for these inevitable changes? What can individuals do to help their unit successfully undergo a major change process?
   b. In many work groups, at least one or two members are critical of change and tend to resist a proposed innovation. Is there a positive role critics can play within the organization? What kind of decision-making processes can best include the critic's input in a positive, productive way?

c. Many innovations live or die depending on the energy and leadership of a few innovators. How can we come to depend less on the radical innovator and more on collective processes? Put another way, how can an organization get full value from its innovators by encouraging them, tapping their energy, while at the same time minimizing the trauma and chaos involved in many change efforts?

d. Some models of organizational change suggest that innovators and early adopters are motivated by different things than are resistors or reluctant users. If this were true, then how would you motivate and support each of these groups of individuals in a change process?

Diane King

BY RONNI HENDEL-GILLER
AND DONALD A. STEPICH

Diane King, a seasoned instructional designer with IDEAL Solutions, a performance consulting group, hung up the phone. Stan Smith, her client from the automotive insurance division of Delta Financial Group, had called to tell her that he would like her to design and develop training materials for team leaders ("leads") in the collections departments of Delta's branch offices.

BACKGROUND

About a month earlier, Diane had completed a course for Delta's phone representatives ("reps"), which covered issues associated with customer handling. The audience for this course had been reps who were new to Delta and had limited experience with collections work. These new reps needed to develop an approach to customers that was assertive without being aggressive and alienating. Most new reps had difficulty finding the right balance. This balance was needed to help customers find ways to bring their accounts current and to show them the importance of doing this.

Diane and her team developed a model for handling calls and designed a three-day course that helped participants achieve the desired balance in their calls through the use of this model. The "soft" skills required to support the model (listening skills, negotiation skills) were developed and practiced, using very specific role plays and case studies. Diane had been excited about the work she'd done—she had a great team of designers and knew the course was well designed. She had received great support from her subject matter experts (SMEs) and she knew that the course was built from a deep understanding of Delta's business challenges and priorities.

Early on in the project, however, Diane and Stan began to realize that the ultimate impact of the course would be limited. While new and recent hires were being trained to be appropriately assertive when handling calls, their colleagues and managers were not aware of what was included in the training. And, to make matters worse, most of the current supervisors and team leads had learned their jobs by trial and error. According to Diane's SMEs, the team leads and the more veteran reps were generally too aggressive or too passive with customers, which was one reason that Delta had a problem with delinquency. It was clear that the new reps would not be supported in implementing what they had learned in the course.

To complicate matters further, the team lead job was relatively new. Recently, the entire collections function had been redesigned and the team lead role established. The team leads had been promoted from the ranks of advanced reps. Now, instead of being responsible for handling the difficult calls themselves, their job was to coach and monitor a team of reps. A new system had been installed that tracked measures, such as call time. Until now, no tracking devices had been used. In addition, a call monitoring system was put in place that allowed team leads to record and listen to calls and provide feedback to reps. When the new systems were rolled out, Delta provided about two hours of systems training for the team leads, but no training was provided on how to use the data that the systems generated to give feedback to the reps.

Diane and Stan had asked to develop team lead training concurrently with the development of training for the reps. At the time, however, Stan had been unable to convince members of the operations group to make this investment. The rep training had already been budgeted, and the team lead training didn't fit into anyone's budget. The restructuring and new systems had been expensive, and there just wasn't any money left.

THE PRESENT PROBLEM

When Stan called to ask Diane to design a team lead course, they both almost had to laugh. Finally, the organization had realized that it had to start with the team leads. It was apparent, in every Delta branch, that the team leads were not performing their jobs as they had been defined. They were reluctant to give feedback to people who had only recently been their peers, they weren't sure how to use the data they received, and they didn't necessarily handle the calls in the most effective ways themselves. Most team leads had slipped back to their previous behaviors and were spending the majority of their time taking the hard calls and ignoring their leadership and management roles. Their supervisors were at a loss—they really weren't much better than the team leads at managing the new processes and tools. Most supervisors had minimal guidance, support, and training in their own roles as coaches and leaders.

Stan and Diane, although frustrated that it had taken this long, were excited that they finally had the opportunity to "do it right." They even hoped to include supervisors in the training process and start from the top down. At the same time, there were a number of challenges that would make this project difficult. Delta was now concerned about what was happening in its branches and had determined that this training was a high priority, meaning the timeline would be very aggressive. It needed to be deployed as soon as possible. Also, Delta had a minimal budget for this effort.

Stan understood that this meant that they'd need to find ways to speed up the ID process. IDEAL Solutions had previously prepared materials for Delta that were robust—participant guides that were graphically impressive and facilitator guides that were highly detailed. Diane knew that Stan would have trouble with any materials that were less than polished and with any approach that appeared to short-circuit the design process. IDEAL Solutions was known for the quality of its process and its deliverables. "Fast and cheap" was *not* its motto.

Nevertheless, Diane was not discouraged. She knew the work environment at Delta, had met with several team leads during the design of the customer rep training, and thought that she understood the organization's culture. She also knew that a quicker, less labor-intensive design process was something that IDEAL needed to develop. More and more clients were emphasizing speed, and more and more vendors were developing training to support organizational change initiatives that were being implemented at a rapid pace. If Diane could succeed with this project, she'd be helping IDEAL become more competitive in the marketplace, as well as helping her client meet its goals.

THE EXISTING ID PROCESS AT IDEAL

Diane decided to try to figure out ways to speed up the existing ID process at IDEAL and to reduce labor costs. The existing process consisted of the following steps:

1. A commitment to a thorough needs analysis: IDEAL told its client that analysis was key to training effectiveness and that a thorough analysis was critical. Typically, IDEAL spent three to four weeks conducting research, including interviews, focus groups, and surveys of the training audience. An assessment report was generated and discussed with clients before proceeding to the design phase.

2. Development of a detailed design plan with clear and well-defined performance objectives was a must. The timeline for design plan development was usually about two weeks (for a two-day workshop), with a week for client review and a full-day client review meeting. Another week was allotted for revision to the design plan and final sign-off on the design.

3. First-draft development was allotted about a month, with a full-time designer assigned to the project; Diane served as primary client contact and occasionally did some development herself. This included the development of participant and facilitator guides. Role plays and case studies were very detailed, incorporating specific work situations to ensure better transfer to the job. When necessary, the designer talked with SMEs to gather additional data.

4. The first draft review and pilot draft development usually took about three to four weeks and included walkthroughs of activities to gain formative feedback from SMEs, accuracy checks by SMEs, and the involvement of a desktop publishing team to develop a polished product for the pilot.

5. A pilot was held with a representative sample of end users. Once the pilot was held, about a month was allotted for pilot revisions and the production of the final materials.

Based on this process, a 2- to 3-day course, such as the team lead course, would take about 20 weeks or 5 months, from start to finish. In some cases, IDEAL could speed up the process by increasing manpower—which reduced the timeline but did not impact the cost of the project.

RAPID ID STRATEGIES

Diane had heard about rapid design and decided to do some research. She wanted to develop some strategies for reducing the time and cost of the design and development process while continuing to deliver training that would meet the needs of the learners and would achieve the desired organizational results. From her research, she learned that there were several key assumptions underlying traditional design and that many of these assumptions were being challenged by those suggesting rapid design strategies. Key assumptions included the following:

- All components of the design process are required to deliver a robust product.
- Design is a linear process, in which each component of the design model appears once and is not reconsidered unless revision is required.
- Effective design requires a commitment to the full execution of each component of the design process.
- Failure to complete a component of the design process will reduce the effectiveness of instruction.

Diane recognized that these assumptions were at the heart of IDEAL's design process and were assumptions that she herself had made in her work as an instructional designer. She also knew that these assumptions were often hard to live by. There had been times when she had tried to short-circuit the traditional design process and had often felt as though she were "cheating." She discovered that proponents of rapid design methods were challenging these traditional assumptions and suggesting new approaches and strategies. Some of the rapid design principles that Diane discovered included the following:

- A belief that instructional design is a nonlinear process and that there is no one right way to design. Different stages can be completed in tandem and then revisited in an iterative manner. Initial budget constraints can result in an initial set of lean materials, which can, if necessary or desired, be enhanced at a later stage.
- Analysis and design are thought of as a collaborative process. Designers work with key stakeholders to quickly complete the analysis and design work. The end user is often a key player in the design process, both contributing to the development of materials and testing prototype materials as they are developed and refined.
- Analysis is completed rapidly by making full use of extant data and by limiting the quantity of data collected with a limited but targeted analysis.
- Budget and time constraints are addressed by focusing on content and instructional strategy, rather than on level of production. Minimalist facilitator and participant materials can be developed—especially for an initial pilot. If necessary, these can be expanded and enriched at a later stage in the project.
- The use of participant input in the actual training session can eliminate some of the need to develop full-blown role-play and case-study scenarios. Sharing real issues and concerns in an action learning type of model, in which participants work with real issues and concerns, can reduce design time and increase value and relevance.

Using these strategies, Diane set out to define a project plan that would allow her to conduct the first training of the team leads within two months of the start of the project and, then, be able to train the rest of the team leads within two weeks after that.

PRELIMINARY ANALYSIS QUESTIONS

1. Review each step of IDEAL's instructional design process in light of the rapid design principles described in the case study. What suggestions can you make to speed up the process and reduce labor costs?
2. How receptive do you think Delta might be to these suggestions? What concerns or objections might be raised by the client? What might you do to sell your rapid design strategies to the client?
3. How can Diane ensure that the training she develops using a rapid design methodology is consistent with the quality for which IDEAL Solutions is known?

IMPLICATIONS FOR ID PRACTICE

1. In this case, the use of rapid design is important because of a request to speed up the process used to design and develop instructional products. What other factors might push instructional designers either toward or away from the use of rapid design?
2. What are the risks and benefits of a rapid design approach? In what kinds of situations would rapid design be most useful? Are there situations in which rapid design should be avoided?
3. How does using a rapid design approach change the knowledge and skills required of the designer?

Terry Kirkland

BY M. ELIZABETH HRABE, VALERIE A. LARSEN, AND MABLE B. KINZIE

"Needs analysis! Why should we want a needs analysis? We already know what we want to do!"

Five heads nodded in agreement as I looked around the table. I tried to read the expressions on the faces of the members of the Workplace Readiness Project Committee: irritation? speculation? boredom? hostility? This was my first meeting with the committee, and my hopes for it going well were rapidly collapsing.

I had been hired as an instructional designer, exactly one week before, by Dr. Jim Cranston, the new assistant superintendent for instruction and vocational services. The Dundee County school system had obtained a small grant for the development of a series of workshops that would introduce high school students to the workplace readiness skills most desired by employers. The workshops were intended to serve as a pilot project for later implementation in all three of the county high schools. The project had been "in committee" for a year and had never gotten off the ground, and the school board had made the decision to bring in an instructional designer to structure the plan and ensure its successful execution. Although this was only my second job as an instructional designer, Dr. Cranston seemed to like my ideas. "You haven't had any experience working with teachers," he cautioned toward the end of our interview, "so it will be important that you take command right away. I know you can do it." His confidence in me, and his enthusiasm for the undertaking, had been contagious. I left his office looking forward to working with this committee in creating an effective and dynamic design for instruction. Now I was not so sure.

MAY I SUGGEST . . . A NEEDS ASSESSMENT?

I arrived at Dundee High School in the afternoon to attend this first project meeting and learned from Mavis Barrett, the assistant principal, that Dr. Cranston had

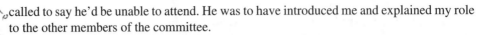

called to say he'd be unable to attend. He was to have introduced me and explained my role to the other members of the committee.

Mavis was pleasant enough but appeared harried by the constant interruptions and distractions that constitute much of the job of a front-line administrator. We had little time for coherent conversation, although she did manage to give me a brief description of the teachers I would be working with in creating and implementing the project.

Jane Pruitt, lead teacher in the business department, had been highly involved with trying to get the project off the ground the year before. The rest of the committee tended to defer to her knowledge of the proposed workshop content, the authority that came naturally with a dominating personality and her 25 years of experience in the trenches. Suzanne Fuentes, the English teacher, and Len Gold, social studies, were holdover members of the committee and supported the concept that all students would benefit from learning skills that would make them employable in the future. Finally, Dwight Harris, the technology education teacher, had been newly assigned to the committee this year. Although he and the others received a small stipend for the after-school work, he had been blunt in expressing his unhappiness at having been pressed into service.

When Mavis finally introduced me to the committee, I had the feeling that they were somewhat underwhelmed by my presence. They had only recently been told that an outside instructional designer was being brought in to design the workshops. Proving myself might be a little more difficult than I had anticipated.

Armed with the committee recommendations from the previous year, I had carefully prepared my presentation. I began by explaining that it would be necessary to begin the design process with a needs assessment. My announcement was greeted by a stony silence, which soon gave way to a litany of protests.

Jane was vehement. "Look, Terry, didn't they tell you when they hired you? We decided on the content for our school-to-job workshop last year. We are going to teach students how to write résumés and fill out applications. I have done a unit that includes these skills in my Intro to Business class every year, and I know exactly how to do it."

Suzanne added, "Also, I really don't think we have the time for such a thing. We're starting late as it is."

"Yeah," chimed in Dwight. "What the hell is a needs analysis, anyway? Sounds like a bunch of jargon!" He did not say more, but I could feel him thinking, "Is that what they're paying you for? Fancy words?"

"Whoa! Folks! Calm down." Mavis invoked her role as committee chair. "Don't bite our designer's head off. Remember, we have a mandate from above. The powers downtown think this is important and they have sent us help. Let's use it."

BLEEP! BLEEP! The chirp of Mavis's ever-present beeper punctuated her observation. "Sorry, gotta go," she said, rising. She shot me an apologetic smile and then addressed the others, "Seriously, give Terry a chance to explain." And she was out the door.

As I reluctantly turned back to face the lions, Len laughed. "Okay, Terry. Do your thing. We'll listen."

Grabbing the friendly invitation, I quickly explained the reasons for doing a needs analysis and the design process itself. As I warmed to my topic, the others seemed to be listening—with the exception of Jane, who sat, leaning back from the table with arms folded

across her chest. Even when the others agreed to my conducting a nee[...]
remained silent. She was not so passive when the meeting broke up[...]
loudly to Dwight, she swept out of the room, "Maybe if they had give[...]
used to hire this Kirkland person, we could have gotten this project g[...]

LATE NOVEMBER

Two weeks later, immediately following the Thanksgiving holiday, the project committee reconvened. I presented my findings:

"And so I think that we should reconsider the objectives for the workshop instruction. It seems clear that résumés and employment applications, though clearly important, are not what potential employers indicate they most want to see in their new employees."

Surveying my fellow committee members, I wondered how they felt about the needs analysis I had just presented. I felt confident that my report was comprehensive and the information accurate. Even though the results conflicted with the expectations of the group, I sensed a surge of interest in my assertion that the employers I interviewed had expressed a desire to see students develop skills in conflict management, cooperation with others, and problem solving. They had also laid great stress on the importance of a good attendance record.

Both Suzanne and Len agreed that these were important attitudes and skills for all of the students to possess, even those in the most academic advanced placement track. Jane, however, remained adamant, insisting that first impressions were most critical and that it was well-done applications, résumés, and job interviews that would get them the jobs they wanted.

BLEEP! Once again, Mavis was summoned from our midst.

"And there's another thing to consider, Terry," Jane continued, not missing a beat. "I know when my students can write good résumés and fill out applications properly. It's measurable. How can you measure such soft skills as 'cooperation' and 'managing conflict'?"

"Good point," I admitted. "Actually, there are two things to be considered here. First, we have asked representatives of the business community what they consider most important. They have responded, and, in good faith, we need to address their concerns—not substitute what we want simply because it is easier and more convenient for us. Besides, as it turns out, these are the same skills listed by employers in a national study commissioned by the Department of Labor." I showed them the latest SCANS report.[1] Recommendations included, in addition to basic academics, that students be prepared in critical thinking, problem solving, decision making, self-management, and responsibility.

"And, second, as far as evaluation is concerned," I continued hastily, since Jane seemed to have shut down momentarily, "we don't have to use pencil-and-paper tests to find out if students have developed these abilities."

"I use observation check-off lists and team evaluations with my classes now," added Dwight, suddenly thoughtful. "Those work pretty well."

---

[1]The Secretary's Commission on Achieving Necessary Skills. (1991). *What work requires of schools: A SCANS report for America 2000.* Washington, DC: U.S. Department of Labor.

"Yes," Len jumped in. "We can devise activities that will allow us to observe students using these skills in practice—role play, group task completion, things like that. And then, perhaps, we teachers could have follow-up discussions and class projects that would show how well their learning lasted over time."

For the next hour, we proceeded to hash out our major goals, objectives, and assessment possibilities in this manner. I could scarcely breathe when finally I asked, "Then, we're all agreed?" Everyone nodded in approval except Jane, whose impassive silence I decided to take for assent.

Our plans shaped up. We wanted to include all of the junior class in our workshop. Since there were approximately 180 students involved, we had to schedule the workshop to be repeated four times, with about 45 students attending each session. We agreed that each workshop would last for three hours, with morning and afternoon sessions repeated over two consecutive days. The workshop dates were set for March 4–5, and a note was written for Mavis to add these activities to the school calendar.

I spent the next few days developing the schedule of tasks and assignments we would have to complete to meet the March deadline (see Figure 21–1).

Develop Workshop Activities	
Create facilitator's guide	Terry, Suzanne, Len
Get resources, materials	Terry, Dwight
Design and produce program	Terry, Suzanne
Workshop Arrangements	
Arrange dates	Mavis
Arrange for room, equipment	Mavis, Dwight
Contact and train facilitator	Terry, Len
Contact guest speaker	Terry, Jane
Invite guests	Mavis, Suzanne
Evaluations	
Design formative evaluation	Terry
Set dates, arrange logistics	Jane
Arrange for facilitator (formative)	Jane
Select student sample	Jane
Carry out formative evaluation	Terry, Len, Suzanne
Write up results of formative evaluation	Terry
Make changes	Committee
Design workshop evaluation	Terry
Conduct evaluation	Terry, Len, Suzanne, Jane, Dwight
Write up results of workshop evaluation	Terry

FIGURE 21–1   Committee Tasks/Assignments

Since we had (nearly) unanimously agreed on the content and activities for our workshops, I went on to complete a design that incorporated our goals and objectives. Later, Len called to tell me he had secured Don McKay as our facilitator. Don, he assured me, had an outstanding reputation and was known to have a way with teenagers.

MID-FEBRUARY

On February 18, I was summoned to an emergency meeting of the project committee. A severe winter storm had shut down the school system for the past week, and that, together with several days missed in January, had really pushed back our work schedule on the workshop project. However, it was the undertone of worry in Mavis's voice when she called to schedule today's committee meeting that had set off a silent alarm bell in my head. What was the matter now?

As I rounded the corner of the corridor that led to the small conference room where the committee met, I could hear the murmur of conversation. I recognized Jane's voice rising discordantly above the others. "I'm telling you, she doesn't know what she's doing. I've heard that she's had only one other job before this. If you ask me, this is going to be a disaster and who will they blame? Little Miss Fix-it will be long gone. It's us, that's who!"

I hesitated before entering the room. I recognized how imperative it was to demonstrate decisive leadership so that the committee would continue to believe in this project. I decided a positive attitude might help to counter Jane's negativity.

Everyone was there, except Mavis, who was closeted with an angry parent. Len waved hello and Dwight shouted, "Well, hello, Ms. Designer! Guess what? We've got a problem. Sorry, make that problems!"

Suzanne, who had been huddled over a paper with Jane, looked up and said, "Hi, Terry. I'm afraid Dwight's right about the problems." Her face betrayed worry and her greeting was tentative.

"Hey, guys," I said, assuming as bright a smile as I could muster, "we're the A-team here. There's no problem we can't handle!"

As it turned out, the first difficulty was easy enough to deal with. In spite of my memo, Mavis had scheduled activities that conflicted with our first workshop session. The school's calendar was jammed, and the only other available time was an afternoon three days sooner. "Terry, are you sure we can do this?" asked Suzanne.

I was calm and reassuring. "Yes, of course. But we really have to get cracking."

The other problem was somewhat more complicated. Jane had not been able to round up a representative sample of students and a willing facilitator for the formative evaluation. "Oh, you know how kids are, they've always got too much to do. Besides, you've done such a superior job at designing your workshop, I'm sure it's just perfect. There's nothing to get all bent out of shape about."

I wanted to bend Jane out of shape, but I bit my tongue. She remained on the committee after her own plans for the workshops had been overruled, but her contributions were casual at best.

"Well, actually, we really do need a formative evaluation of our materials and procedures. We have to know what works and what does not," I addressed the rest of the group, ignoring Jane. "This is a really important project, and a lot of people are invested in it. You all know that."

"I have an idea," offered Len. "My second-period history class would be a good test for the workshop."

"Oh, yeah. Your remedials!" This from Dwight.

"Not all of them. But, certainly, some are," Len continued, his enthusiasm beginning to grow. "These kids are a hard audience. You really have to sell them. If they don't like something, they are not polite about letting you know. They would give us a real shakedown cruise."

Dwight remained somewhat dubious, but Suzanne and Jane were warming to the idea. After all, with little more than a week before our first scheduled workshop, what else could we do? It was, therefore, agreed to use Len's class for the formative evaluation, with Len himself acting as facilitator.

CONDUCTING THE FORMATIVE EVALUATION

The formative evaluation session took place in Len's classroom, February 23–25. I hadn't realized it before, but he was a master teacher. He came alive in a roomful of kids. Perhaps some people considered these kids remedial and at-risk, but they clearly loved being in this class.

No doubt about it, the workshop hummed under Len's capable delivery. The students responded well and clearly benefited from the concepts presented in just the ways we had planned. It couldn't have gone better. I wished Suzanne had been there. She'd sent me a note saying she had to beg off to take care of some other things that had come up unexpectedly. Since Dwight and Jane were not free during second period, I had to carry out the evaluation by myself. The results were so good (see Figure 21–2), however, that with just a few minor changes in presentation order and the reformatting of two overheads, we had it!

I was really beginning to get excited about this. In spite of all my initial doubts, perhaps my first school-based instructional design was going to work! I even looked forward to our workshop presentation next week.

MARCH 1, 3:15 P.M.

Finally, after months of work, our first workshop was grinding to a close. I had been watching the clock for the past half hour and I knew that I was not the only one.

The strawberry blonde girl in the seat in front of me was loud in her complaints to her seatmate, "Man, this is so-o-o boring! Why have they got us in this meeting when we're going on to college? What we need to know is how to do well on the SATs and write the best essay on the admission form. Not this junk!"

Her friend returned, "Oh, it wasn't that bad. Got us out of the witch's class, anyway. But I guess you're right. I need to get a job this summer. I hear Mrs. Pruitt's students at least do job applications and all that stuff."

"Are You Ready?" A Workplace Readiness Workshop – Formative Evaluation Results

Dates: February 23–25   **Time**: 2nd Period   **Facilitator**: Len Gold

The purpose of the formative evaluation was to provide an assessment of the effectiveness of workshop activities in producing gains in student learning outcomes. The pilot workshop was presented over a three-day period, 50 minutes per day.

Goal: Students will be able to describe and demonstrate interpersonal communications skills suitable for the workplace.

Learning Outcomes:

Students will be able to:

- Describe the principles of teamwork
- Work as a team to solve a problem
- State steps the team used to solve the problem
- State different roles people assumed within the group
- Recognize personal contributions to group process

Students will be able to:

- Determine a process that can be used to resolve conflicts with others
- List steps in conflict resolution
- Practice listening and speaking skills used in conflict resolution
- Practice mediating a conflict

Workshop Activities:

Part 1 Problem Solving Activities and Teamwork Evaluation
The 28 students in Len Gold's class were divided into five groups of 5 and 6 students each. All teams satisfactorily resolved the problem-solving tasks that included completing 3 stations: Crossing the Alligator River, Knots, Survival in the Desert

Part 2 Conflict Resolution
All students participated in role-playing activities both as mediator and disputants. Seventy-eight percent of the students could list all the steps in conflict resolution process.

(continued)

FIGURE 21–2 Terry's Field Notes

Part 3 Guest Speaker

This section of the workshop was not presented during the pilot due to time limitations. These students will attend the formal workshop in March and will hear this presentation at that time.

Part 4 Overall Workshop Assessment

Results from Student Evaluation Form

A Likert Scale was used with ratings from 1 (Strongly Disagree) to 4 (Strongly Agree). The average rating for each question is given below:

	$n = 28$
Overall, I thought the workshop provided useful information that will help me in my future work.	3.55
The activities held my interest.	3.63
The workshop was well organized.	3.76
I think that this workshop will be helpful to other students.	3.76

Summary of Responses to Open Ended Questions:

(Note: Student responses are reproduced in their own language and spelling.)

1. Please comment on the different sections of the Workshop. Which part of the Workshop did you like the best and why?

A majority of students (73.2%) selected the group problem-solving activities as the one they liked best. Almost all students said that they enjoyed these activities. Comments:

- "Way cool"
- "Let's do this all of the time"
- "This is gooffy, but OK"
- "I wish all of my classes could be like yours, Mr. Gold"
- "Dum"

The conflict resolution portion of the workshop was seen as valuable by a majority (83%) of the students, with 5.6% listing it as the most important. Comments:

- "I need to medate with Calvin and Veronica so they will leave me alone."
- "Its OK. Maybe we can help stops the fights"
- "Dummer."
- "We need to know how to get along better."

FIGURE 21–2 *Continued*

---

2. Do you have suggestions for improving the workshop?

Comments were largely positive, suggesting that most students felt that the workshop was all right the way it was. Comments:

- "Good work, Gold. No changes."
- "Let's have the workshop during my business accounting class."
- "Have food."

Recommendations

1. Redo the overheads giving the expert's solution to the Survival in the Desert. Use larger type. Use fewer lines per page.

2. Change the order of the activities in the problem-solving section. Put the Survival in the Desert activity between the Alligator River and Knots (the two-out-of seat activities)

FIGURE 21–2   *Continued*

Looking around the room, I could see that students were doodling, passing notes, and looking out the windows. Several had their heads on their desks.

Mercifully, the final bell rang, signaling the conclusion of the school day. The students didn't wait to be dismissed. They took off in a stampede for the doors. The facilitator, Don McKay, caught my eye and shrugged. Well, I knew he wasn't to blame.

The difference between this and the formative workshop run in Len's class was like night and day. Why had so many things gone wrong?

PRELIMINARY ANALYSIS QUESTIONS

1. What were important issues for each of the workshop project committee members? How might a designer in Terry's position get cooperation from the committee and support from the administration?

2. Terry's needs assessment was strong in describing the input from employers. What other stakeholders might have been consulted? How might their ideas have differed from the authorities Terry cited? What ramifications might this have had on the outcome of the case?

3. In what ways might the formative evaluation in this case be seen as problematic? What events led to these difficulties? What possible outcomes may have resulted?

4. At the conclusion of the case, Terry thinks, "Why did so many things go wrong?" Knowing what you know about the needs assessment, the formative evaluation, and Terry's management style, suggest the kinds of things that might have gone wrong.

5. There are three more workshops due for presentation within a matter of days. List ways in which the situation can be improved to assure that these workshops are more effective in achieving their objectives.

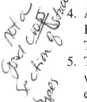

IMPLICATIONS FOR ID PRACTICE

1. List ways to ensure that all stakeholders have been included in a needs assessment.
2. Describe effective strategies for encouraging positive participation from all stakeholders.
3. Describe ways to carry out an in-depth contextual analysis.
4. Describe ways to conduct useful formative evaluations under imperfect field conditions.

Haley Lawrence

BY DIANE EHRLICH

Over the past seven years, Kadence Communications (KC) has been one of Haley Lawrence's major clients. Her expertise is in health care, and she consults as an instructional designer for sales training and management development projects. She recently returned from a national sales meeting in Arizona and was looking forward to a well-deserved break when her phone rang. She listened to a request from Bob Williams, the account executive she usually works for at Kadence Communications. He explained that KC had been asked to develop sales training for GNA Healthcare, a major player in the highly competitive managed care field. He wanted Haley to fly out to a meeting this Friday, September 12.

Haley agreed and Bob faxed her a list of GNA people recently brought together by corporate headquarters to spearhead a major training effort (see Figure 22–1).

The meeting was hectic, and Haley was busy asking questions and taking notes. On the flight home, she reviewed her notes and highlighted the following information:

GNA is committed to training. Brought team into corporate headquarters to spearhead training effort.

Currently, 450 sales representatives and 40 district managers. Plan to expand sales force when new product is launched.

Formal two-week training program in place, but 90% of the existing program deals with product knowledge and sales.

Existing training materials include chunks of skills (e.g., one hour on active listening). Doesn't seem to be a coherent, logical design. Lots of paper—little structure. Looks like everyone put in his or her pet ideas. Lynn Katz (current trainer) does not seem to have bought into the need for improving training.

James Sumida wants to design and develop a three-day sales training workshop for GNA. He wants to use video, audio, and print materials. Doesn't have an extensive budget and isn't quite sure what things cost.

GNA wants the material ASAP but has allotted about three months for the project to be designed and developed.

SEP 09 '01   **11:17 AM**   **Kadence Communications**   **P.1**

Fax Transmittal Cover Sheet

To: Haley Lawrence
From: Bob Williams
FAX Number: (555) 788-5483
Date: Tues., September 9, 2001 11:17 A.M.

Transmitting two (2) pages, including cover sheet. If there is any difficulty with this transmission, please call (555) 788-5484.

Note:
Haley: Here is the GNA list we talked about. Good luck on Friday!

- James Sumida, VP of Human Resources, has been with GNA as a district manager for 10 years but has only been VP for 6 months. He has final project approval, since training comes out of his budget. Sumida has worked with KC on other projects. This is a high-visibility project—has been given top priority by the president.

- Lynn Katz, currently trains new district managers in the field. She has been with GNA 6 years and taught English prior to that. GNA feels that her teaching experience qualifies her as a trainer, even though she has no experience in sales.

- Larry Paulsen, has been with the company for 20 years and is considered an expert in managed care.

Not expected at the meeting but who will be involved in the project, is

- Carol Califano, a new training specialist, who will not start until November. Although she has strong presentation and facilitation skills, she has little knowledge of how to design instruction. She received a President Club Award for District Sales Manager of the Year three years ago.

FIGURE 22–1   Fax Outlining GNA Project Team

James wanted the sales force to have ownership in any new training initiatives and had already assembled a task force made up of regional managers. The task force had been asked to generate ideas for training needs and had produced a list of desired content. However, James failed to mention either the task force or the list discussing content during the meeting with Haley. Two days later, Haley was surprised to receive a fax, detailing the content developed by the task force (see Figure 22–2).

Haley quickly called James to clarify the project. She had questions about various items on the list, but her primary concern was the amount of information GNA wanted cov-

---

INTERPERSONAL SKILLS

External-internal customer relationships; treating customers as business partners; working with different customer personality types; working as part of a sales team; understanding one's own style; looking at sales from a "total office call perspective"; developing new relationships for the future; observation skills; listening skills versus a "how to pounce" attitude; continuity and stages of a sales call; coaching

SATISFYING CUSTOMER NEEDS

Listening; probing; pre-call planning/post-call analysis; "selling the sizzle"; value-added; benefits orientation

TARGETING KEY CUSTOMERS

Using data to identify key customers; case studies; 20/80 rule; paradigm shifting for customer base

STRATEGIC SALES

Service; formularies; selling as a process; tailoring to the customer; positioning products; rewards

PLANNING

Time management; electronic data support

FIGURE 22–2 Content Outline

ered. James assured her that this was a wish list for all GNA's training needs, and she breathed a sigh of relief. GNA wished to develop a *series* of training sessions but planned to start with the one on building customer relationships. This sounded better to Haley; however, the list of material was endless and she realized she needed not only to define terms but also to learn more about the organization. She wasn't sure what a "total office call" was, and she had questions about the existing program.

James assured her that she could rely on Carol Califano when she came on board in November, and he suggested that she call Lynn in the meantime so they could get started on the project. Lynn thought that the training in the field worked well and wasn't sure why James and Carol were redesigning what she did. She mentioned that her training had been well received and resented outsiders intervening on her turf. Haley reassured Lynn that field training would still be an important part of the process, but they were looking to make the training more consistent. Haley thanked Lynn for her help and told her that she would be in touch with her later.

Based on her visit to GNA headquarters and her subsequent telephone conversations with James, Haley suggested that the following content should be included in the *Building Customer Relationships* module: quality relationships, personal interaction styles, active listening, and observation. James listened to her suggestions and agreed that the topics sounded good. Haley wanted to develop a design document, and James thought that was fine, but he also suggested that Haley come back to GNA headquarters because they were going to conduct a sales training the following week. Although she thought her time might be more efficiently used, she recognized the advantages of seeing a current sales training session and agreed to attend.

When Haley got to GNA, she sat through several hours of training on GNA's major new product initiative. She had a 15-minute meeting with James, and he mentioned that he was reading a book he'd like to see incorporated in the training: Covey's *Seven Habits of Highly Effective People.* She had already noticed that, when James addressed the group, he had overheads made from this book and recommended it to the group. He also referred to a book on consultative selling. Haley also noticed that only about half of the audience knew this book; the other half looked confused.

Haley questioned him later about the book, and he mentioned that part of the original group had gone through training on this consultative sales model. When she asked for the title of the book, James provided it. However, he didn't think she needed to read it—he thought she should just start designing the program because time was short. She also noticed several effective role plays that were part of the training, and James mentioned that GNA videotaped and reviewed these "clinics" during each of their training sessions. He requested that similar videotaped role plays be included in the proposed training. Haley thought that was an excellent idea from an instructional point of view but expressed concern about cost.

On the flight home, she listed several concerns she had with the project. She decided to discuss these with James during their next telephone call, but, after two days, he still had not called. He had left on a two-week vacation. Carol mentioned that James was out of town and that Carol was in charge. Haley asked if she could send a design document to Carol for review (see Figure 22–3). Carol thought the design document looked fine and told Haley to go ahead with the units.

Three days later, Haley sent a copy of the unit on active listening to Carol for review. Although it was only 15 pages, Haley wanted to see if the format would work for the other units in this module on interpersonal skills. Carol agreed to review the materials but told Haley that she might not get to it until the following week.

With less than five weeks before the training was to be presented, time was increasingly becoming an issue. Haley continued writing the unit on observation skills without either Carol's or James's feedback on the previous unit. She then sent the second unit to both and waited a few days before calling. James thought it was great. Carol sent a few pages with grammatical changes but said she liked the format. James sent copies to Lynn, Larry Paulsen, and three other people to review. Each had suggested changes—some minor, some major. Lynn had major concerns about the whole approach to teaching observation skills. She also questioned the decision to have role play as the primary method of teaching lis-

Objective	Materials	Time
Participants will define what a quality relationship is from their own perspective.	Worksheet Flip chart	20 minutes
Participants will learn how others define a quality relationship.	Print and video	1 hour
Participants will identify their personal styles.	Personality profile Worksheets Discussion	1.5–1.75 hours, including debriefing
Participants will demonstrate active listening skills.	Role play	1 hour, including debriefing
Participants will demonstrate their ability to be perceptive observers.	Observation model exercise	45 minutes

FIGURE 22–3 Module 1: Building Customer Relationships

tening skills. Larry didn't like many of the self-assessment questions in the unit on observation skills. Tim Anderson, who had been part of the task force of district managers, liked the questions but thought they should be formatted differently.

Haley became increasingly frustrated and decided it was time to set up another meeting with the team. This time Larry, Carol, Lynn, and James were all there. Haley presented an overview of the project and mentioned that they had only four weeks before the first sales school. She suggested that they do a run-through in two weeks, so that any changes could be made. At this point, James brought up the idea of the video again and asked who in Haley's group could produce a video. Haley mentioned that production costs would be at least twice what it would cost to produce in-house and suggested that they use their own video department. She suggested using their own people, instead of actors, as experts on how to sell to further reduce costs.

Haley and James disagreed as to the number of sales representatives to be interviewed and who they would be. He asked whom she was planning to interview, and she suggested a cross section of reps, in rural and urban territories, as well as both newer and experienced reps, so that they all would have buy-in to the quality relationship idea. James and Carol eventually agreed on five people and then found a sixth. Haley and James also disagreed on how the tape should be used during the training. Haley suggested they table that discussion until after they saw the tape. James agreed.

A week later, he called Haley and suggested she come to their home office and see the tape. Given the limited budget available for the project, she was surprised at the suggestion of another trip to view the videotape. She suggested that they send a copy of the tape to her and pointed out that they would save money on her plane fare, and her time could be better spent finishing up the last two modules. James assented.

When Haley viewed the tape, she suggested condensing it. James proposed that the group meet. She suggested a conference call. The videotape was not part of their original contract, and she was concerned about the amount of time and attention this was taking from the original project agreement. After a phone discussion, the group finally eliminated one of the interviews and edited one of the interviews and some of the interview questions. James seemed content with the video.

There was only one week left before the project deadline, and Haley had yet to receive comments on the final two units. She spoke to both James and Carol; neither seemed to see the urgency. They weren't too concerned until she discussed the consequences of making last-minute changes. They decided to have the material copied by their copy center and sent out. Haley was relieved not to have to worry about making and shipping copies.

The night before the project, James was still making changes. Haley was upset but had been in the consulting business long enough to know that was par for the course. She suggested that, instead of running off the 500 copies he had wanted, they print only enough copies for the pilot sales class, in case they needed to make changes. She would spend the three days at GNA with a colleague, evaluating the program and discussing its effectiveness with participants. Although reluctant at first, James agreed.

During the pilot, some of the trainers didn't follow the schedule because they didn't seem to know how to limit the discussion. Haley made careful notes on how to target the discussions so that the program could be adapted and still fit within the allotted time. The pilot test provided a lot of information, and the team decided to meet and make one last set of revisions before duplicating an entire set of materials. At that meeting, James looked at Haley and suggested that they start on the second module. She said she was interested in continuing to work with the group but she had several concerns.

PRELIMINARY ANALYSIS QUESTIONS

1. What are the major problems in this situation, from Haley's point of view? How could Haley have avoided these problems?
2. Discuss Haley's performance as a consultant. If you were at the first meeting with the client, what advice would you have given her as to how to proceed?
3. Discuss Haley's performance as a designer. Using any instructional design (ID) model of your choice, describe how she addressed the various elements of the design process.
4. What suggestions do you have for Haley, now that the client wishes to move on to the next stage of the project?

IMPLICATIONS FOR ID PRACTICE

1. What information might an instructional designer need to decide if the scope of an ID project is realistic and achievable?
2. What strategies can an instructional designer use in dealing with a client who is constantly changing the scope of a project?
3. How can an instructional designer educate a client as to what designing instruction involves without using too much instructional design terminology?

REFERENCE

Covey, S. R. (1989). *The seven habits of highly effective people.* New York: Simon & Schuster.

Ricardo Martinez

BY PATTI SHANK

Georgina Bates, a respected professor of human resource development at West-ern College, sat at her desk, checking student e-mails, and sighed. She was be-coming increasingly concerned and anxious about the frustrated tone of these and previous student e-mails. Students in her graduate-level online course, *HRD 512: Organizational Psychology,* did not seem to be getting the hang of learning online, and they had just completed week 6 of the 12-week course. She expected a little confusion at first, as many of the students had never taken an online course before. Her close colleague, Dr. Ben Wu, who had taught in the school's online MBA program for 2 years, promised her that the students would soon get the hang of it, even though there was often some confusion at first. She grabbed her phone and put in a call to Ben. "I'm upset and it's all your fault!" she yelled into the phone. "Good day to you, too, Georgina," answered Ben. "What's up?" Georgina sighed. "Ben, you said my students would be getting the hang of learning online after a few weeks, but it's been 6 weeks and that's clearly not happening." "What exactly is the problem?" Ben asked. "Geesh, Ben, if I knew, I wouldn't be calling you!" she exclaimed. Ben offered, "How about I come over around 2:00 and we look at it together?" "Yes, please," she answered.

BACKGROUND

Previously, all human resource development (HRD) courses had been in-person, on-campus. In the past year, some department faculty members discussed using Internet technologies in their courses in response to directives from Western's president. He had publicly declared his desire to provide more technology-based and technology-enhanced courses in order to keep up with other higher educa-tion institutions. Additionally, many graduate students complained about having to come to campus two or three nights a week, and student travel could easily be reduced through online or hybrid (online/in-person) courses.

Georgina saw the value of using technology in the HRD program. She believed that using technology was a necessary skill for students and faculty and was frustrated with faculty resistance to the idea, so she offered to teach HRD 512 online. She expected that her successes would help the more reluctant faculty members in her department consider online or at least hybrid courses. The pressure to succeed was high.

Georgina had dabbled in website development using *FrontPage*™ and she found the development of her course website only slightly more complicated than the development of the small personal site she had developed a few months earlier. The biggest difference, to her, was that the course website had far more pages. The authoring, though, seemed much the same.

Students in the graduate HRD program usually got to know each other pretty well, as they often attended classes together in somewhat of a lockstep fashion. For most of them, HRD 512 was their first experience with an online course. Despite some anxiety, many felt positively about giving the new format a try.

Georgina's courses had always been popular. She typically received extremely high student evaluations and was known by students to be a hard but excellent teacher. Even though some students were nervous about the new course format and expectations, they were excited about the course and the benefit of not having to drive to class. Georgina explained in an introductory e-mail to the class that she had very high expectations around online participation, the use and evaluation of online learning materials, and online discussion.

2:15 P.M.

Ben read through a few student e-mails that Georgina had displayed on her computer screen. "These *are* troublesome," he admitted (see Figures 23–1, 23–2, and 23–3).

Subject: Re: interview assignment

Arial | 10 |

Dr. B: Huh? I didn't know I was supposed to do an interview. Where does it say this? Do I have to do it over?

Sharonn

Georgina Bates wrote:

> **Sharonn,**
>
> **Your opening description was excellent. Good description of the factors involved.**
> **Question: You did online research rather than an interview, per the directions. Why?**

FIGURE 23–1   E-mail from Sharonn Concerning an Assignment

Subject: Re: assignment due

Dear Dr. Bates,

The paper was due yesterday? I didn't see a due date posted so I thought it was open ended. I'll work on it this weekend. I hope you aren't going to take off points for it being late...

Kent

Georgina Bates wrote:

> **Kent,**
>
> **I haven't received the paper that was due yesterday. Please advise.**

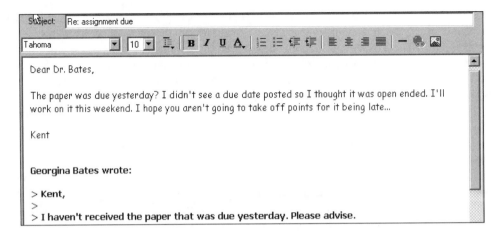

FIGURE 23–2 E-mail from Kent About the Assignment Due Date

Subject: Re: participation in discussions

Dr. B - Where is it? The discussion thing, I mean.

R.

Georgina Bates wrote:

> **Rodney,**
>
> **I notice that you haven't been participating in the online discussion and are wondering**

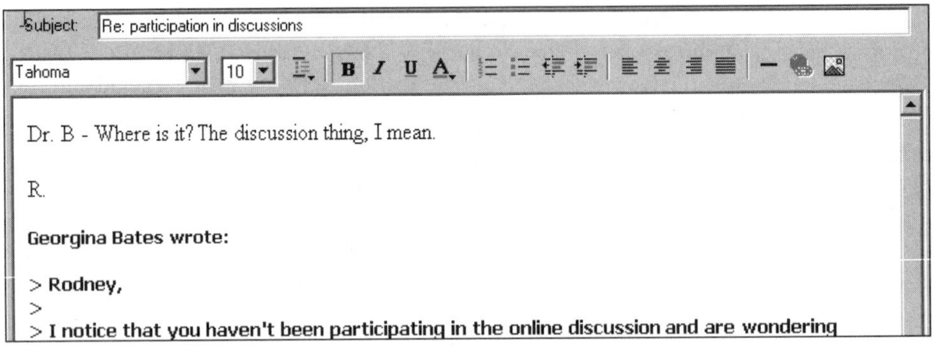

FIGURE 23–3 E-mail from Rodney About the Discussion Forum

"These folks sound confused," Ben declared. "I know I had some difficulties with students feeling confused the first few times I taught online. Maybe that's your problem here. Didn't you just have mid-semester evaluations? Are other students confused?" Georgina showed him the list of comments from the recent mid-semester evaluations (see Figure 23–4).

"Look, I'm an expert in finance but I'm certainly no expert in developing online courses, so I got help when I started to see problems," said Ben. "I guess I figured I could do this myself, since I know how to use *FrontPage*™," she answered. Ben put his hand on Georgina's shoulder and said, "I think this is a pretty specialized skill, and even a reasonably tech-savvy person like you might not know all the ins and outs. It can't hurt to get some advice from someone who designs and develops online courses for a living, right?" He recommended that she meet with the instructional designer he worked with at the business school.

Georgina wondered aloud if she should just forget teaching online to avoid these kinds of problems and potential embarrassment. Ben assured her that she just needed some help

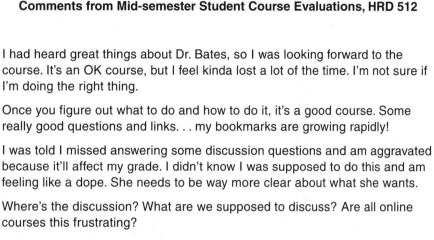

Comments from Mid-semester Student Course Evaluations, HRD 512

I had heard great things about Dr. Bates, so I was looking forward to the course. It's an OK course, but I feel kinda lost a lot of the time. I'm not sure if I'm doing the right thing.

Once you figure out what to do and how to do it, it's a good course. Some really good questions and links. . . my bookmarks are growing rapidly!

I was told I missed answering some discussion questions and am aggravated because it'll affect my grade. I didn't know I was supposed to do this and am feeling like a dope. She needs to be way more clear about what she wants.

Where's the discussion? What are we supposed to discuss? Are all online courses this frustrating?

Dr. Bates needs to tell us what she wants for the assignments. I thought I was doing the right thing but I wasn't. Discouraging.

When is the final project due? Do you want assignments emailed to you or brought to your office?

Once I found everything I was fine, but it wasn't clear where to find instructions for the assignments.

Help! Too hard to take this course online! Can we meet in person?

Great topics. A little hard to follow at times.

FIGURE 23–4   Mid-semester Course Evaluation Comments

tweaking the course in order to make it great. Georgina wasn't so sure but agreed to meet with Ricardo Martinez, an instructional designer and web developer for the business school, if Ben could arrange it. She was feeling somewhat frantic and hoped that Ricardo could meet with her soon.

4:40 P.M. RICARDO'S OFFICE

Ricardo was in his office, troubleshooting a *JavaScript*™ quiz he had developed for one of the school's marketing courses. He wanted to make sure it worked right before he left for the day. Ricardo had been working for Western's business school for almost 2½ years. After graduating from the online master's program in instructional technology, he was hired just after Western decided to build an online MBA program. Although he could make more money working in corporate training, he found that his laid-back style fit better in an academic setting. He especially enjoyed working with the faculty.

Ben peeked around the corner and saw Ricardo hard at work in his office. "Hey, Ricardo! I'll buy you two boxes of your favorite milano cookies if you'll share some of your amazing insight about online course development with my friend, Georgina Bates. She really needs your help." Ricardo agreed. "And I will *definitely* take you up on the cookies!" he chuckled.

NEXT DAY, 11 A.M.

"Ricardo, I really appreciate your willingness to help me," said Georgina. "Dr. Wu has sung your praises, and I'm hoping you can help me figure out how to fix my problem." "Glad to help. Dr. Wu told me a little about what's going on," replied Ricardo. "Sounds as if both you and the students in your course are pretty frustrated. Tell me more about the problem." Georgina showed Ricardo the e-mails from students and a list of problems she had compiled (see Figure 23–5).

"Yep, looks like frustration alright," commented Ricardo. "Let's take a look at your course, OK?" he asked. Georgina brought up the course homepage on Ricardo's computer (see Figure 23–6).

"Let me get a feel for how students actually take the course, OK?" Ricardo asked. Georgina nodded her head in agreement. Ricardo clicked on the link for Week 2 and pulled up the Week 2 page (see Figure 23–7).

Problems with HRD 512

1. Some students aren't regularly participating in online discussions. When I e-mail them to find out why not, the most common reply is "What discussions?"

2. I'm chasing after too many students who haven't handed in assignments on time. Some students complain that they didn't know when they were due. Due dates are listed on the site!!!

3. Some of the assignments that are completed on time do not match the criteria specified for the assignment. Some students have complained that they don't know what I want them to do.

4. Students continually e-mail me with questions that are answered in the online course materials.

5. I need to look for a new job. :-(

FIGURE 23–5   List of Course Problems Compiled by Georgina

HRD 512: Organizational Psychology

Welcome to HRD 512! This course provides a survey of organizational psychology and will help you gain knowledge and skills in a variety of important areas, including motivation, group dynamics, organizational communications, and organizational culture.

Click on these links to get more information about the course:

- Introduction to the course
- Readings
- Week 1
- Week 2
- Weeks 3–4
- Weeks 5–6
- Weeks 7–8
- Weeks 9–10
- Week 11
- Week 12
- Slides

E-mail me with questions

FIGURE 23–6 Homepage for HRD 512

Motivation and Attitudes

This week we'll begin by asking. . .what makes people do the things they do? Pretty big question. Take a look at the slides for this week and see what a number of experts have to say about this question. Then check out the following websites for additional information:

Motivation and the workplace (make sure to check out the audio interviews. . .they're good!)
Systems thinking about workplace problems
Making sense out of chaos

This week's discussion questions:

1. Think about people you work with (or have worked with). Use the slides and this week's readings to consider why people sometimes appear to behave in ways that seem counterproductive. Provide some examples and insights.
2. What's the difference between intrinsic and extrinsic motivation? Why is this distinction important?
3. What recommendations would you make in your organization to use the information gained in the slides, websites, and readings?

Search for and post one additional resource related to this week's topic in the discussion area.

E-mail me with questions

FIGURE 23–7 Week 2 Course Materials Page

"Dr. Bates, if I'm a student in your course and it's Week 2, is everything I need to do for Week 2 here?" Ricardo asked. "No, my slides for the week are available on the "Slides" page, which is accessed from the homepage," she explained. She went back to the homepage and clicked on the link to the "Slides" page to show him how the slides for each week were accessed (see Figure 23–8).

"Any place else students need to go other than the Week 2 link and the "Slides" link?" asks Ricardo. "Hmm," Georgina thought for a moment. "They should go to the readings link, too—that's also available from the homepage." She returned to the homepage and clicked on the link to the "Readings" page. "And," she added, "they get to our course discussion forum from the "Readings" page, too" (see Figure 23–9).

With Georgina's help, Ricardo checked out the materials for the other weeks and saw that they were all accessed the same way: a general page that started off the week, readings listed on the "Readings" page (and a link to the discussion area), and *PowerPoint* slides accessed from the "Slides" page. "I'm thinking that students just aren't finding the information they need," explained Ricardo. "Does this hunch make sense, given what you're experiencing?" Georgina asked, "It's all there on the site, isn't it?" Ricardo clarified, "It's there, but, in my line of work, we assume that, if the learner can't find it, it really *isn't* there." Georgina considered his statement and then nodded her head in agreement.

Ricardo then asked Georgina to show him where the information that Sharonn and Kent needed was located. Georgina went back to the homepage and clicked on the "Introduction to the Course" page. "Here's where they find detailed assignment instructions and due dates," she said, pointing to the link to the "Assignment Instructions" page (see Figure 23–10).

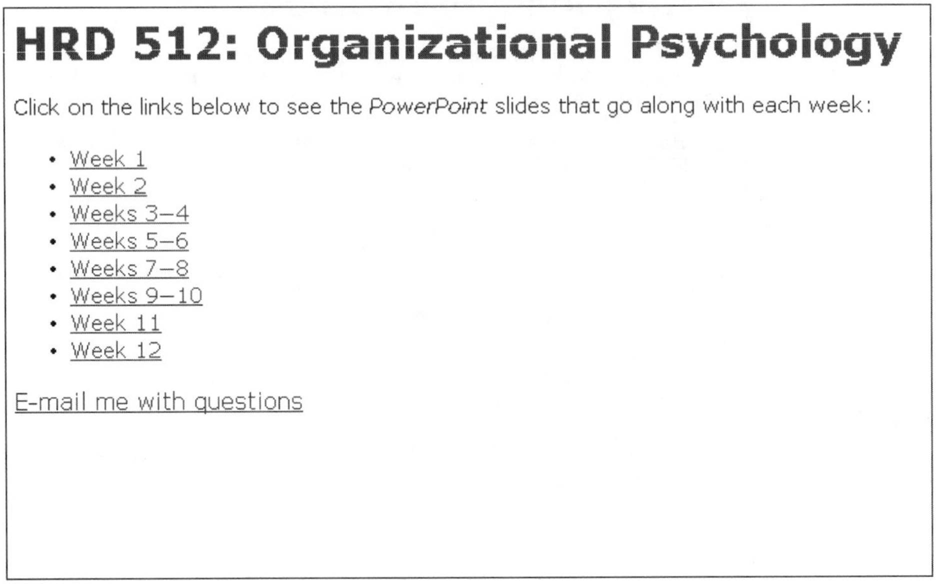

HRD 512: Organizational Psychology

Click on the links below to see the *PowerPoint* slides that go along with each week:

- Week 1
- Week 2
- Weeks 3—4
- Weeks 5—6
- Weeks 7—8
- Weeks 9—10
- Week 11
- Week 12

E-mail me with questions

FIGURE 23–8   "Slides" Page

HRD 512: Organizational Psychology

Below are the readings from your text for each week of the course.

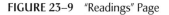
Go to the discussion forum

Week	Reading	Focus questions
Week 1	Bradley and Moore, introduction and chapter 1	• What are the most critical organizational issues in organizations today? • How urgent are these issues? • Compare these issues to the issues of the mid 20th century. What has changed? Why?
Week 2	Bradley and Moore, chapters 2, 4 Tomlinson, pp. 15–45	• What does motivation mean? • How do the authors recommend that you think about intrinsic and extrinsic motivation? • What understanding does Tomlinson want you to have regarding the Cole case?
Weeks 3–4	Bradley and Moore, chapters 3, 5 Tomlinson, pp. 46–112	• In what ways are cooperation and conflict alike? • What were the main issues in the Ferana case?

FIGURE 23–9   "Readings" Page

HRD 512: Introduction to the Course

The following information will help you gain the most from this course.

Welcome!

This three-credit course is a survey of the field of organizational psychology. We will cover theory and application in the following areas: work attitudes and motivation, group dynamics, organizational communication, organizational structure, and organizational culture. I want students to actively participate and highly encourage you to interact with me and your classmates in the discussion area.

Course Structure

Each week starts on Sunday and ends on Saturday. You'll notice that sometimes two weeks are together, on the same topic. Each week (or double week), we will have readings from the text, online activities, and *PowerPoint* slides. We will discuss these items in the discussion forum.

Assignments

Click here to get information about each of the assignments, including a rubric for completion and due dates.

All assignments are due on or before the due dates unless alternate arrangements have been made beforehand.

FIGURE 23–10   "Introduction to the Course" Page

"I think we can take some of the frustration out of this for both you and your students, Dr. Bates," Ricardo suggested. "Let's make a flowchart of how your site currently works, and then we can determine what arrangement might work better, OK?"

PRELIMINARY ANALYSIS QUESTIONS

1. What is causing the frustrations Georgina and her students are facing?
2. Develop a flowchart of Georgina's site as it currently exists. Develop another flowchart with your recommendations of how to solve the current problems.
3. What other improvements would you recommend for the existing pages in order to decrease student frustration?
4. If you were Ricardo, how would you work with Georgina to fix these problems?
5. What options are available for salvaging this course at this point? Which course of action do you recommend?

IMPLICATIONS FOR ID PRACTICE

1. Discuss the impact of interface and information design on the usability of online courses.
2. How can problems such as those that arose in this course be averted in the development of online course materials?
   a. How can instructional designers work with faculty members to address these issues?
   b. What overall guidelines might you provide to the faculty to avert these problems?
3. Develop a set of guidelines to help the faculty address the issues of interface and information design.

Austin McGwire and Ken Casey

BY I. ANDREW TEASDALE
AND SEAN R. TANGNEY

Brian Joseph, manager of a newly restructured engineering department in a major manufacturing company, initiated a request to his company's training department for a new course. Brian's department was charged with building large dies for manufacturing-formed sheet metal. The dies range in cost from $1 to $3 million. The training was intended to update the die engineers on information they needed to perform their jobs, to provide guidelines for keeping projects on time and within budget, and to provide recommendations for managing projects that had time or cost overruns. There were two principal reasons for Brian's request. First, the restructuring had caused a significant change to the department's tools, people, and processes. Second, several projects managed in his department had significantly overrun their allotted budgets. Brian had identified some causes for these overruns and wanted to present solutions to the cost overrun problems.

Austin McGwire worked in the training department and was the lead designer assigned to the project. The training department had traditionally focused on developing classroom training. Now the management of the company was encouraging "e-business" (i.e., using the company's intranet and the Internet to make work processes more efficient); Austin was charged with integrating web-based components into interventions developed by the training department. The plan was that Austin would have primary responsibility for the instructional design as well as contribute to interface and content design. Ken Casey would be the developer for this project. His principal role in the project would be to develop all paper-based and online materials. Ken had experience developing classroom-based courses but was new to web-based development. He was completing his master's degree in training and development and was contracted to the manufacturing company from an outside firm that specialized in training.

WEEK 1

Ken and Austin learned about Brian's training request from their director who wanted an intervention that would implement some of the corporation's e-learning initiatives (the corporation seemed enamored with anything "e"). These initiatives included a push to reduce the amount of class time by delivering content asynchronously over the company's intranet as well as a move toward blended approaches—interventions that combined classroom-based instruction with other delivery methods, such as intranet-based and videotaped delivery. The director had scheduled a strategy meeting for the following week between representatives from the training and engineering departments to sketch out a rough plan for the intervention.

WEEK 2

The meeting consisted of Austin, Ken, Brian, and three subject matter experts (SMEs) from Brian's department: a program timing expert, responsible for overseeing the events and deliverables associated with the various stages of the die development process; an investment report expert, responsible for managing the spreadsheet that tracks spending on a project; and a part management system expert, responsible for tracking various parts in a die.

In the meeting, Brian agreed to an intervention that blended classroom-based instruction with an intranet-based performance support system. The classroom portion would serve dual purposes: (1) provide instruction on the new tools and processes and (2) introduce course participants to the performance support system to which they would have access on the job. The performance support system would have all the content necessary for the course, plus additional information that could be accessed back on the job as needed.

Austin and Ken pressed for access to the die engineers to conduct a preliminary needs analysis and to identify a few engineers who could become part of the development team. Brian's response was that, essentially, he already knew what they would say and that their participation would not add any value to the project. He also added that there weren't any engineers who had time to participate. Ken and Austin emphasized that the intervention would be successful only if it addressed actual needs. Brian assured them he knew what the engineers needed and commented, "The process is new to many in our organization, and we need to tell them how to do their jobs."

Ken and Austin feared that there were other factors, not related to a lack of knowledge or skill, that were significantly impacting the performance of Brian's department. For example, Ken asked Brian what an engineer should do if he or she learned that a project was exceeding its budget. Brian's response was, "Manage the project better." When pressed for more detail, Brian responded that he would deal with project management issues elsewhere.

Ken and Austin expressed other concerns during the meeting. Foremost was their concern about Brian's aggressive project timeline. He wanted an intervention ready several weeks earlier than they had estimated would be possible. They told Brian they could meet the deadline he proposed only if a strict schedule were developed for Brian's team to deliver content and if the team adhered to the proposed schedule. Brian assured them that this would happen.

Ken and Austin also had additional timeline issues, which they did not express in the meeting. They were concerned that the timeline didn't allow for technology problems that could be expected to surface with an innovative (for their company) approach that included a web-based component. In addition, they were concerned that Ken, an untested designer/web developer, would not have ramp-up time to learn web technology. Finally, they were concerned that the nature of the development environment would cause too many delays in transferring information among members of the team. As a contract employee, Ken did not have access to the company intranet and would have to rely on other team members to shuttle information back and forth between Brian and his team.

Given the short project timeline, Austin suggested that the development team use a rapid prototyping approach to designing the intervention. Brian, Ken, and Austin had agreed that weekly meetings would be necessary to review the progress, and this meeting schedule appeared to Austin to be a perfect scenario for rapid prototyping. In addition, Austin believed that a rapid prototyping approach would have two significant advantages. First, it would reduce the risk of spending time on a design that was not satisfactory to the client, since the client would have the opportunity to review the design each week. Second, rapid prototyping would allow the client to be more involved in the design, leading to a corresponding feeling of ownership in the intervention.

WEEK 3

Austin was beginning to think about the project in terms of the two main components: design and content. He believed that both parts would evolve as the project continued, with a heavier emphasis on design toward the project's start and more attention to content as the project progressed. Ken and Austin were working on the design of the classroom instruction as well as the design of the performance support system.

Ken had already roughed out a prototype of the performance support system organized around timelines, tools, and supporting information (see Figure 24–1). The timeline sections ("Program Timing" and "Event-Based Procedures") were intended to help the learners understand project flow, key milestones, and the deliverables. The tool sections ("Investment Report" and "Part Management System") were designed to provide information on using the tools necessary to perform project tasks. The supporting information section included a FAQ (frequently asked questions) page and course outline. In the weekly meeting, Brian reacted enthusiastically to the preliminary design, making suggestions on how content could fit within the different areas. The discussion around the performance support system occupied nearly all the allotted time, so not much was said about the classroom component.

WEEK 4

Austin and Ken both brought laptops running the performance support system to the weekly meetings. Austin displayed the performance support system and led the presentation. Ken also had a copy of the performance support system on his laptop. As changes and suggestions were

FIGURE 24-1   Preliminary Design for the Main Page of the Performance Support System

made, Ken made updates on the fly. At breaks and when conversation shifted to noncontent discussions, Ken provided Austin with the updated content, allowing the meeting to continue with the changes already active. In addition, they audiotaped each meeting. The tapes proved to be very useful in developing the participant guide for the classroom component.

Austin and Ken experienced some unexpected benefits of their approach. Due to the time pressures on the project, they never made the effort to fully develop a content document and accepted the risk of some possible gaps in the content because of this lack of attention. As the project progressed, they realized that the performance support system was functioning as a pseudo-content document. In the weekly meetings, the review of the performance support system provided a structure for identifying missing content and refining the existing content. When missing content was identified, assignments were given to the various SMEs. They provided the content to Austin; then he entered it into the performance support system for the following meeting. Ken also added a button to the main page of the performance support system: "Brian Click Here." Since the performance support system was available on the company's intranet, Ken was able to place preliminary designs for Brian to review. This allowed Ken and Brian to communicate about ideas between the weekly meetings, so the initial work on the design of the performance support system was, in some respects, analogous to framing a content document.

WEEK 5

By week 5, the excitement of the initial project launch had faded. In the initial strategy meeting, Brian committed his people to provide content quickly to Austin and Ken. Now, however, already late on delivering the content they had promised, Brian and his team were beginning to realize the scope of their commitment. During the previous week's meeting, Ken and Austin reemphasized that, considering the aggressive timeline, they could not be responsible for identifying and gathering content and that a late delivery of content would postpone the course pilot and the roll-out of the performance support tool.

In this week's meeting, Brian acknowledged that the initial project timeline was unrealistic and that the project timeline would slip (i.e., the course pilot date would have to be pushed back). Austin and Ken were both relieved. Both had suspected a slip in the timeline, but allowing Brian to come to that realization on his own worked much better than Austin or Ken telling him. Ken whispered to Austin later in the meeting, "We just need to be sure that we aren't the cause of any delays later in the project!"

Even with the delays in getting content, the development of the performance support system was moving along fairly smoothly. Ken was becoming much more comfortable with the web development and graphics software. He hadn't had the opportunity to take formal classes on using the software but had learned from experience and a never-ending flow of questions to other web developers in his building. Ken's technical prowess was improving, but he had to deal with other problems somewhat out of his control. Because he was a contract employee, he did not have access to the company intranet and had to receive messages by way of other team members who were employees of the company. For example, once Ken learned that someone had sent content to a co-worker (usually, the content was sent as an attachment to an e-mail message) he needed to figure out a way to get the information from his co-worker's computer to his own. If the file was under 1.44 MB, he could save it on a disk and transfer it to his own computer. However, if the file was larger than 1.44 MB (which was commonly the case, due to *PowerPoint*™ files with large graphics), he had to either compact the file or resend the e-mail message to one of the other employees in his building with both access to the company intranet and a larger-capacity drive. The transferring of data was very cumbersome in this organization.

Ken and Austin left the weekly meeting feeling a little better. They were waiting on the SMEs to provide the needed content. The performance support system was reviewed and Brian was happy with the progress. The performance support system was functional, but it still lacked a great deal of content.

WEEK 6

From a development perspective, this week was very productive. Ken and Austin made some changes to the performance support system that considerably enhanced its usability. One enhancement was a new method for navigating. Ken and Austin browsed the Internet for a few hours and considered ideas from other sites. In the previous version, users had to navigate to the main menu (review Figure 24–1) to get from one area of the performance support system to another.

FIGURE 24–2   The Redesigned Navigation Bar

Based upon designs they saw on the Internet, Ken and Austin created a navigation bar, which appeared on most pages. The navigation bar contained tabs which allowed the user to navigate from one area to another with one click (see Figure 24–2). The framework for the performance support tool was nearing completion, but there remained considerable content gaps.

This week's meeting took a slightly different tone. The SMEs had been slow in providing information to Ken, and the delivery deadline was again pushed back. In addition, for the first time, Brian began trimming the material he wanted to include in the performance support system and in the classroom instruction.

Ken and Austin were comfortable with the changes in the timeline. After all, this only made their work easier, allowing more time for design, for changes, and for Ken to learn the technology. However, the reduction in scope that took place this week was troublesome. Austin and Ken were already worried that they might not be addressing the real (or complete) problem. Now that the scope had been reduced, they became even more concerned that the intervention would not address the problem that Brian presented initially.

WEEK 7

Several times during the meeting this week, Austin displayed content that was not the current version, and Brian expressed some frustration. Somewhere in the process of getting content from the SMEs to Ken, there had been problems, and either Ken didn't get the proper version or something unknown had happened. Ken realized that they were too informal in defining how they wanted content sent to him. In their after-meeting debrief, Ken and Austin decided that on the next project they would be sure to develop a process for communicating content and make that process explicit to their client(s). They even went as far as to rough out a spreadsheet they would use to track content as it moved through the development process.

Nevertheless, the performance support system was functioning well, and the gaps in content were being filled. The classroom component was nearing completion and would be ready on time. Ken and Austin tested the performance support system on the computers in the classroom. There were a few small problems, which were quickly corrected. Brian was pleased with the progress. This week, he admitted that he initially had some serious reservations about the performance support system, but now he believed that it would provide real benefit.

WEEK BEFORE PILOT

In the meeting this week, the team decided that Ken would drive the performance support system during the pilot (i.e., run the computer that is projected to the front of the classroom). Brian would be the instructor for the pilot. He wanted to personally gauge the reaction of the audience he had selected. He also wanted to answer any questions and determine the changes to be made for the subsequent classes. Brian was comfortable with the content, and, given the circumstances, Ken and Austin were satisfied with the design.

Somewhat surprisingly, Ken and Austin were not in a panic over last-minute technology problems. Early in the development, they had put together an implementation plan and had identified most of the areas needing attention. They had tested the support tool in the classroom before the pilot, and it had worked as designed. They even went as far as to create a CD-ROM version of the performance support system to load onto individual computers in the classroom in the event that the company's intranet was not functional.

PILOT

The pilot was two months later than Brian initially desired and, interestingly enough, precisely when Ken and Austin predicted. Brian was frustrated with the delay but recognized the source of the problem. The pilot went well. The technology worked flawlessly. The only problem was that Austin forgot to put together an evaluation form for the participants. The training department had a standard evaluation form, but Austin wanted to target some specific areas dealing with the performance support system. He hastily created an evaluation form (with no time for testing) and had it ready on time. However, the evaluation form suffered from the lack of testing and refinement. Austin made a mental note to be sure to add an evaluation section to his implementation plan and to review his implementation document more regularly in future projects.

Twenty students registered for the pilot (many were handpicked). The pilot was held in a computer classroom, each student with his or her own computer. Ken drove the performance support system during the pilot and encountered only one glitch (a bad hyperlink). With Ken driving, Brian was free to elaborate and move somewhat at will in response to questions and other feedback from the audience. The design of the performance support system was such that Ken had no problem keeping up with unscripted changes in course flow. Most content could be accessed with three mouse clicks.

While Ken was driving, Austin was surreptitiously observing the audience and their interaction with the support tool. Several people refused to touch the computer. They gave their full attention to Brian and viewed the content as Ken displayed it. The majority followed Ken's lead and clicked through the content on their own computers. A few spent a portion of the class exploring the entire site (not paying much attention to Brian's lecture). Austin noted that the elements that seemed to generate the most interest were the support tool's visual areas: graphic representations of the major processes.

The class participants' responses to the performance support system were, for the most part, what Ken and Austin had expected. However, they were surprised that some refused to touch the computer. The results from the smile sheet evaluation forms (a series of questions about the classroom experience) placed this course on par with other courses. The questions on Austin's supplemental form specifically addressed the performance support system and its future applicability to their work. The responses were favorable but not outstanding. Several participants wrote that the tool should not be used in lieu of a paper-based guide.

Brian was satisfied with the intervention. He felt the pilot went well and enjoyed the discussion the class generated. He had several recommendations for improvements, which he promised to send to Ken within a few days.

SIX MONTHS LATER

Things were quiet, too quiet. The classroom instruction was going well. Every other week, 20 students took the course. The evaluations remained consistent with other courses hosted by the training department. The performance support system continued to serve its purpose in the course. The course instructor had only positive things to say about the performance support system, and all of the links were still working. The course instructor had received some feedback from students that there had been some process changes that need to be reflected in the support system. He promised to assemble the suggestions and forward them in a few weeks.

However, the feedback from the instructor was the only feedback Ken and Austin were receiving. There had not been any requests for additional information. There had been no requests for clarifications or corrections. Austin suspected one of two things might have been happening. Either the performance support system was designed so well that it was functioning perfectly, or no one was using it. He suspected the latter. Without the ability to speak with the engineers, Austin and Ken had worried that the intervention would have little value. The lack of response to the performance support system seemed to confirm their fears. The silence was almost deafening. A spider web is as good as a cable if no load is placed upon it—and they feared there was no load on the performance support system.

PRELIMINARY ANALYSIS QUESTIONS

1. Early in the project, the instructional design team was denied access to the target audience. What would you do in that situation? If you had the choice, would you have continued with the project? Why or why not?
2. Ken and Austin were concerned about Brian's aggressive timeline. Placing the responsibility for meeting the deadlines on Brian worked, in their case. How might they have handled the situation differently?
3. As Ken and Austin realized the project timeline was going to change, what might they have done differently?
4. Austin found some class participants unwilling to use a computer in a learning situation. What are some strategies he could have used to help those in the target audience who were not comfortable learning from computers?

IMPLICATIONS FOR ID PRACTICE

1. Ken and Austin were asked to provide a blended intervention: one that combined classroom instruction with a web-based component. What do you think would be important in designing such an intervention?
2. Ken and Austin used a new (for them) instructional design approach in this project. What might be the benefits and drawbacks to trying new approaches?
3. Often, people or organizations see a need for training only after a problem has been identified—often with a need to have the training completed immediately. How might ID practice be made quicker and more responsive to customer demands in such situations?
4. Many companies now outsource their training and training development to companies that specialize in training and e-learning. Ken found some disadvantages to his situation as a contract employee because his client had not provided sufficient technology support for his activities. What do you think are some of the benefits of outsourcing training? What might be some drawbacks?
5. If you were asked to implement a new technology in a training intervention, what would you do to ensure a smooth transition to using the technology?

Clare Morris

BY JOANNA C. DUNLAP

Clare Morris stared at the television screen, shaking her head. Feeling an overwhelming need to verify what she had just seen, she rewound the videotape and pressed "play" again. There was no question about it. She made notes on her pad, indicating what could be salvaged and what could not. Unfortunately, many of the segments would have to be reshot—field shots at that! She tried not to think about how much time and money had been wasted. She also tried to control her anger: Why hadn't Mark followed her directions? The content of that day's footage had been clearly defined, scripted, and storyboarded to avoid this very problem. She finished writing her notes, ejected the videotape, shut down the equipment, and walked out of the editing suite.

BACKGROUND

Clare is the instructional designer for the distance learning program at Clarkstone University. Clarkstone's distance learning courses are designed to provide professional, working adults with a more convenient way of completing undergraduate and graduate degrees. All of Clarkstone's distance learning courses have an asynchronous broadcast/video component. Because Clarkstone does not have in-house video production facilities, Clare contracts video producers, equipment, and facilities from local television stations and video production houses. Her responsibilities include working with content experts to design the video content, scripting and storyboarding all video segments, and managing the overall production process.

Clare's first project at Clarkstone, nine months earlier, was a videotape component for a senior capstone course offered through Clarkstone University's distance learning programs in business administration, computer science, and elementary education. The video needed to present the requirements for a senior project, demonstrate the necessary steps, and provide real examples of senior capstone projects from three recent graduates—one from each major. The business administration graduate was a stockbroker, whose senior project involved the development of an expert system that helped him create electronic portfolios for clients. The computer science student owned his own desktop publishing company and had developed a technical manual and website for a client's new telecommunications product. The elementary education student was a third-grade elementary school teacher. For her senior project, she developed a miniaturized model of the "perfect" classroom-based learning environment for young students, complete with teacher, students, furniture, and computer equipment, which she used to demonstrate how the classroom would be set up and used. After editing these segments and finalizing the other elements, Clare previewed the video and believed that she had accomplished the project's goal: to create a video that could be used by all three distance learning programs. However, when she showed it to an audience of Clarkstone's program faculty, the associate dean jumped out of her chair and exclaimed, "We can't show this! It makes it look as if men work on computers and women play with dolls!" Clare hadn't even seen the footage as potentially gender-biased until that moment. To fix the problem, she interviewed another business administration student who had developed an electronic performance support system for her company and added the new segment to the video. It was a costly lesson, and Clare vowed to be more sensitive to how things can be interpreted, especially when they are committed to video.

THE CURRENT PROJECT

Currently, among other things, Clare was working on the video courseware for an undergraduate accounting course that would be used by the business administration distance learning program. Because most of Clarkstone's business administration students were not planning to pursue careers in accounting, Clare, in consultation with the accounting faculty, decided to present the accounting material within the context of how project managers, marketing and sales managers, and operations/production managers use accounting information to make and support business decisions. By placing this information within these types of authentic activities, it was expected that it would be more relevant to the learners. Therefore, each lesson was designed to begin with a day in the life of a real company to illustrate how accounting information helps businesspeople make day-to-day and long-term strategic decisions; the company would help establish instructional relevancy by showing students how accounting information is used to make business decisions in the real world. Real cases and scenarios would also take advantage of the strengths of the medium—realism, demonstration, attention getting—and avoid the dreaded "talking head" mode often typical of instructional video delivery.

Luckily, one of the accounting professors working on the project had a friend who owned a company called The Gemstone Puppet Theater. The company, owned by successful entrepreneur Jill Boyd, designed custom-made puppets for retail and ran a puppet theater, with weekly performances. Jill also took the puppet theater on the road, doing shows for schools, libraries, and special events. Her company had recently incorporated; a building was purchased to house the puppet theater, and five people had been hired to help with puppet designs and theater productions. This put The Gemstone Puppet Theater in a perfect position to demonstrate how accounting information is used to make business decisions.

With the course content mapped out and The Gemstone Puppet Theater lined up, Clare needed to select the video producer and production facilities. The facilities were easy—she had established an ongoing partnership with one of the local public television stations and was always happy with its work. A producer was more difficult; she was currently working on multiple projects and really needed a producer who could work autonomously and follow her scripts and storyboards to the letter. When she told the station's production coordinator that she still hadn't lined up a producer, he recommended a well-known producer—Mark Alexander—who had done a lot of documentary work for PBS. In fact, Mark had produced three award-winning documentaries for PBS, and his list of accomplishments filled Clare with confidence. And, as it turned out, Mark was very interested in expanding his video production work into the educational market. Clare met with him right away, and a contract was negotiated and signed.

During their initial planning meetings, Clare was struck by Mark's enthusiasm and commitment to doing a good job. When Clare walked him through the scripts and storyboards for the video segments, he was forthcoming with video, graphic, and audio production techniques that would improve the video by gaining and holding viewers' attention and interest: animation, upbeat music, multiple cutaways, multiple camera angles, and humor. In awe of his accomplishments and extensive production experience, and in order not to stifle his enthusiasm or creativity, Clare neither agreed nor disagreed with his suggestions. Instead, she reiterated the importance of taking into consideration the demographics of the target audience (adult working professionals), the importance of the course content, and the need to portray The Gemstone Puppet Theater scenarios as authentically and professionally as possible.

On the first day of field shooting at The Gemstone Puppet Theater, Clare was scheduled to work on another project and therefore was not able to go on the field shoot with Mark, so, before her scheduled planning meeting with him the following morning, she went to the station to view the previous day's footage. Included with the waiting videotape was a note from him:

Clare—

The shoot went great! Jill and the rest of the Puppet Theater staff were so easy to work with, and the puppets really added a lot of splash to the shots. I'm really excited about getting your feedback on the work so far. I think this is some of my best work! I think you'll be really surprised at how well it's turned out. See you at 8:30!

Mark

Clare inserted the videotape and pressed "play." The introductory footage of Jill Boyd and her staff at the theater looked great: It showed them working on a production line and building puppets, working on sets in the theater, and putting on a puppet show in front of a live audience. Next, Clare examined the footage of Jill's various financial dilemmas, which highlighted how accounting information is used to help make good decisions. The first segment was supposed to show Jill working on an inventory problem. Instead of showing her thinking aloud about how much it was costing her to stock various materials for puppet construction, she was shown conferring with Conroy the Coyote—one of her puppets. To top it off, the puppet was actually giving her advice! Although it was creative and made the scene more colorful, it was anything but professional or authentic; in fact, it took away from the authenticity of Jill's inventory dilemma and nullified the reason for using a real company. It also made light of her dilemma and her company. Clare couldn't help but reflect on the similarities between Jill's getting financial advice from a puppet and the elementary education graduate "playing with dolls." Hoping that Conroy was featured in only this one scene, Clare fast-forwarded through the rest of the tape. Unfortunately, Conroy played an active, advisory role in every scene. Clare reviewed the footage and took notes. Looking at her watch, she realized she had an hour to figure out how to communicate, clearly and constructively, her requirements to Mark without interrupting the flow of production or bruising his creative ego.

PRELIMINARY ANALYSIS QUESTIONS

1. How could some of the problems in this case have been avoided?
2. Given the differences in Clare's and Mark's ideas about "authentic experiences," how can Clare gain buy-in from Mark for her ideas?
3. What are the strengths and weaknesses of the use of Conroy the Coyote? Under what conditions would the use of Conroy the Coyote be instructionally effective?
4. When planning and carrying out future projects, what strategies should Clare use to avoid these types of misunderstandings with production personnel—producers, graphic artists, computer programmers, and so on?

IMPLICATIONS FOR ID PRACTICE

1. Discuss the relationship between front-end analysis and instructional strategy selection.
2. Recommend appropriate instructional techniques for adult learners.
3. Identify appropriate instructional strategies when using video as an instructional medium.
4. Discuss the instructional value and limitations of using video to depict highly authentic settings and problem situations for instructional purposes.
5. Suggest strategies that an ID manager can use to optimize the quality of work produced by project developers.

Catherine Nelson

BY LINDA LOHR AND LAURA SUMMERS

Insulware, a major manufacturing company, had awarded Instructional Media Solutions (IMS) a contract to redesign a two-day instructor-led course for online delivery. As part of the contract, IMS was asked to convert supervisory skills training to web-based instruction for Insulware supervisors worldwide. Because this first course conversion was successful, a bigger contract between IMS and Insulware had been awarded to develop an entire web-based university for 66 Insulware facilities.

The lead instructional designer for the Insulware project was Catherine Nelson, a confident young woman in her mid-thirties, who was one of the five managing partners of IMS and one of the company's four vice presidents (see Figure 26–1). However, Catherine wondered if IMS would actually be able to fulfill the bigger contract. Although IMS had completed the project successfully, the entire development of the first Insulware course was fraught with internal problems. Catherine thought back through the project history.

EARLY APRIL

At the start of the project, Catherine was full of positive thoughts regarding her work at IMS. Though long-term job security wasn't a given in a start-up multimedia learning company like IMS, the excitement of potential success more than made up for the risk of working there. Every day was new and exciting. Catherine remembered the thrill of walking into the conference room when Carlos Martinez, the chief operating officer (COO) and project manager for the Insulware project; Dan Layton, the computer programmer; and she, had first met Patricia Morrison, the Insulware training director. The room was bright and cheerful and the mood relaxed. Dan was wearing jeans and had his feet propped up on the edge of a nearby bookcase. Catherine and Carlos were dressed in casual business attire.

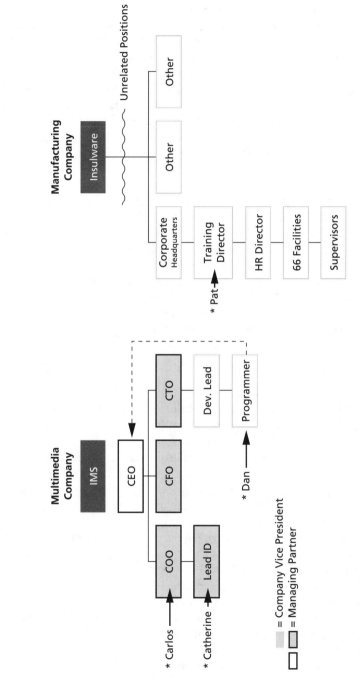

Manufacturing Company

Insulware

Unrelated Positions

Other | Other

Corporate Headquarters

Training Director
* Pat

HR Director

66 Facilities

Supervisors

Multimedia Company

IMS

CEO

COO | CFO | CTO

Lead ID

Dev. Lead

Programmer

* Dan

* Carlos

* Catherine

= Company Vice President
= Managing Partner

FIGURE 26–1   Organizational Flowchart

When Carlos introduced Pat, Catherine stood up and extended a courteous handshake. Dan simply nodded his head to acknowledge Pat. At the time, Catherine was mildly annoyed at this subtle disrespect toward Pat, but she was too interested in the project to think much about Dan's behavior. As she reminisced, though, she realized his behavior was a red flag that should have alerted her to problems ahead.

Prior to the meeting that day, Dan had sneered when Catherine mentioned one of her classes in her Ph.D. program in instructional technology. Dan commented, "In our field, education doesn't mean a thing—it's what you can do that counts. I was self-taught; I didn't need a Ph.D." Catherine thought that the way he said "Ph.D." mocked her and her efforts.

Dan's confidence was somewhat understandable; his father was the CEO, and at the age of 23, he had just been offered a six-figure salary to join another highly successful technical company in the Pacific Northwest. Everyone, Catherine included, didn't want Dan to leave IMS, so the company let him get away with behaviors that wouldn't have been tolerated from others. Dan believed that his technical skills gave him the right to be condescending and often rude.

There were other red flags that day as well. Carlos started the meeting with his usual charismatic flair. He put everyone at ease and had a magnetism that made people feel confident in his abilities. He passed out a tentative project schedule, listing major dates and deliverables. He mentioned to Pat that he didn't want unnecessary detail to clutter their first meeting, since the objective of the meeting that day was to discuss the big picture and to make sure that the overall goals for the project were identified. He assured Pat that she could expect to see a comprehensive project plan sometime the following week. The red flag, Catherine thought now, was the lack of detail in the project plan. Looking back, Catherine now realized that she, Dan, and Pat never did receive a more detailed project plan.

The final red flag was Pat's attitude toward any type of instructional analysis. "I just want you to put our existing training online. You really don't need to change the training much. It should be easy; everything is right here," she said, pointing to a stack of training manuals. "Besides, I don't want to go over budget here. We need to keep the costs of this project down. I'm really concerned about that," she added with emphasis.

Catherine persuaded Pat to consider a front-end analysis of the existing training. "Pat, we want to give Insulware a high-quality learning experience. We try to shape your training to fit the needs of your learners and the special requirements of web-delivered instruction. Although your training is probably very good now, we will try to discover if we need to add new information or change any of the existing information. I'll be able to do that by visiting some of your facilities to talk with the very people who will be using this training."

Pat hesitated, clearly not excited by this news. She responded, "I really doubt you'll find much need for any visits. This training has been very successful in the past. Besides, it is important for me to keep costs down."

"Well," Catherine responded with a warm smile, "you have already paid for the site visits. It was part of our contract, so that shouldn't be a problem."

Pat half-heartedly agreed to go ahead with the site visits. "OK, I'll set those up for you next week," she said, making a note in her calendar.

ONE WEEK LATER

A short time later, Catherine stopped Carlos in the hall. She was concerned with the aggressive deadline shared in the initial projected plan. She wanted to check out how he had arrived at his deliverable dates.

"Based on my calculations, Carlos, a 150:1 development ratio has been used to estimate the time it will take to create and test the Insulware training," she said. When Carlos looked confused, she added, "You know, 150 hours of development time for every hour of deliverable instruction. In my experience, I've found a 300:1 ratio to be more realistic."

Carlos motioned Catherine into his office and asked her to take a seat. "I know it is probably not realistic, but I really wanted us to get the Insulware business, so I bid low. If we do a good job on this project, we are almost assured of many more projects in the future. We essentially use this to get our foot in the door. In a way, you can consider it a marketing expense."

"I understand," Catherine responded hesitantly, thinking that she would be the one putting in the extra hours. The next four months would be long ones for her. "I'm just wondering if we could call a meeting and talk about what needs to be done in order to work efficiently with the time we have."

Carlos smiled at Catherine and said, "Catherine, you didn't get our communication award for nothing. Why don't you set up the meeting?" he suggested.

After jotting down several dates that worked for her and Carlos, Catherine entered Dan's office to ask him to identify the dates that would work for him. Dan replied, without looking up from his book, "Just e-mail them to me." However, Dan never returned the e-mail, so Catherine met only with Carlos. During that meeting, they created a rough schedule designating deliverables for the site visits, the design document, and the storyboards. Catherine remembers thinking that Dan's lack of communication wouldn't hold her up for a while at least.

MID-APRIL

Catherine had been excited about being the lead instructional designer for this critical project because it would finally prove to Dan that she really knew what she was talking about and that her education was an asset to the company. Dan commented frequently on the futility of her degrees in instructional technology. Just last week, he told her at the water fountain, "If I had more education, I would be laughed at by my co-workers."

In mid-April, Catherine traveled to Insulware headquarters to meet with Pat. After waiting in the lobby for a few minutes, Pat appeared behind the security-glass doors. She wore a navy blue suit and briskly walked down the narrow hall to her office overlooking the city. Catherine listened to Pat talk about the 100-year history of the company. In a male-dominated industry, Pat felt lucky to be one of nine women at the corporate managerial level. Pat had visited the installation facilities often and knew most of the managers, who had been in the company since high school.

Catherine's first site visit would be to Miami, Oklahoma, a small agricultural and manufacturing community in the northeast corner of the state, where she would visit three installation facilities. It was decided that Catherine would meet with the human resources assistant, who would drive her to the different plants to see operations and to meet with six selected front-line supervisors. The goal of the trip was to gather enough data for the design document. Catherine expressed her concern, "Will one day of interviews be enough?" Pat assured her that the three plants in Oklahoma would provide the best representation of the 66 facilities and that one trip would be adequate for Catherine's analysis. "Use this material. Everything you need is right here." Pat handed Catherine the two large binders of current instructor-led training that she referred to in their first meeting at the IMS office. Catherine then left the meeting to talk with the technical group responsible for hosting the web-based courses.

Back at IMS, Catherine spoke with the chief technical officer and requested that he follow up with the appropriate technical people at Insulware to confirm server requirements. Catherine also spoke with the art director and assured him that she would take several pictures of the Miami sites to give an idea of the company "look-n-feel." This would provide the basis for the web course interface design and architecture. The next few weeks were spent coordinating with the facilities' schedules to see when Catherine could make a site visit with Pat. When Pat became sick and was unable to fly, it was agreed that Catherine would make the trip alone and meet the human resources assistant at 8 A.M. at the first installation facility.

EARLY JUNE

Catherine had a positive visit with the supervisors in Oklahoma. "I am here to listen. You are the experts, and I am here to absorb as much as I can about what you know," Catherine explained to the six designated supervisors after her brief demonstration of samples of previous web-based courses. Based on her sincere, enthusiastic approach, Catherine felt accepted. The supervisors, all men, started telling Catherine about their experiences with the current corporate-initiated training.

They explained that the training was infrequent and did not pertain to their everyday operations. In addition, the competency ratings were not practiced at a local level, so they did not feel the evaluations applied to them. Also, the training did not transfer to their real-life situations. "When I go back and try to work with my crew members, they do not respond the same way my peer did during the role plays," stated Ben, one supervisor. "My crew members are 18 years old, with no work ethic. They come in late and just don't care."

Ted, another supervisor, piped in, "I came off the floor after 12 years and, all of a sudden, I have to reprimand men who have been my peers for years. They resent the change in authority." Ted continued, "The training we get doesn't help with these kinds of things."

After the meeting, Catherine incorporated the supervisors' requests into the design document and noted how the current training material did not meet the needs of the supervisors. Catherine also requested several training documents from the plant manager, since he had done a good job addressing the plant's training needs on his own time.

A week later, Pat called to express her approval of the design document—except for the change in curriculum. She didn't want to change any of the training material. She wanted a uniform corporate approach that would benefit all the facilities. She requested that Catherine not use any of the individual facilities' materials gleaned from her interviews with the supervisors. When Catherine asked why they weren't looking at what the facilities were doing on a local level, Pat explained that the politics were different everywhere and that Insulware needed a generic approach. Catherine decided that, if she couldn't change the curricular material, she would at least make the learning as interactive as possible.

MID-JUNE TO MID-AUGUST

After returning from her site visit, Catherine didn't interact very much with Carlos, since he was distracted by other projects. In his haste, he did not read the storyboards and did not calculate enough development time in Dan's schedule. From June until August, there was only one storyboard meeting, in which Dan yelled about the number of interactive components in the modules. When they couldn't calmly discuss the storyboards, Dan and Catherine agreed to meet later, when they were both more relaxed. Catherine continued with her original plan for storyboards, seriously attempting to cut out any unnecessary animation but not eliminating the interactivity altogether, as Dan requested. Dan, however, never responded to the request for meetings. Catherine stopped by his office, frequently reminding him that they needed to meet. Each time, Dan kept his eyes on his computer and muttered something like "I'll get to it." Catherine was counting on Dan to allow enough time in his development schedule to talk with her about the importance of the interactive components.

Meanwhile, Insulware's technical team could not agree on whether or not the web-based courses would be internally or externally hosted. In addition, the technical team confirmed that not all of the installation facilities had web access, and a temporary hybrid solution would need to be implemented. The web-based modules would be placed on CD-ROMs temporarily until web access could be added.

Once Catherine finished the storyboards, Carlos sent them to Pat for her sign-off without consulting Dan first. Unfortunately, Dan had not had time to look through them before they were due to the client. Pat approved of the instructional design, content creativity and clarity, and number of interactive, multimedia components. Throughout the design process, Catherine continually explained to Dan and Carlos the need for the interactivity based on the dry nature of the content and the audience's need for simple, audio-based screens. Catherine double-checked with Dan to make sure he had read through the storyboards and asked for clarification. Catherine remembered stopping by his office several times, trying to be friendly and open.

"Dan," she had politely said, "I'm wondering how far along you are with the development." When he wouldn't respond, she mentioned, "The storyboards were approved by Pat. We are all set to go. If there is anything you do not understand, please let me know."

Despite Catherine's attempts to be a cooperative team player, Dan remained noncommunicative, rarely adding any information to the conversation. As time passed, Catherine learned that Dan had not kept up with the project plan and, rather than asking for an extension, had cut out some of the interactive strategies and feedback elements suggested in her storyboards.

LATE AUGUST

Catherine had started her final review of the course when she recognized that Dan had made unapproved changes to the practice activities for Module 8. "Dan," she confronted him, "Why did you change the Module 8 practice activities? Pat signed off on those when she approved the storyboards."

Dan started yelling, "There's no way I could put in all the interactivity in those storyboards. Those are completely unrealistic for the time I've been given to develop them. Besides, the practice activities you've designed are worthless."

Catherine felt despair, since it was too late to restore all of the interactive components before the deadline. In a reactive mode, Carlos, the project manager, met with Dan and Catherine to fix the practice activity errors. Dan refused to make any alterations to what he had already developed. "No, I am not going to make any changes until Catherine looks through the module to see the mistakes she has made in designing these activities. This is the only way she can prove to me that she knows what she is doing."

EARLY SEPTEMBER

Pat quickly reviewed a few modules and enthusiastically approved the course design. Her only question concerned the changes to the Module 8 activities that Dan had made. "What happened to the parts where the user gets to pick an appropriate and inappropriate comment?" she asked. "Those practice activities made this really good. Why aren't they here? I'm afraid I can't accept this. These multiple-choice items just aren't cutting it. They aren't realistic, and they are hard to understand." When Dan received Pat's feedback, he made the changes without further protest.

The web training was then implemented in several Insulware facilities where the supervisors took part in using it. IMS conducted a focus group evaluation of these facilities to determine the effectiveness of the training. One supervisor complained about having to take time out of his day to critique the training since he would be retiring soon and didn't like computers anyway. For the most part, the comments were neither positive nor negative. Catherine decided that the supervisors were not used to critiquing instruction and were unfamiliar with the focus group process. She concluded that, as part of a future focus group effort, she would explain in greater detail how to critique web-based instruction.

ONE MONTH LATER

Catherine remembered how strained the atmosphere was at IMS following the Insulware deliverable. Catherine, Dan, and Carlos attempted to conduct a postmortem meeting, but Catherine and Dan still blamed one another for the mistakes. As a result of the project mismanagement, however, IMS discussed new internal processes to keep the same mistakes from happening again.

Unfortunately, the instructional designers in Catherine's group were nervous around Dan, based on what they had observed during the past months. They were afraid to approach him with any multimedia questions. If IMS were awarded other Insulware projects, how would Dan cooperate with her team?

PRELIMINARY ANALYSIS QUESTIONS

1. Given her front-end analysis, critique Catherine's design decisions.
2. If you were the project manager for this project, what would you have done to improve team dynamics?
3. Develop a project management plan that would improve the instructional development process in this case.
4. What strategies would you suggest to improve IMS team interactions in the future?

IMPLICATIONS FOR ID PRACTICE

1. Discuss the challenges of implementing standard ID models in real-world settings.
2. How might poor project management affect the quality of an instructional product?
3. Explain how dynamics within an instructional design team can influence organizational performance.

Michelle Nguyen

BY JOANNA C. DUNLAP

Michelle Nguyen went to work on Monday morning, feeling optimistic and looking forward to the week's work ahead. Walking into her office, she looked at the project Gantt charts that covered one whole wall. She smiled as she reexamined the time line for the hematology computer-based instructional (CBI) project she had been working on for the past nine months. Although there had been some delays throughout the project due to the complexity of the content and the design, as well as the busy schedules of the two physicians serving as subject matter experts on the project, Michelle had been able to keep the project within budget and on schedule, a fact of which she was very proud. Having completed the formative evaluation and made the necessary changes, she was ready to begin implementing the program for student use—just in time for the spring semester.

The product Michelle was implementing was a CBI program on hematology for third-year medical students. The program would replace an existing classroom-based course covering such topics as the hazards of giving and receiving blood products, indications for transfusion, transfusion products, and the diagnosis and treatment of diseases that impact blood production and functioning. Developed as part of a medical education grant, the program was the medical school's first big CBI program and was, therefore, designed to be the flagship in a line of proposed CBI programs to be integrated into the third-year curriculum. Instructors and administrators had expressed some healthy skepticism regarding the quality of the learning experience in a CBI environment and the strain on scarce instructional resources that CBI projects can have, so Michelle had taken it upon herself to make sure that the program alleviated those concerns and went to market without a hitch.

Ever since she took the project over nine months ago, she had been looking forward to completing the program. She had accomplished a lot during the course of this project. Although it was not the first time she had developed computer-based instruction, it was the first time she had used constructivist instructional methodologies to structure the CBI. In addition, Michelle was a novice when it came to the content domain of hematology. She was far from being a hematologist and, therefore, had to rely extensively on the subject matter experts assigned to the project. Her skills at mining for knowledge from subject matter experts were constantly challenged; the two physicians, serving as experts, were enthusiastic about the project but had trouble expressing their expertise and their decision-making processes in ways that would be appropriate for instructing third-year medical students. In addition, the physicians' schedules were almost prohibitive, especially given that Michelle worked from 8:00 to 5:00, during which time the physicians were busy teaching, conducting research, working with patients, running a blood center, and being on call for the hospital. And, if that weren't enough, Michelle had also spent nine months listening to the physicians' "Dr. Stab" jokes and, whenever they noticed her getting squeamish, being subjected to their detailed descriptions of their own medical school experiences, such as bumping into cadavers in dark hallways and encountering the unexpected surprises that can occur during an autopsy.

The project had required her to do a lot of work in a short time with a limited budget, dealing with sophisticated subject matter experts and applying complex instructional methodologies to an ill-structured content domain using computer technology as a delivery vehicle. Thinking about how it was almost over, she mimed wiping her brow with her hand. Michelle was proud of her work and knew that, once the program was implemented and the students were actually using it, the hematology program was going to be a feather in her cap. Still smiling, she walked to her desk to answer the ringing telephone.

"Hello. Instructional technology department. This is Michelle."

"Hey, Michelle. This is Tom DiBona over in academic computing. Are you sitting down? We've got a problem."

NINE MONTHS AGO

After being assigned to the new hematology CBI development project, Michelle set up a meeting with the project's feasibility team—the people who had developed the original grant proposal. Alex Wheeler and Susan Martin had conducted a front-end analysis for this project as part of the initial grant proposal; the front-end analysis, in fact, helped sell the project to the selection committee and secure the award. Michelle already had some information: The new hematology course had to be "real world," CBI, self-guided, and something that students could easily access, given their busy clerkship schedules. Before she began work on the design of the product, she wanted to meet with Alex and Susan to go over how their front-end analysis recommendations were derived, so that she would fully understand what the final product needed to be. From experience Michelle knew that, regardless of how instructionally sound or innovative her design was, the program would fail to be an effective instructional tool if the front-end analysis recommendations were not reflected in the final product.

After Michelle, Alex, and Susan were settled in the conference room, Michelle asked them to describe the instructional motivation for the project. Alex started the discussion by talking about why the hematology course needed redesigning. Their findings indicated that the current hematology course was failing to meet the needs of the students for three reasons:

1. The hematology content was delivered in a classroom setting via lecture. These lectures took place during the day to fit into the professors' work schedules. However, the students' clerkship schedules required them to be at their assigned hospital or clinic during the day. Therefore, it was difficult for students to attend lectures; students needed an instructional intervention that they could access during hours not spent in their clerkships.

2. Now that they were in their clerkships, the students did not see the relevance of the hematology content, especially since it was presented in a decontextualized way. That is, the content was usually presented by professors using a lecture format, defining concept after concept in sequence, prototypically, simplistically, and in isolation. Under these conditions, students failed to learn how hematology related to other medical content domains or how it impacted the decisions doctors make on the job.

3. Students were so stressed about being in their clerkships that the last thing they wanted to do was "learn more content." Susan described the problem to Michelle in the following way: "As you know, Michelle, this medical school is really no different from most. Our students begin their clerkships during the third year. Suddenly, students who are really good at taking lecture notes, studying textbooks, and passing exams are required to perform tasks they haven't practiced. They're required to use all of the facts they have memorized in biology, pathophysiology, chemistry, anatomy, and so on in an interdisciplinary way to solve a real patient's real-world, real-time problem—a leap that is very stressful and not always successful for students who've never been asked to perform that way and have never had a chance to practice."

The rest of the information Alex and Susan provided had to do with environmental issues that would impact her design:

- Students needed to be able to use the program in the library's academic computing labs.
- The library's computer resources consisted of Macintosh computers networked to laser printers.
- Students were fairly computer literate, using word processing and online reference search tools.

Using her notes from her meeting with Alex and Susan, Michelle made the following design decisions for the hematology program:

- According to the front-end analysis, there is a need to create a program that would not only cover the appropriate hematology content but that would also help bridge the gap between what and how students learn in a conventional medical school environment and how they are expected to function and apply their knowledge and skills to a medical emergency in a hospital setting. To do this, the program would be a case-based instructional environment that would enable students to practice applying what they had learned in the classroom to solving real problems in a safe, nonthreatening environment.
- Using appropriate instructional methodologies, Michelle knew she could develop a structure for presenting hematology cases that encouraged students to think, research, solve problems, and ultimately make the types of decisions regarding hematology issues they would be making in their clerkships. This would address the issues of relevance and practice brought up during the front-end analysis.

■ The program would be self-guided and self-contained, so that students could access the instruction when it fit into their busy schedules. This would address the time constraint issue students had with the classroom-based hematology course.

Using these macro-level design decisions to guide her work, Michelle worked with the subject matter experts to develop a CBI product that fulfilled the requirements of the front-end analysis conducted by Alex and Susan.

TODAY

"What do you mean, Tom?"

"Well, Michelle, I've been going over the results of the academic computing needs survey we've been having students fill out over the past four weeks. We've had a really good response—65% so far. What I'm worried about is that the students have indicated that the library's hours are not sufficient; specifically, the third- and fourth-year students are saying they are working in their clerkships during library hours and, therefore, need us to have extended hours. So, if you're planning on using the library's computer labs for the hematology program, you're going to have an access problem for the third-year students."

"But, Tom, hold on. When I took over this project, I met with Alex and Susan to go over the front-end analysis for this project. Their data indicated that making it available in the library was the best solution. I don't . . ."

"Michelle, that front-end analysis was conducted over a year ago. Last year, we had the budget to hire folks to keep the library open after hours. With the new fiscal year, that budget was cut. No more extended hours. Alex and Susan know this—haven't you been meeting with them throughout the development process?"

Michelle was silent, feeling paralyzed by the news. "No, not really." As Tom continued to describe what the students were writing on the survey, Michelle pulled her file on the academic computing needs survey to review the questions for herself.

"OK. Tom, what if—if we can't provide library access for students to use the program, what about making the program available for home use? Don't most of our students have computers at home? Didn't I see a question on the survey that gets at this?"

"Yes, Michelle, that's covered in questions 3 through 6 on the survey. But you know that anything related to computer technology can change overnight. Those students who didn't have a clue how to use the Internet are now on the Web constantly. But here's the rest of the bad news. The majority of our students do have access to computers at home. But they have PCs, not Macintoshes. I don't suppose it's easy to convert your program to run on a PC platform?"

Staring at the front-end analysis report on which she had based many of her design, development, and implementation decisions, Michelle examined the data summary for questions 3 through 6 (see Figure 27–1).

For the first time, she realized that the survey did not ask for enough detail regarding computer platform and home availability. The rest of her conversation with Tom was a blur. The project was now in trouble, and, if she wanted to make sure it was available for the

		Yes	No
3)	**Do you know how to use a**		
	Macintosh computer?	711	223
	Windows computer?	587	336
	printer?	806	137
	CD-ROM?	254	539
	modem?	223	647
4)	**Do you have access to a computer at**		
	home?	519	314
	work?	475	588
5)	**What software applications do you use:**		
	word processing?	847	166
	database?	154	779
	presentation?	127	857
	spreadsheet?	188	736
	Internet/World Wide Web?	285	566
	MedLine?	247	619
6)	**Do you use a computer to**		
	write papers?	687	156
	conduct research?	263	658
	deliver presentations?	127	684

FIGURE 27–1   Data Summary

spring semester as promised, she needed an immediate solution. Pulling the project files from the filing cabinet, Michelle asked herself how this could happen to her "perfect" project. She had done everything by the book, using the front-end analysis findings to guide her design decisions. She had paid especially close attention to the environmental analysis results: access, platform, and so on. How could she get to the implementation phase of the project and suddenly have all these problems? How would this setback impact the project's budget, resource needs, quality, and timeline? Michelle closed her office door, forwarded her phone, and began to think about how she might salvage her project.

PRELIMINARY ANALYSIS QUESTIONS

1. At the end of this case, Michelle is asking herself how there could be surprises this late in the instructional development process. What would you tell her if she asked you this question?
2. Evaluate Michelle's actions and identify what she might have done differently.

3. Describe the relationship among the front-end analysis, design, and implementation phases of the instructional development project described in this case.
4. If you were Michelle, what steps would you take now to salvage the project? How would those steps impact the project's budget, resource needs, quality, and timeline?

IMPLICATIONS FOR ID PRACTICE

1. Create a diagram to illustrate the relationships among front-end analysis, design, and implementation.
2. Discuss the importance of context analysis and its relationship to front-end analysis.
3. Describe how problems not discovered until the implementation phase of a project can impact budget, resource allocation, and the timely release of a product.

Beth Owens

BY MICHAEL L. WRAY AND BRENT G. WILSON

CHARGE FROM THE DEAN

It's a rainy day as Beth Owen arrives to meet with Dean Carlton Jacobs. Stepping into the dean's suite, she laughs as she shakes the remaining water from her raincoat. "I always enjoy the rain, especially in the West. We don't get enough of it!" Beth has lived the past 10 years in Colorado, first as a stay-at-home mom, more recently completing a master's degree in instructional design at a nearby state university. Eight months ago, she accepted a faculty consulting position at State College, a four-year, open-enrollment college in the downtown metro area. State's academic programs are always changing, and faculty members appreciate the instructional design support that Beth provides. At any given time, Beth is consulting on 12 to 15 projects, with only an occasional need for in-depth analysis and evaluation. Technology leadership is a part of the job, but she sees her primary role as helping faculty members make the transition from traditional teaching methods to more constructivist kinds of teaching activities.

Dean Jacobs welcomes Beth into the office. "Thank you again for meeting with me. Your study of our programs is one of my highest priorities right now, and I know your findings will make a big difference to us." The School of Consumer Technology was recently divided, with the always growing Management Information and Office Systems moving out to create their own school, leaving the remaining half of the students in a wide array of service-oriented programs: cosmetology, fashion merchandising, hospitality management, and culinary arts. The Dean is anxious to develop a growth plan for his remaining programs and to make improvements at all levels. His first goal is to review the culinary arts program, the smallest within the school.

"As you know," the dean continues, "information and office systems was something of a cash cow for us, to some extent subsidizing our smaller programs. Now every program has to stand on its own legs, both quality-wise and by the raw numbers. We're starting our analysis with culinary arts. The program is small but self-sustaining. We're having a few problems, which I'd like you to look at."

Beth is looking forward to jumping in on this project but just a little anxious about the prospects. In her eight months at State, she has heard occasional rumors about the program director. Chef Gerhard Reiner is known to be something of a taskmaster and disciplinarian. Beth turns to the dean, "I understand that the program director of culinary arts, Gerhard Reiner, teaches both the introductory class and the upper-level culinary classes. His teaching and leadership must be important to the program."

The dean responds, "Yes, he's a major figure. Reiner gets very good teaching ratings, although you'll always find the occasional student who can't stand him. He is well known within the school for being a challenging instructor. He maintains strict rules in his lab; any student can tell you that!"

"What kind of rules?" Beth is curious about this instructor. She doubts that this chef has even heard of such things as constructivist teaching methods.

The dean leans toward Beth. "I've had a couple of students in my office in tears, feeling overwhelmed by the demands of the program. They feel Chef Reiner is too strict. With enrollments more of an issue now, I don't want to lose any students unnecessarily. It's all about including all students and growing enrollments."

The dean leans back in his chair, continuing, "My problem is complicated. I want the program to produce quality graduates, but I also want to retain students and grow the program. I'd like you to figure out how we can be more inclusive, improve retention, and maintain a quality program at the same time!"

"Piece o' cake!" Beth jokingly replies. "Thanks for your time, Dean Jacobs. I think I would like to see the classroom and visit with Chef Reiner." The dean smiles, "I'll give you much more than that. How about a personal tour and lunch in our student dining room?"

Beth agrees, "I think that would be wonderful; please lead the way." Dean Jacobs shakes hands with Beth and escorts her from his office to the culinary labs.

TOUR AND LUNCH

Beth is eager to see the students in action. Dean Jacobs shows her the student culinary lab, where students are preparing the meal before service. She is impressed to see everyone in crisp uniforms, each busy and involved in food production. It is easy to see who is in charge. Chef Reiner, in his tall white hat, has an air of authority, his name clearly embroidered on his starched chef whites, with his culinary title and a patch from the school he attended prominent on his breast pocket. The students rush from their work areas, receiving instructions from the chef. She notices him sampling the students' work, tasting and checking temperatures.

Following the tour, the dean and Beth take a seat in a small dining room adjacent to the culinary lab. The room is filled with administrators and staff members, who pay a small fee to attend the luncheon. The dean explains, "The restaurant serves meals three days per week, offering a sample of the students' accomplishments. It continues to be a popular event on the campus and attracts the general public." Beth smiles as she is served an inviting meal of roast chicken with a light cream sauce. "The plate is so elegant," Beth remarks. The garnish on the plate captures Beth's attention: roasted tomatoes pierced by rosemary stems. Beth sighs, "It smells wonderful." The dean nods in agreement as they both begin their meal.

During lunch, Beth begins to think about her approach toward advising the chef. She wants to introduce constructivist teaching principles but thinks it may be difficult to convince Chef Reiner of the benefits of constructivism. Reiner's approach to teaching seems antiquated and somewhat confrontational.

Beth declines the dessert, although it does look delicious, a five-layer chocolate cake with a rich frosting and mint leaves—decadent, indeed. Beth keeps imagining how nice the dessert would have been as she watches other guests enjoy it. But she settles for coffee and enjoys the pleasant service by the students.

After the meal, Beth concludes her tour with the dean and is anxious to get a chance to meet Chef Reiner and talk to him about the course. She thanks Dean Jacobs for his time and shakes his hand firmly.

MEETING THE CHEF

Beth knocks on Chef Reiner's door with a sense of anticipation. What is he like, really? As the door opens, Chef Reiner extends his hand, saying, "Good morning, I'm Gerhard Reiner. I've been looking forward to meeting you." Beth is relieved to see a tentative smile on his face. Stepping into the office, the two engage in conversation aimed at breaking the ice.

When Beth takes her seat, she is immediately impressed by the order of the room. The desk is clear, all items in their places. Beth's eyebrows rise as she notices that the books on the shelves are in order of height, smallest to the tallest, and the edges of the books are in line with the shelf. She smiles and thanks Chef Reiner for a great lunch. "It was a true pleasure," he returns. I'm glad you had the chance to see the students working."

He gets to the point. "When the dean told me that you were coming, I immediately thought of how you could help us increase program enrollment. I'm looking forward to our work together. How can I help you get started?"

Beth reflects for a moment and responds, "Perhaps you could start by telling me about the successes the program has had. Tell me about your history with the college and what you consider the strengths of the program to be."

Chef Reiner begins a lengthy recital of his qualifications and the program's strengths. He has been at State College for five years, following a career as an executive chef for a major cruise line. He had also worked in fine dining in France and Germany. He speaks several languages and has had the opportunity to work with many fine chefs. He is also the president of the local chapter of the American Culinary Federation. His students have a chapter as well and participate in local competitions. The program's greatest accomplishment is the quality of the graduates. Before his arrival, the prior dean was concerned about the reputation of the program. They hired Chef Reiner to develop prestige for the school and produce quality graduates capable of obtaining high-level chef positions throughout the metropolitan area.

"Since I arrived," Chef Reiner explains, "I have instituted a student dining room, which produces meals three days a week, as you saw today. Before that, we had no outlet for the student work; most of the food production was in the classroom only. I have found that students like to see the public enjoy the meals they create."

Beth agrees, "I certainly enjoyed it!"

Chef Reiner continues, "We have had problems with student professional standards, and I have worked hard to reverse that problem."

"What do you mean, professional standards?" asks Beth.

"We are in a metropolitan area," Chef Reiner explains. "Our students don't like to wear uniforms and maintain hygiene standards. We have had problems with long hair, nail polish, jewelry, and body piercings, which are not part of a professional and sanitary kitchen."

"How have you solved that problem?" Beth asks. Chef Reiner shows her his culinary laboratory evaluation sheet (see Figure 28–1). "Following each class, the students are evaluated on their appearance, quality of work, attendance, and so forth."

Beth studies the performance criteria and behavioral categories. Something in this grading sheet conflicts with her constructivist principles. Beth ponders how effective a point system like this would be. She sees the value of meaningful experiences, such as the student lunch, but wonders how such strict behavioral monitoring can be effective.

Beth looks up from the sheet. "Hmm. Neatness, organization, teamwork, ability to follow instructions. Does this work? How do the students respond to this evaluation?"

"It is quite effective," the chef explains. "Before our daily evaluations, I would get frustrated with student uniforms and professionalism in class. They would not behave professionally and respect uniform standards. I would give them low grades and they would get angry and not understand why they got bad grades. It is almost as if they expected to get an *A* for just being here."

Beth's mind is racing with ideas and conflicts as she asks, "How does the checklist evaluation change that?"

Chef Reiner is resolute in his response. "I get better performance from the students because the evaluations tell them what I expect. If they don't behave professionally, they can see how many points they will lose for not meeting standards. It is also less stressful on me."

"How do you mean?" Beth wants to understand what's going on in the chef's mind.

"At first, I would do the same as I was taught in culinary school. If a student didn't show up in uniform or behaved unprofessionally, I'd send him or her home, with a zero for the day."

Beth chuckles, "How did that go over?"

Smiling, Chef Reiner responds, "Not well at all! Students got frustrated, and I quickly realized I'd lose most of my students, so the daily evaluation gives them more immediate feedback on my expectations. They can choose to change their behavior on their own, knowing the penalty. I'd say the daily forms are less forceful than how things were before."

Beth is skeptical. "Less forceful?"

Chef Reiner explains: "Most students actually like getting a grade each day—and they don't blame me as much for their grade. At least they know where they stand. The bottom line is, my students now wear their uniforms and act like a team. I do have some who still don't respond, but overall it's much better."

Timeliness

On time
Stays entire time
No idle time

Uniform

Hat
Clean whites
Black slacks
Nonskid shoes
Closed-toe shoes
Ironed

Appearance

Hair clean, pulled back
Fingernails trimmed 1/4″
Hands and nails clean
Jewelry: two rings, watch, stud earrings only

Equipment

Chef's knife sharp
Paring knife sharp
Apron
Kitchen towel

Production

Listens well
Tastes all food
Takes direction well
Displays knowledge
Observes others, stays involved
Respectful of speed, timeliness
Quality of food production
Respectful of waste and food cost

Sanitation

Aggressively cleans
Cleans/sanitizes well

Teamwork

Volunteers to work
Is supportive of leader
Offers suggestions
Provides constructive criticism

FIGURE 28–1   Chef Reiner's Behavioral Checklist for Student Performance

Beth is trying to process this approach. "Do you think the evaluation is causing some students to drop out?"

Chef Reiner sighs, "No, they make this decision themselves. I view my role as preparing them for success in the industry. Kitchens require a distinct chain of authority and rules. The students need to learn how to survive in that environment while in school. If not, they won't succeed in business. I'd rather they fail here than later on the job."

Raising her eyebrows, Beth responds, "Are you saying, if they can't stand the heat, get out of the kitchen?"

"Exactly!" Chef Reiner continues, "I realized that these students had never learned to take school or work seriously and professionally, so I created a performance system that takes me out of the picture, almost entirely. Instead of blaming me when they don't get the grade they want, they look at the point totals and see where they can change."

"Sounds as if it worked," Beth admits.

Chef Reiner continues with enthusiasm, "You wouldn't believe the difference. Before, I had students refusing to complete a cooking assignment, afraid it would wreck their nails. Nail polish, clothes, hairdo, whatever the excuse, I had students who were not doing the work. Now, everyone shows up on time, in uniform, ready to work. And word has spread around campus. The students take a great deal of pride in their accomplishments. Employers see the difference, too. We have a 96% placement rate, with starting pay up 60% in five years."

Beth stands to leave. "You've given me a lot to think about. Let me get back to you with some notes and observations; then we'll figure out where to go from here."

"That sounds fine," answers Chef Reiner as he stands to see Beth out. "If I can be of further help, please feel free to ask." Shaking hands, Beth leaves the office with a lot to think about. "Maybe I should have had that dessert!" she muses, returning to her car, umbrella in hand. The rain is gone and the sun is shining again.

On the drive home, Beth continues to turn over these ideas in her mind. She is unsettled about the strict behaviorist approach used by the program, but it seems to be working. She had wanted to suggest more constructivist ideas but didn't quite see where they would fit. In fact, the situation is something of a challenge to Beth's beliefs about good teaching.

PRELIMINARY ANALYSIS QUESTIONS

1. Identify the "problem" in this case, as perceived by the dean, Beth, and Chef Reiner.
2. What is causing the conflict within Beth? How do her preexisting ideas about constructivism and behaviorism relate to her observations of the culinary arts program?
3. What suggestions do you have for Beth for how to deal with her conflict between constructivist and behavioral approaches to instruction?
4. Beth has only begun her review of the culinary arts program. What further data should be gathered to address the dean's concerns and provide suggestions for improving the program?

IMPLICATIONS FOR ID PRACTICE

1. Constructivism and behaviorism are often presented as competing philosophies, yet many designers seek to include elements of both approaches in their practice. How can that be done while maintaining some underlying integrity or cohesion in philosophy?
2. Professionals such as Beth develop their expertise by paying close attention to both theory and practice. What kinds of conflicts have you experienced between textbook approaches and everyday concerns of practice? How can instructional design professionals learn to respect both sources of knowledge and incorporate them successfully into their outlooks and practice?

Case Study 29

Mary Robbins

BY BRENDA SUGRUE

The Cuts-R-Us hairdressing school hired Asgard Training to redesign its entry-level course. The famous hair stylist, Hugo, has always been responsible for this course, which lasts 12 weeks and covers the basics of cutting and coloring. Twenty students take the course at one time, and the course is run three times a year. The reason that the consulting company was hired was that, usually, 50% of the students who begin the course do not finish. The positive consequence of the high failure rate is that the course is regarded as one of the best in the country. The negative consequences are that (1) the company makes only half of the money it could make on this course, since it refunds tuition fees to anyone who does not complete the course, and (2) there are fewer students for the advanced courses that the school offers. Cuts-R-Us wants to increase its graduation rate from the basic course. The director also believes that the school could run more than three basic courses per year, and, if the course were better documented, instructors other than Hugo could teach it.

Mary Robbins from Asgard Training conducted a needs analysis and came to the conclusion that the existing course materials were incomplete, disorganized, and badly sequenced. The course content was mostly inside Hugo's head, and he covered topics in whatever order he wished. Mary recommended that a thorough cognitive task analysis be done, using Hugo as the expert, and that a set of print-based job aids (laminated cards in a notebook-size looseleaf binder) be created for each technique that trainees would learn. Each week would focus on one cutting and one coloring technique, beginning with the simplest techniques. She convinced Hugo that the basic strategy for teaching each technique would be a demonstration of the technique by him and many opportunities for the trainees to practice the technique and get feedback on their progress. Since Hugo could not personally monitor all of the practice, it was decided to group students in pairs and have one person practice while the other coached, switching roles back and forth. Every Friday, each student would be videotaped performing the techniques of the week, and Hugo would assign pass or fail grades to each student for the week, based on his viewing of the videotapes. If a student fails three weeks in a row, then he or she must drop the course. In addition, it was decided to pretest all students on their level of fluid ability (generally conceived of as novel problem-solving ability and often measured by tests of nonverbal reasoning), because this is known to be a good indicator of the amount of structure and feedback a student will need during instruction.

Mary will carefully monitor the first offering of the new course in order to make adjustments during the course and to make revisions for future offerings. Part of this formative evaluation involves tape recording conversations among four students who are taking the course. The first taping takes place on the first day.

DAY 1

Roberto: So, are you guys looking forward to this?

Krystal: Of course. I can't wait to get started. I've always wanted to be a hairdresser, and I can't believe that they accepted me into the program with my low high school GPA. School was so tough for me—all that reading and writing—but I'm really good with hair; I worked part-time in a salon last year. I spent all my time just washing hair, but the cutting and coloring seem just as easy. I don't even know why we have to train for three months. But at least it's a break from real work. I'm going to treat it like a vacation. How about you?

Roberto: Well, I'm a bit nervous myself. I hear that it's kind of like a boot camp here and, if you don't pass the weekly tests, they throw you out. And they don't give you much help. But the good thing is that, if you train here, you can get a job in any salon; this is supposed to be one of the best hairdressing schools in the country. You know, Tony Ronato, the guy who cuts the president's hair, trained here.

Philip: Yeah, but then he went off to France and worked with Pierre LeBlanc; that's where he really got trained. You won't get a good job with just this course. I wanted to go to the Sidel Academy but didn't get in, so this is a last resort for me, and, if I could go right into a salon without it, that's what I'd do. But, unfortunately, all salons require some basic training, so I'll suffer through this. But I can't wait for it to be over.

Donna: Me, too. I already know all this stuff; I've been working at my dad's salon for a year now, doing everything—cutting, coloring, perming, the lot. My dad's Frederiko. But I want to open my own salon, and you have to have a certificate and this school was the quickest way I can get that. What a drag.

Roberto: Wow, you're Frederiko's daughter! Do you think I could meet him? He's my all-time hero. I just love the way he did Liz's shaggy cut.

Philip: What did you think of their making us take that stupid "pick the next picture in the series" test on the computer this morning? They said it was some kind of fancy IQ test. I'm glad that they gave us our scores right away. I got 90%! I wish I could show that to my old high school teachers. They thought I was dumb because I never did any work and always failed their silly tests. But I knew I was smart all along.

Roberto: Well, I got only 60%. I was confused when the patterns got so complicated. I hope that doesn't mean they'll be watching me closely all the time. How smart do you have to be to cut hair, anyway? And what does picture matching have to do with cutting hair?

Donna: I agree. I think that they were just trying to scare us. I got only 65 on the test this morning, and I've been doing great cuts at my dad's salon.

Krystal: Well, I liked the test. You didn't have to study for it, just figure out the patterns. I got 85, and I could have done better if I hadn't been distracted by that gorgeous guy sitting in front of me.

WEEK 5

At the beginning of the fifth week of the training, Roberto has failed Weeks 3 and 4. Donna and Krystal have failed Week 4. Philip has passed in all four weeks. Roberto and Donna have been working together as a pair. Krystal and Philip have also been a pair.

Roberto: I don't know what I'm going to do. If I fail this week, I'm out. I wish I could ask Hugo for help, but he's so impatient, and I'm scared he'll think I'm even worse than I am. I'm trying so hard. I was doing fine the first two weeks, when we were doing basic trims and layering. But the coloring is so hard—matching the chemicals to the customer's hair and getting the time right. I felt so bad for that woman when her hair came out green. I wonder if I could hire my own tutor. Donna, you're great, but you don't tell me what I'm doing wrong, and last week your own coloring was a disaster.

Donna: Now, listen here, Roberto, I'm not here to teach you. You're just holding me back. I wouldn't have failed last week if you hadn't been watching me like a hawk and telling me I was doing things wrong when they were right! I wish I could just work on my own.

Philip: I don't know what your problem is, Roberto. It shows you exactly what to do in the manual. It even has pictures of what a cut or color should look like at every stage. When I'm watching Krystal, I put an *X* beside each step she does that does not match the picture in the book and then show it to her after. Roberto, if you like, I'll help you in the evenings this week. We can practice on some cheap wigs.

Krystal: Roberto, if you let Philip help you, you'll pass this week. Philip is almost as good as Hugo, and much more patient. Philip, if it weren't for you, I'd have failed every week. The only reason I failed last week was because of that terrible woman I had to work on for the video. She kept telling me what to do with her hair, so that I couldn't practice what we were supposed to be practicing. It's so unfair and so much work. We can't relax for a minute. If I'd known the training was going to be this hard, I might not have enrolled.

Roberto: Thanks, Philip. There may be hope for me after all.

Philip: Of course, there's hope. They're packing a lot into 12 weeks; that's why you're having trouble. But I like it this way. I'm glad that they leave us alone most of the time. And I like having a partner. I'm a lot happier than I expected to be when I started. Hugo says I'm one of the best students he's ever had!

Donna: Just because you're always asking questions and showing off. Just wait until I have my own salon and am inventing new styles, like my dad. I hate the boring old styles they are making us learn here; they are so eighties. And they make it all seem so complicated. I'm not going to remember any of their stupid rules, anyway. I'll do what it takes to get the certificate, but then I'll wipe it all from my mind and go back to the way I was doing things before I came.

Roberto: But Hugo says that all new styles are just variations on the basics and that you have to know the basic rules before you try experimenting.

Donna: But hairdressing is about experimenting, not about sticking to rules. I feel stifled with all these rules and steps.

Philip: Well, you'll never have your own salon if you don't pass this course.

Donna: There are plenty of other training programs. If I don't pass this one, I'll just enroll somewhere else, somewhere where they value my creative talent and don't make me learn all this stupid stuff.

PRELIMINARY ANALYSIS QUESTIONS

1. Create a profile of the abilities and motivational characteristics of each of the four learners in the case at the beginning of the training course and one month later.
2. Identify the key source of poor performance for each of the three learners who are failing. Why did the fourth student succeed with the course as designed?
3. What strategies would you recommend for each of the failing students, so that they don't have to drop the course?
4. What changes to the training would you recommend, so that all four learners have a chance at succeeding?

IMPLICATIONS FOR ID PRACTICE

1. Discuss what kinds of data can be used as indicators of ability and motivation before and during instruction.
2. How can learner analysis be used before and during instruction to optimize the chances of learner success in a course?
3. Identify the characteristics of learners that are most influential in predicting learning.

30

Michael Sanchez

BY DONALD A. STEPICH AND
TIMOTHY J. NEWBY

Michael Sanchez, training project manager for Universal Electronics, a large consumer electronics manufacturing company, left his boss's office with a new assignment. Suzanne Manning, Universal's training director, had asked, "Can you show that Differences is really making a difference to the company?" Differences Among People (Differences for short) is the company's diversity training program. If this course is going to stay on the books, and Suzanne thinks it should, now is the time to demonstrate its value, because next year's training budget is being considered. The company is looking to cut unnecessary courses, and this course may be on the chopping block. This is a different kind of project for Michael. He's helped design a large number of training programs, but this is the first time he's done this kind of evaluation project.

Suzanne had explained that Universal's management has been taking a more critical look at training, challenging the value of every training course. It isn't that management doesn't believe in training. Over the years, the company has invested heavily in training, and there are no signs that this investment will be reduced anytime soon. However, just as with new marketing strategies or manufacturing techniques, management wants to see tangible evidence that a particular training course is working to the company's benefit. Management wants to be able to base the decision on information rather than opinion. So far, the emphasis has been on technical training (for example, courses on engineering standards and quality-control methods), and some courses have been eliminated or substantially revised. However, the focus has been shifting to the "soft skills" courses (for example, courses on teamwork and coaching skills), which present a more difficult problem.

Suzanne's opinion was that Differences was valuable when it was first offered and is still valuable today. Curricular decisions were being made in 60 to 90 days, and she would have to make a recommendation about this course and to back up that recommendation. If the course were still valuable, she would need more than her opinion to convince management to keep it on the books for the next year. She'd need some hard evidence. And, if the course were no longer valuable, then maybe it was time to scrap it. Michael knew that this, too, would require hard evidence. He knew Suzanne well enough to know that, regardless of the situation, she liked to be thorough in backing up her recommendations. He also remembered that she had been one of the initial promoters of the course. She had worked hard to get Differences going in the organization. He knew that she wouldn't recommend dropping this course lightly. Either way, Michael knew that whether the employees learned anything wasn't really the issue. For the evaluation to be useful, he would have to find out whether what they learned was having a positive effect on the company as a whole.

Michael had asked about the original purpose for the course. It had started out as a "bandwagon" course. Especially with the passage of the Americans with Disabilities Act (ADA), it seemed as if everyone was doing diversity training, and Universal's management saw this course as a way to "keep up with the Joneses." In addition, although the company hadn't been in any legal trouble, management wanted to keep it that way. The course was designed to show that the company was treating all of its employees in a fair and equitable way and encouraging them to treat one another in the same way. The expectation was that this would help keep the company out of court, or at least lessen the impact of any lawsuit. Michael thought there were significant problems with these arguments. Diversity didn't seem to be the hot topic it had been a year or two ago, so the bandwagon argument wouldn't carry the same weight. The legal argument was still valid but seemed relatively weak because it was presented in negative terms—avoiding lawsuits. To assess the value of the course, Michael thought it would be important to approach it from a positive perspective—to determine whether the course was having a positive effect, rather than simply helping avoid a negative effect.

After some thought, Michael came up with two approaches that he thought would work. The employee development approach was based on the fact that, because of Affirmative Action (AA) and Equal Employment Opportunity (EEO) guidelines, the company had been hiring and promoting an increasing number of women and minorities. A substantial investment had been made in these employees, an investment the company would want to protect. The argument was that, if employees (all employees) better understood their unique backgrounds and perspectives, then these minority and women employees might have a better chance of succeeding on the job. As a result, they might be more likely to want to stay with the company, giving the company a greater return on the investment it had made in them.

The productivity approach was based on the fact that consumer electronics is a very competitive business. Innovation and productivity were critical to the company's continued success in the market. The argument was that, the more employees understood about one another, the easier it would be for them to communicate with one another, which would result in better problem solving. As a result, both innovation and productivity would increase, helping the company maintain a competitive edge in the market.

Michael reviewed the course materials. Differences is a two-day course designed to improve the communication among the company's employees by making them more aware of the ways communication is influenced by the age, gender, and cultural background of the people involved. The course attempts to accomplish this by teaching some basic listening and conflict-resolution skills; providing information about the common differences among various age, gender, and cultural groups; and describing the impact stereotyping has on communication between groups. The course format includes a combination of lectures, videos, discussions, self-assessment exercises, and experiential activities. Response to the course has been generally positive. Based on course evaluations completed at the end of every training course, employees seem to feel that the information in Differences is interesting, clearly presented, and useful.

PRELIMINARY ANALYSIS QUESTIONS

1. Identify the key issues from both the management and training department's perspectives.
2. Develop a list of indicators of employee development (e.g., what are employees doing differently?) and productivity (e.g., how is this affecting the company's performance?).
3. Develop a plan for obtaining information related to the employee development and productivity approaches.
4. Discuss the relative value of both approaches from management's point of view.
5. Identify Michael's dilemma in this situation. What is Suzanne's attitude toward the training program? How might her attitude affect Michael's evaluation?

IMPLICATIONS FOR ID PRACTICE

1. Describe the purpose or value of evaluating a training program from the broad perspective of organizational effectiveness, in contrast to the perspective of training effectiveness alone.
2. Specify measures for evaluating the impact of a training program on the organization as a whole.
3. Describe methods that can be used to obtain information needed to make decisions about training impact. Discuss the relative merit of information obtained from different sources.
4. Identify potential situational influences on the process and outcomes of an evaluation.

Andrew Stewart

BY STEVEN M. ROSS AND GARY R. MORRISON

Dr. Andrew Stewart looked forward to his meeting on Tuesday with Dr. Lois Lakewood and her staff at Rainbow Design. Aside from wanting to see Albuquerque again (it had been about 10 years since he last visited), he viewed his assigned role as program evaluator, in Rainbow's design project as something he not only was well prepared to handle but would enjoy as well. Andrew was a professor of instructional design (ID) at a large university in Boston. He was knowledgeable about many aspects of design theory and practice and was considered a national expert in educational evaluation.

THE BTB GLOBAL TRANSPORT CONTRACT

For Andrew, the professional challenge and opportunity seemed tremendous. Rainbow Design had been awarded a $1 million contract from BTB Global Transport (a large and profitable shipping firm) to develop a user support system for a new computer system, called Galaxy, being developed for BTB. The new system would support nearly all business functions, such as inventory management, accounting, billing, and ordering, and would require substantial changes in employee job functions and specific tasks.

On Tuesday, Andrew arrived early at Logan Airport in an effort to escape some of the office distractions and to gain additional time to review Rainbow Design's plan of work. By the time the airplane boarded, he had become thoroughly reacquainted with the "meat" of the plan. Rainbow Design would need to develop varied types of user supports, using a learner-control-type format. Specifically, for each job task (e.g., accessing a customer's order number), the employee would be able to select online support when needed from a menu of options, including, for example, cue cards (brief definitions, reminders, or directives), computer-based instruction (CBI), wizards (intelligent demonstration/application functions), and coaches (response-sensitive correction/feedback). Andrew's main responsibility would be to conduct a formative evaluation—first of the overall design approach and later of the individual support tools as they were developed.

Engrossed in his reading, Andrew barely noticed the smooth take-off of the plane as it left Boston behind and cruised toward the West and Albuquerque. The effects of his early morning wake-up made him drowsy, but, before allowing himself to drift off, he wanted to study one additional part of the plan—the staffing section. It looked good. Rainbow Design had a project manager, Cecilia Sullivan, who would perform necessary administrative functions but remain removed from ID decisions. Lois Lakewood, a talented and experienced designer with a doctorate from a nationally recognized graduate program, would head a diverse team of seven designers, including experts in text instruction, computer programming, CBI, and technical graphic design. In a vague, semiconscious way (especially in his sleepy state), Andrew experienced some discomfort with the role of a second, external design team housed in St. Louis. Because BTB Global Transport had a large satellite division in St. Louis, Cecilia thought it wise to hire local designers who could interface with the computer programmers in St. Louis to acquire a better understanding of how the Galaxy computer system would work when completed. A formidable challenge in this project was that user support prototypes would need to be developed based solely on impressions and draft models of Galaxy because the real system wouldn't exist for an indeterminate time. The St. Louis team consisted of three young designers, all having master's degrees in instructional design from Davis University in St. Louis. Their leader, Alicia Rosenthal, in her early thirties, was completing her dissertation for a doctoral degree there.

THE PLANNING MEETING

After arriving in Albuquerque, Andrew made good time while taxiing to the Rainbow Design office, which was located in a suburban strip mall about 10 miles from the airport. The meeting started as scheduled at 1:00 P.M. All the major participants were there, including the Rainbow team, the St. Louis team, and the BTB project manager, Carlton Grove. Lois did an excellent job briefing the group on the purposes of the project. Carlton described his expectations and, despite his lack of much formal ID training (his background was human factors), displayed an excellent intuitive grasp of how user support should be employed and how to increase attractiveness and utility.

Several times during the discussions, Andrew observed that the St. Louis team, through facial gestures and side comments, was inattentive and disapproving of the orientations being proposed. The team had prepared a set of detailed flow diagrams, which, according to their brief description, established a support selection model based on the works of Gagné, Mager, and other theorists. However, there was little time to study the selection model sufficiently, and, as Andrew observed, the St. Louis team members themselves had little interest in it, since they appeared to be primarily a practitioner-oriented group. Lois, he noted, frowned in response to the antics of the St. Louis team, and, when speaking, seemed somewhat tense and guarded.

Andrew closed the day with a clear and forceful overview of his formative evaluation plan. He described it as involving progressive stages of increasing focus and comprehensiveness, as the support prototypes evolved from early drafts to near-final products. In all phases, the evaluation would include multiple data sources (different instruments from different participant groups) to provide triangulation and increase the amount of feedback regarding the quality of the design and its products.

PROJECT PROGRESS

Over the next two months, the Rainbow staff generated several user support prototypes for various employee job functions. Disappointingly, the St. Louis group, given the same assignment, was slow to produce any materials and still seemed constrained by their strict adherence to textbook models they had studied in their ID courses.

In several conference calls among Andrew, Lois (Rainbow), Alicia (St. Louis), and Carlton (BTB), there was obvious strain in the discussions. Provoked largely by Alicia's frequent resistance to the directions proposed, each stakeholder increasingly pursued an individual agenda for his or her team's work. Andrew's agenda, however, was already clearly defined by the current status of the project. With the first series of user supports developed and substantive costs already incurred (as Carlton frequently reminded the group), it was time to initiate the formative evaluation. Carlton wanted it done "yesterday," but "next week would be OK." Andrew mused that this was exactly the type of real-world situation he had recently warned his graduate students to expect.

DEVELOPING AN EVALUATION PLAN

Over the next few days, Andrew drafted questions and rough instrument plans and faxed them to Lois, who turned them—almost magically, it seemed—into a professional, polished set of materials. The final product was an "evaluation manual," consisting of a complete set of instructions, prompts, and instruments for guiding the evaluation step by step. In brief, the basic orientation, as designed by Andrew, was one-on-one trials, in which each participant (interviewee) would: (1) describe his or her background and job activities; (2) walk through a simulation of a computer-based job function in the transportation industry (specifically, scheduling rail shipments); (3) examine sample user support tools made available for specific tasks; (4) rate each tool on various utility, user-interface, and aesthetic dimensions; (5) "reflect aloud" on its possible application; and (6) make recommendations. The manual was directly coordinated with the computer simulation and provided (so Andrew and Lois believed) tight control over the data-collection process, as well as an efficient data-recording system.

The final steps before launching the evaluation were to arrange for interviews and to train the evaluators. Interviewees would be approximately 10 employees at 6 national BTB sites. The evaluators would consist of designers from Rainbow Design and would include, to a more limited extent, Andrew (given time and travel constraints) and St. Louis staff (given Lois's concerns about their commitment and orientation).

Three days before the first set of interviews were to take place in the Minneapolis division, Lois received a call from Alicia, who said, "Given that we've been kind of impeded in our work with the BTB tech types here, I am very interested in taking a lead role in collecting evaluation data from the users. This would give me and my staff a really good feel for who's out there in BTB. User analysis is really our strength." Lois felt a tinge of anxiety about this proposal, but the idea did have some merit. It would occupy the St. Louis group (finally!); it would be good politics with her boss, Cecilia, who had hired the St. Louis team; and it would free the Rainbow staff, who now wouldn't have to travel as much, to work on the design task with their increasing demands. An agreement was reached whereby Alicia and staff would do the bulk of the user interviews (about 40 out of 60). They flew into Albuquerque, met with Andrew and Lois, and, along with the Rainbow crew, received training on the evaluation procedure.

IMPLEMENTING THE EVALUATION

Data collection began. Over the next few weeks (through the end of March), Andrew and Lois each administered a few interviews and felt good about the procedures and materials they had designed. Alicia called Lois intermittently to give status reports from the field (they were always positive). Carlton from BTB called Andrew on April 2 to request that an evaluation report be submitted as a "deliverable" on April 15. "This can be done," Andrew thought, but he'd need Alicia to wrap things up in a week or so and get the data to him. Alicia, in a call to Lois, agreed.

On April 10, a large package with a St. Louis return address arrived at Andrew's Boston office. He opened it with anticipation. He would now need to contact his graduate student assistants, who would code and analyze the data. Pulling up the flaps of the box, he immediately saw a cover memo from Alicia ("Here are all of our data forms—42 interviews!!"). He then removed a stack of about 10 evaluation manuals from the top. All seemed to have the top page correctly filled out—interview name, employee name, time, date, and so on. When he turned to the second page, he noticed that it wasn't filled out. There were no user ratings of the first support tool, only the evaluator's handwritten notes. The same was true for the rest of the manuals—no ratings, only brief, often illegible comments. "Perhaps this one just didn't go right," he thought. "Really, can't use it." Looking at the next manual, his pulse increased, and then at the next manual and then two more, while his heart raced even faster. He dug into the middle of the box and grabbed a stack of three manuals—same thing. All were filled out in the same informal way that completely omitted the ratings.

TRUTH AND CONSEQUENCES

It was the next day by the time his call to Lois produced the call to Alicia that brought Lois's call back to him—with the bad news. Alicia's group had decided on their own that the evaluation manual was really just a "heuristic" (general guide) and that the rating scales and specific comments weren't actually needed. "For doing user analysis," Alicia explained, "My designers favored a more holistic and qualitative orientation." Thus, they formed global opinions that they were certainly willing to share. (Andrew, too, had some opinions, but "share" would be too gentle a way to present them.)

The aftermath in the next few days was that Alicia and her group were severely reprimanded by Cecilia and put on probation in the project. But Andrew had a report to submit. Carlton, from BTB with his scientific orientation in human factors research, would be expecting at least some quantitative results (bar charts and the like), and Andrew had only about 13 correctly completed evaluation manuals—the ones from him and Rainbow Design. The report was due in three days.

PRELIMINARY ANALYSIS QUESTIONS

1. Discuss each issue in the case from the perspective of the four key roles featured: evaluator, design manager, external design team, client project manager.
2. Evaluate the actions taken in the four key roles in terms of making the final product (the evaluation study) successful.
3. Discuss what actions you might have taken in each of the four roles to avoid the problems that occurred.
4. Create a scenario in which the evaluation study is successful and the four key stakeholders are satisfied with the results.

IMPLICATIONS FOR ID PRACTICE

1. Describe the role of formative evaluation in the instructional design process.
2. Describe how instructional design practices can be impacted by unexpected variables and events in real-life contexts.
3. Differentiate between the roles in a design project of a project business manager, a project design manager, an instructional designer, an evaluator, and a client project manager.
4. Describe the importance of a good management system for coordinating the activities of various consultant groups on a design project.

Frank Tawl and Semra Senbetto*

BY PEGGY A. ERTMER AND WALTER DICK

About 10 years ago, the government of a Southeast Asian country (referred to here as SEA), in cooperation with a major U.S. electronics corporation, began to plan the development of a training design center in SEA, in which participants would be trained to design instruction using a systems approach. The hope was that SEA would obtain the long-term capability to determine the need for, and then to develop, appropriate training programs for its workforce. At the time this decision was made, there were no instructional design (ID) training programs being offered in SEA, although there were various training institutes in operation (e.g., the Teacher Training Institute, the National Training Center, and the Vocational Education Center) and numerous government employees who provided training for local businesses. Although these employees served as trainers, they themselves had received little, if any, formal instruction in design theory or practice, and, furthermore, they had never participated in a curriculum that used a systems approach to the design and development of training. Although SEA trainers often delivered instruction on specified content, they had no formal experience with, or knowledge of, adult learning principles or the use of interactive teaching strategies. The instruction they created typically depended on their own content expertise or revolved around instruction that had been imported from the United States and then adapted.

A pair of U.S. designers was hired to plan and develop a curriculum for preparing SEA instructional designers. One of these designers, Frank Tawl, was a university professor and a noted expert on the use of the systems approach for designing instruction. Frank had developed a number of courses at his U.S. university that related to ID topics and issues, and he felt fairly confident that these

---

*Based in part on a 1991 article by Walter Dick, which appeared in *Performance Improvement Quarterly, 4*(1), "The Singapore project: A case study in instructional design," pp. 14–22. Used with permission of the author and publisher. Note that information from the original case was altered in order to increase its educational value for our readers. Readers should not consider this case to be a true representation of the Singapore government.

could be modified to fit the SEA learners' needs. Frank's teammate, Semra Senbetto, was a private consultant who had worked with Frank on a number of previous projects and was noted for her ability to recognize and address culturally relevant issues in situations involving learners from diverse backgrounds.

As part of their front-end analysis, Frank and Semra conducted interviews to determine the current perceptions of professors at the national university, as well as training staffs at the Teacher Training Institute, National Training Center, and the Vocational Education Center, regarding the proposed ID training curriculum. Among other things, they were interested in determining the following: What kinds of training experiences were currently in place at the existing training centers? What procedures did SEA trainers follow when designing and presenting new instruction to fellow Asians?

In these initial interviews, it became clear that the professors at the national university were supportive of whatever the U.S. Americans thought best—teaching whatever content Frank and Semra thought was appropriate, as well as using whatever strategies the Americans typically used. During follow-up interviews, they posed virtually no opposition to Frank's and Semra's ideas; after a suggestion was made, the professors would simply nod in agreement. Although Frank and Semra made a concerted effort to uncover any culturally sensitive issues that should be taken into consideration in the design of the curriculum, they identified almost none. If the SEA professors had any culturally related concerns, they didn't acknowledge them.

Additional interviews were held with potential students for the ID curriculum—namely, the current trainers. Frank and Semra asked questions to determine the following: What did the SEA trainers already know about the design process? What beliefs did they hold that reflected possible acceptance of the systems approach and/or findings from current research regarding the teaching and learning process? What beliefs seemed contradictory to these current theories about teaching and learning? How motivated were they to participate in this new training program? Although, on the surface, these potential students seemed to accept Frank's and Semra's ideas about interactive delivery strategies and alternative assessment measures, they were obviously unclear as to what was expected of them. They wondered how similar this training would be to the imported training they had become accustomed to modifying. Was this instruction going to be more or less effective with their students?

The SEA trainers indicated that they preferred lecture-based instruction and memory-based assessment measures. Interestingly, it was discovered during the interview process that SEA trainers had been modifying "imported" instruction by *eliminating* the built-in interactive activities and changing the assessment techniques to be more memory-based, as opposed to performance-based. The SEA trainers indicated that, although they "mostly" liked these training programs, they were concerned that their students would be uncomfortable performing in front of their peers and mentioned that losing face was something to be avoided at all costs. There was an additional concern that students over 40 years of age may not be sufficiently motivated to perform under the nontraditional conditions advocated by the imported programs. These students would be retiring when they turned 55 and mentioned that the time spent learning new skills, at their "mature" age, was "a real waste."

The majority of the trainers interviewed expressed little motivation to attend this new training when it became available. Those who were interviewed mentioned the following concerns:

- Additional time commitments involved in completing a degree program (all worked full-time)
- A need to learn a new way of designing and delivering training
- The lack of job advancement, salary compensation, or other rewards or recognition being tied to the completion of the program
- A lack of confidence in convincing clients to let them use these new skills

If these concerns were adequately addressed, the trainers indicated, perhaps, they would participate.

Frank and Semra decided to observe a few training programs currently being offered by the National Training Center. Additional time was spent with the instructors of these courses to determine how their training courses had been developed. In essence, the observations supported what had been suggested in the interviews. SEA trainers were accustomed to presenting and attending instructor-led training. They did not like being put on the spot (performing or responding in front of their peers); they liked assessment measures that provided a quick indication of how much they had learned. Also noted was the fact that they used very few media during instruction and did not engage in either needs analysis or formative evaluation procedures when developing instruction. It was difficult, if not impossible, to determine if any of the training being offered was making a difference on the job.

In contrast to the opinions and preferences mentioned by the SEA trainers, the SEA government strongly supported a move to more "modern" training—it was more than eager to imitate the U.S. Americans' approach to the systematic design of instruction. Although Frank and Semra agreed that appropriate teaching methods, such as simulations, role plays, and case studies, should be used when such methods support the instructional objectives of the ID curriculum, they were concerned about motivating the learners to engage in these activities.

Frank and Semra realized that the typical ID competencies needed to be included in a way that fit the needs of the SEA students. Some modifications to a typical ID curriculum would be required. Finally, the question of who should teach the new courses, U.S. or SEA trainers, needed to be addressed. There did not seem to be any easy answers to the many questions facing this experienced design team.

As Frank and Semra labored to design a blueprint for the ID curriculum, including the identification of the strategies and approaches that should be used, they were faced with a number of difficult decisions:

- How to help the students master factual information and develop intellectual skills and positive attitudes regarding the systems approach to ID
- How to motivate the students to use effective learning strategies, including interactive techniques, when appropriate
- How to design and evaluate alternative assessment measures (project-based assessments, simulations, role plays, etc.)

- How to teach the students to use mediated instruction effectively
- How to get buy-in for the use of needs assessment and formative evaluation methods
- How to build the students' confidence to respond and perform in front of peers when appropriate
- How to motivate the older employees
- How to build confidence to work effectively with clients

PRELIMINARY ANALYSIS QUESTIONS

1. Make recommendations for the design decisions facing Frank and Semra.
2. Discuss the trainers' rationale for modifying existing programs. How can their concerns be addressed? Can you suggest modifications and/or improvements that are culturally sensitive?
3. Discuss the previous training experiences of the students in the new design program. What will their expectations be for the new curriculum? What kind of adjustments will they have to make? How can you facilitate this?
4. Provide a recommendation and rationale for selecting instructor(s) for these courses. How much should the instructor(s) be involved in decisions affecting classroom instructional strategies and assessment techniques?
5. Consider evaluation as a sensitive issue in this case. How should the effectiveness of the methods, materials, activities, and media be assessed? How should the students be evaluated?

IMPLICATIONS FOR ID PRACTICE

1. Describe how an instructional designer might deal with issues related to the use of interactive instructional strategies in contexts where such strategies are not common and might not be welcomed.
2. Describe strategies for meeting the needs of older employees, as well as students who work full-time.
3. Outline strategies for promoting needs analysis and formative evaluation techniques.

Maya Thomas

BY CHANDRA ORRILL AND JANETTE R. HILL

Subject: Math ideas
Date: Wed., April 21 08:10 GMT
From: r.ponten@middlecity.k12.ga.us
To: m.thomas@middlecity.k12.ga.us

Maya,

Next year, I will be teaching pre-algebra to at-risk, low-level 7th grade math students. For self-survival, I have got to find an innovative way to reach and teach these kids. I am open to trying ANYTHING! I envision making this like a laboratory class, where we "do math" by doing activities and lots of different things. Obviously these kids are not pencil-and-paper learners. They have got to learn by doing. In my classroom I have 7 student computers and 1 teacher station with Internet connection, so the possibilities are not limitless but are promising.

What do you think?

Ruth Ann Ponten

Maya Thomas, the staff development and instructional consultant for the Middle City school district, looked up from her e-mail and remembered her most recent science class with similar kids and knew that there had to be some way to help Ruth Ann succeed with her students. She picked up the phone to call Ruth Ann and set up a time to talk.

The next afternoon, Maya drove out to Middle City Middle School. As she drove through the rural area, she reflected on the changes that had occurred in the past decade. The community was in a major state of transition. This once quiet community of farmers and working-class folks was changing. College-educated professionals were moving in because they were attracted to the community's tight-knit feeling and immaculate old houses. This physical change was also bringing other modifications, such as different expectations about education and a willingness to try new ideas for teaching and learning. These changes made Maya's job exciting as well as challenging.

Maya arrived at the school at the beginning of Ruth Ann's planning period. Maya entered the room, dodging a couple of students who were rushing off to their next classes. She quickly got inside and sat down at a desk. Ruth Ann, who was writing something on the board, turned and greeted Maya, then resumed what she was doing. After she finished writing, she came over to talk. She explained to Maya that she was so frustrated the last time she taught the pre-algebra class that she just couldn't bear to do it the same way again. Maya listened patiently, knowing that often teachers need time to vent before being able to get to work. Maya found herself thinking about the last class that she taught before becoming a staff development specialist after seven years of teaching. They were a bright group but simply were not motivated to succeed in school. She remembered the helpless feeling of knowing there must be better ways to help her students learn and the frustration of not knowing what those ways were. She empathized with Ruth Ann's stress and feeling of helplessness—this was a tough case.

They talked for about an hour, and, as they talked, Maya took notes identifying some of the assumptions and beliefs that Ruth Ann seemed to hold. Maya began asking Ruth Ann questions about her previous class and about the students she expected next year. Ruth Ann explained that the previous class had been very difficult because the students were out of control. A few of the kids just did not care about what was going on in the class and distracted the rest of the students. Ruth Ann continued to say that, even when the students were on task, they were so deficient in their basic mathematical abilities that she just was not sure where to begin with them. She also mentioned that some of the kids seemed really interested in the technology, which is why she had mentioned that in her e-mail. But Ruth Ann also pointed out that other students seemed to not like the computers at all. She finished by noting her extreme frustration that the students simply would not do their homework.

During the conversation with Ruth Ann, Maya asked about the kinds of students that tended to be enrolled in the class. Ruth Ann commented that it was almost never the farmers' kids or the kids of the college-educated professionals who were tracked into these classes. In fact, these were the kids of the unemployed or blue-collar parents; they tended to move between parents and between schools, and they tended to be latchkey kids. Maya added that these were kids who probably did not have parental support when they got home in the afternoon. Maya pondered how these factors might influence students' reactions to being immersed in a laboratory setting such as Ruth Ann envisioned.

As Ruth Ann talked, Maya realized how often she mentioned getting the kids to work more math problems. Even though Ruth Ann had originally said that she would be open to doing anything to help her kids, Maya realized it might not be as easy as just *saying* it. It was apparent to Maya that Ruth Ann typically taught from the front of the room, giving assignments with many problems, so that students had a lot of opportunities for practice. Learning in this environment meant memorizing formulas and calculating accurately. Ruth Ann had mentioned a laboratory-style class in her e-mail; now she also added that she thought the math needed to tie more to the "real world." Ruth Ann also mentioned that she knew that having students work problems at the board was not enough—that there had to be a better way to teach math. But, she added, she did not know any other way to teach math.

Maya realized that helping Ruth Ann develop a more hands-on, real-world learning environment would be difficult, given the differences in Ruth Ann's desired outcomes and her current practices. Maya knew from personal experience that changing teaching styles was a lot of hard work. She wondered how best to support Ruth Ann in helping the kids succeed.

Maya went home that evening, thinking about Ruth Ann's situation. On her power walk that night, she formulated a plan to help support Ruth Ann: She would talk to some students and teachers to explore the current state of the pre-algebra curriculum, as well as the kinds of things that might improve it. She was determined to begin the next day.

First thing the next morning, Maya started her detective work. She began at the curriculum office to find out which students had taken seventh-grade pre-algebra the previous year and which ones were in the current sixth-grade class. She deliberately selected a few students from each group, dividing them into three subcategories: those who had done very well, those who had struggled, and those who were likely to be in the seventh-grade at-risk pre-algebra class the following year. One-by-one, she talked to about 10 kids over the next week and a half. To round out the analysis, Maya also interviewed each of the teachers about the curriculum and their perceptions regarding students' performances. She also talked with the assistant principal for curriculum about her thoughts on the pre-algebra course (see Tables 33–1 and 33–2 for a summary of student, teacher, and administrator information).

In addition to talking to various people during data gathering, Maya spent time combing through the state and national math standards and the pre-algebra textbook (see Table 33–3 for a summary of curricular information).

Once she had completed the interviews and reviewed the current curricular materials, Maya analyzed the data she had collected. She wanted to be well prepared for her meeting with Ruth Ann the next week. She was surprised to see that the factors working against success in math went beyond those she expected. Maya had anticipated that students of noncollege graduates would be lower performers and would demonstrate lower achievement than other students. However, she also found, among a segment of the population, what looked like a cultural tendency to be resistant to education in general. There was an attitude of "My mom and dad didn't get a high school education and they're doing fine" or "My friends aren't doing well in school" or "My community doesn't care if I succeed here because school isn't an important part of my life" or a combination of these. Maya was saddened by this. She wondered, "How do you help students with these kinds of attitudes see the value of pre-algebra in everyday situations?"

About three weeks later, Maya and Ruth Ann finally got to spend half a day working on ideas for the class. Maya presented a short synopsis of her findings. Ruth Ann was surprised, and like Maya, she was saddened by the poor attitudes of the lower-achieving students. Ruth Ann was also surprised at the discrepancies between what the national standards called for and what her book was providing. She told Maya that she knew the book had problems but did not realize that it neglected so many important skills. Then, Ruth Ann and Maya looked over a variety of new curricular materials and discussed what issues there would be in integrating them into the math curriculum.

TABLE 33–1 *Summary of Field Notes from Student Interviews*

Source	Notes
High 7th grade math achievers at Middle City	– "6th and 7th grade math was boring. They've already covered all this stuff and I want to do something new." – "I just don't see how this math will help me when I grow up." – Many like some group work but don't like being graded in groups because students don't always do their part in a group. – The overwhelming student definition for math is that it means working a lot of problems. – Many students claim to like using the calculator because it makes things easier. – Several commented that their favorite part of math is the puzzles (number and shape) that they get to work on when they have extra time in class. – Most students don't really like the computers because they do only drill and practice.
Poor 7th grade math achievers at Middle City	– "6th and 7th grade math was boring." – "6th and 7th grade math didn't make any sense to me." – "All the teacher did was work problems on the board and expect us to do them at our desks." – "There was too much homework." – "My mom works and can't help me with my homework." – "I hate math." – "Man, my dad says that this math is useless. I don't know why I have to do it." – Students reported liking classes that involve hands-on activities, such as science. – Most of the students said they like working in groups. – Most said that they like solving problems. – A few commented that they used to like math but that it is not fun anymore. – They don't really like the computers because they do only drill and practice.
Poor 6th grade achievers (next year's 7th grade at-risk pre-algebra class)	– None like math—it's boring and hard. – None see connection to real life. – Most like hands-on work in science. – None want a teacher who makes them do a lot of homework. – "I can't get any help with my homework at home." – "This math won't matter when I grow up—just as long as I can add and stuff. I can just use a calculator." – They all hope that the teacher will help them more than just talking at the board because that is boring and because they don't always understand what the teacher is doing. – Most haven't really used the computers a lot. – They all seemed to think that there are too many problems to work in the book. Their homework takes too long, and they don't know how to do it.

TABLE 33–2 *Summary of Field Notes from Interviews with Ruth Ann and Assistant Principal*

Source	Notes
Ruth Ann	– Feels that regular curriculum doesn't work for this kind of learner
	– Hates to teach at the board and let students practice yet does this all the time in all of her classes
	– Believes that low-achieving kids can benefit from doing hands-on activities in authentic situations
	– Worries about class conduct—the pre-algebra kids tend to be rowdy and off-task and often skip class
	– Wants to look at innovative ways to grade, but is bound to the *A, B, C, D, F* policy of the school
	– Doesn't like the current book used for these kids because it is too choppy—ideas are covered in strange orders and for the wrong amount of time
Assistant principal for curriculum	– Supports Ruth Ann in whatever efforts she takes; these kids aren't succeeding, so any success is a giant step
	– Would like to see a more progressive approach to math but stressed that the state standards *must* be met
	– Wants to have a written pre-test, midterm, and post-test
	– Knows that there is little money to support the purchase of materials for the students
	– Wants synergy with other in-school programs, if possible

Ruth Ann: My first reaction to these materials is that I have no idea where to start. I mean, I can see that these problems are really good—they are open-ended and would get the kids engaged. But how would I help them solve these problems when they don't even have the basics? I'm a person who believes that you need the foundations first. Develop the skills—then you can move on to these problems.

Maya: OK. I can understand your point. The students you're targeting do come in with really low skills. But don't you think that we need to explore some different ways to help them? I mean, after all, if the traditional drill and practice worked for these kids, you wouldn't have them in this class, would you?"

Ruth Ann: That's true. And I can see how these materials could really make the kids think. But how do I know I'm meeting the state standards? I don't see how this is going to help them do better on the test.

Maya: I'm glad you see some potential here. Maybe you and I can work together to see how they meet the standards.

TABLE 33–3 *Summary of Curriculum Information from State Standards, National Standards, and Textbook*

Source	Notes
State standards	– Include a lot of computational skills. – Many do not correlate to national tests (NAEP, PSAT) in their focus. – Include some explicit practical links (e.g., calculate sales tax). – Require considerable mastery of concepts involving variable use and graphing. – Include fractions, decimals, and percents. – Include lots of discrete skills—no discussion of integrating or applying many.
National standards	– NCTM breaks into 10 key areas: number and operation, algebra, geometry, measurement, data analysis and probability, problem solving, reasoning and proof, communication, connections, and representations. – Concerned mostly with understanding, with less attention to computational skill. – NAEP calls for students' ability to connect knowledge across mathematical areas – NAEP is centered on five major strands (algebra, number sense, geometry, statistics, and measurement) and three major kinds of abilities (computational understanding, procedural knowledge, and problem solving). – NAEP supports use of manipulatives and assessment using constructed responses.
Textbook	– Includes a lot of practice in computation. – Focuses on the topics listed in the state standards. – Does not focus on communication, connections, or representations. – Is visually appealing and interesting. – Includes a link to everyday life in each chapter, but problems do not come from that. – Includes regular multiple-choice test-practice activities to prepare students for national standardized tests. – Review problems are offered regularly throughout each chapter to review computation. – Includes a technology integration idea in every unit. – Chapter problems include one or two higher-order thinking problems. – There is no explicit call for manipulatives or alternative materials; everything can be done with paper and pencil.

Ruth Ann: Won't the kids panic when they see these? I mean, these kids don't like school—they don't do their homework and they certainly aren't going to like all the writing.

Maya: You might be right about the writing. Do you think that the kids will see these materials as more relevant to their everyday lives?

Ruth Ann: Well, yeah. Still, what if the students refuse to do the work? But what if *I* can't work the problems?

Maya: Maybe we can come up with some incentives to help get the kids interested. As for you not being able to work the problems, we'll make sure that you have some practice ahead of time, so you'll be fine. It may actually be a great way to get the students interested: Have them help you!

Ruth Ann: Well, I can see that the students would at least have answers to some of their questions about how they'll use it in the real world. I worry, though, about the grading. How will I grade this work?

Maya: Yeah, grading will be different in this kind of class. This is something I think we can work on together.

Ruth Ann: I mean, all this writing—how will I know what they're thinking? I'm afraid that I won't see where they are having problems in this. They just don't have to do enough problems to indicate where the gaps are in their skills.

Maya: I think you'll be surprised. I talked to a teacher at a workshop a couple weeks ago who is using this kind of approach. She said she actually knows *more* about her students' thinking now than she did when they were just working problems. She says it's been wonderful.

Ruth Ann: And what about the parents? I know that they'll be screaming at me— this isn't what they know as math!

Maya: I can see your point here.

Ruth Ann: Hmm, I just don't know, Maya. I mean, we just went through textbook adoption a couple years ago, and we were so sure that we chose the best stuff out there. How can I go and change what I do now? I know the kids need something more than the textbooks, but this is a big change. Well, let me keep these materials and look at them more closely. [Ruth Ann is flipping through the notebooks.] Hey, here's an activity for graphing. We'll be doing that in one of my classes later in the week— maybe I can try it there.

Maya: Great. How about if we sit down again next week and talk about this some more?

Ruth Ann: Sounds good!

Maya left feeling hopeful, but there was still no firm commitment to a new approach. Ruth Ann raised a number of issues that Maya thought indicated that Ruth Ann might not be comfortable with adopting a new approach. It appeared that, although Ruth Ann wanted to implement a new approach in her classroom, she was reluctant to jump in. Maya believed that Ruth Ann wanted to change and was working in a system that valued change. However, there was still a strong core in the community that might hold tight to tradition, and Maya thought that Ruth Ann might be a little uncomfortable actually implementing the approach that she had initially said she wanted.

How could she and Ruth Ann work together to create a better math experience, given all these constraints? What kinds of support could she offer Ruth Ann that might help her use these innovative curricula to get the kids interested in math? How could they meet the assessment requirements set forth by the assistant principal and still keep the instruction focused on the learning and development of mathematical knowledge? These were the questions that were going through Maya's head as she reflected on the conversation with Ruth Ann. Although she knew that it would be a lot of work, she felt confident that she could help Ruth Ann. This is what she enjoyed about her work.

PRELIMINARY ANALYSIS QUESTIONS

1. Critique the steps Maya took to identify the needs in the case, including the collection and analysis of data.
2. What are some of the options Maya can explore to support the learning environment Ruth Ann requested?
3. What are some of the critical factors Maya needs to attend to if this effort is to be successful?
4. Consider how the work with Ruth Ann could be used as a starting place for schoolwide mathematics reform. Does that change the way Maya should work with Ruth Ann and the other math teachers? Does it change the options they should consider?
5. How might the community and parents influence the success of this effort?

IMPLICATIONS FOR ID PRACTICE

1. Discuss how characteristics of an organization affect the outcomes of a needs assessment.
2. Discuss how factors such as culture and resource availability impact change management.
3. To what extent should a change manager determine the direction a change should go? Who owns the change process?
4. What are some ways to move people from one stage of adoption to the next?

Elizabeth Ward and Catherine Peterson

BY CHRISTINE L. THORNAM
AND LAUREN CLARK

BACKGROUND

Preparing to teach Culture in Health and Healthcare during the upcoming winter intersession was going to be a new and exciting challenge for Dr. Elizabeth Ward. The Office of Extended Studies (OES) at the university asked her to offer the course to students living in remote parts of the state using the interactive video conferencing system. Elizabeth didn't have much experience with telecommunications but had a passion for teaching and was an expert and a leader in her field of specialization within nursing. The technical aspects of connecting with students at the remote classroom locations was something new to Elizabeth, but she was consciously making an effort to improve her technology-related skills and was up for the challenge. The OES provided support to faculty members who were teaching for the first time with the video conferencing system, and Elizabeth planned to avail herself of that assistance. Elizabeth contacted the OES to set up a meeting with its faculty support and instructional design personnel to discuss the necessary adjustments to her course delivery by video conference.

The meeting went well. Elizabeth realized that reaching students in the remote classroom was more than switching cameras and talking to students on a television monitor. She would need to extend her current ability to facilitate a psychological connection among students and between the students and herself. Following the meeting, minor logistical modifications were made to the course syllabus and assignments to accommodate the students located in the remote classrooms. Also, in an effort to reduce the psychological distance, lectures and teacher-led activities were modified to include more student discussion and small-group activities. The result was a clearer description of learner outcomes and the possibility of a higher level of student interactivity. Elizabeth enjoyed scrutinizing her teaching practice and course design in preparation for delivering her course by video conference because she could see how it would benefit her students. Her early reluctance to teach via video conferencing out of fear that it might reflect poorly on her teaching skills or that she might risk losing her status as an expert in her content area was soon replaced by enthusiasm for the process.

When the registration period for the winter intersession ended, the enrollment in the course was adequate to offer the course locally but was insufficient to support the delivery of the course to students in rural areas of the state. Elizabeth felt disappointment at the missed opportunity to test the changes to the course and to test her confidence in teaching with technology. However, given the option to teach the face-to-face course in the technology classroom, specially designed for video conferencing, Elizabeth decided to turn disappointment into opportunity. She used the technology classroom to teach the course locally as a way to acquaint herself with the equipment and to test changes to the course with students in the face-to-face classroom. The course went well, and Elizabeth and the students both enjoyed the experience. Elizabeth's appetite for teaching with technology was whetted; there was no turning back.

New Possibilities

After the initial disappointment of not teaching on the video conferencing system wore off, Elizabeth began to wonder about the feasibility of ever offering the course on the video conferencing system. Elizabeth wanted to maintain a low enrollment in the course to optimize student–student and teacher–student interaction. However, this desire for low enrollment, combined with the fact that the course was not required, made the possibility of future video conferencing look rather bleak. Elizabeth started thinking about other delivery methods as a way to offer the course to students in distant locations.

The second repurposing of the course began with an opportunity to apply for a small grant. Elizabeth called Catherine Peterson, the instructional designer in the OES and said, "You know, the Office of Education has these grants called *Innovations in Education*. The grants help the faculty develop new ideas, especially related to teaching with technology. Since we have a start on adapting this course for video conferencing, why don't we take the next step and redesign it for the Web? The two of us could apply for one of those grants and use the money to build on the ideas we developed for video conferencing last semester."

Catherine was very excited about Elizabeth's phone call. Catherine's experiences related primarily to multimedia development and telecommunications, including video production and video conferencing. She designed online courses with other professors but typically met resistance when proposing anything but a text-based approach. The excitement she perceived in Elizabeth's voice struck a positive chord with Catherine. Still, she wondered if her experience with Elizabeth would be any different from her experiences with other professors. Was teaching with technology a brief romance for Elizabeth, or was it a reality she was meeting head-on? Was Elizabeth looking for techno-gimmicks, or was she trying to strengthen her instruction through technology? Did Elizabeth want to use technology simply to deliver the course, or did she want to use it to provide advantages that learners would not have in face-to-face instruction?

Elizabeth had a few questions of her own. How could the course be designed to enhance students' personal growth with respect to their cultural identities? Would students be equipped with the necessary hardware and software, as well as the technical skills necessary to access Web-based instruction? Or would redesigning this course for delivery on the Web be an exercise in futility, just as the video conferencing experience had been? Still, after talking about the possibilities, both Catherine and Elizabeth agreed that, although there would be bumps in the road ahead, they were both ready for this adventure.

While they were putting the proposal together, the university administration decided that all courses delivered through OES would be repurposed for delivery on the Web. In addition, all courses would be required to replace current course goals with performance-based competencies. This meant that Elizabeth and Catherine had to find a way to assess students' performances in cross-cultural patient encounters in a Web-based learning environment. Determining whether learners could perform the expected competencies at the end of the course would be difficult, especially since most of the students in the course would never set foot in the same city as Elizabeth. However, Elizabeth and Catherine decided to apply for the grant funds. The application for the *Innovations in Education* grant was written, accepted, and funded for $5,000.

THE COURSE

Elizabeth was eager to make a clear distinction between this course and other cultural competency courses she had reviewed. She did not want the course to be a laundry list of "do this, don't do that" when encountering a patient from another culture but, rather, a more respectful, fuller understanding of how culture influences one's health care practices—including the personal cultural influences health care providers bring with them to their practice. Elizabeth explained to Catherine: "I want students to think about how cross-cultural encounters with their patients are *crucial* to their nursing practice and to the delivery of safe and effective care. How can we get the students to really experience the beneficial effects of care delivered by culturally competent health care practitioners and, just as important, to grasp the potentially damaging effect of care that is *not* culturally competent? And, oh, yes, we need to design something that provides evidence of students' ability to perform competently in a cross-cultural patient-provider encounter."

Elizabeth wanted students to arrive at an understanding of the influence of cultural variation on clinical nursing practice and to use a culturally informed theoretical framework when considering patients' symptoms during a cross-cultural patient-provider encounter. The course addressed theory derived from medical anthropology as a basis for interpreting patients' construction of illness and eliciting patients' symptoms.

Based on Elizabeth's clinical observations and expertise, her experience teaching the course, and previous course evaluations, she wanted to sequence the course conceptually as expressed in the expected learner outcomes: (1) Recognize the broad cultural variation in clinical nursing practice and (2) apply a culturally informed theoretical framework when communicating with patients. The early part of the course emphasized the discovery of one's own cultural heritage. The second part of the course emphasized theoretical perspectives and the application of these perspectives to clinical cross-cultural patient encounters.

Six broad topics were identified and later molded into modules:

1. Introduction to health care in multicultural environments (demographic trends, diversity vocabulary, common clinical challenges in multicultural health care environments)
2. Genogram (a picture of the relationships within a family) skills (self-disclosure, benefits of self-awareness, skills needed to assess patients' heritage)
3. Self-awareness (self-identity exercises, skills needed to assess patients' culture)
4. Theoretical frameworks in nursing practice (advantages of a theoretical approach to nursing care, including cultural assessment)
5. The viewing of symptoms through a theoretical lens (symptoms as merely symptoms, explanatory models, idioms of distress, semantic illness networks, folk illnesses, and the analysis of illness narratives)
6. Cross-cultural communication standards and skills (outcomes of provider-client [mis]communication; implications of differences between patients and providers in terms of language, semantics, and disease classification; and the elicitation of illness narratives cross-culturally)

Design Issues

Beginning early in the design process, Elizabeth was eager to make the online course visually appealing and media-rich. She had observed many online courses that were heavily text-based and had heard student criticism of those courses. She took pride in students' positive evaluations of her face-to-face teaching and wanted to avoid designing an online course that might lead to poor reflection on her teaching practice. Furthermore, her face-to-face teaching strategies consisted of interactive small-group collaborations, so why should her online course consist of lecture notes?

For example, activities such as drawing one's own genogram were deemed effective in the face-to-face classroom and, so, were redesigned as interactive graphics for the Web-based course (see Figure 34–1). This allowed students to construct and culturally code a genogram of their own families.

Existing audio and video recordings that demonstrated cross-cultural patient-provider encounters were located and digitized for use in the course. These recordings approximated the high degree of interpersonal relatedness inherent in cross-cultural communication and assessment (see Figure 34–2). In addition, an excerpt of a lecture by a noted theorist in the field of medical anthropology added special interest to the module that introduced theory. Finally, Elizabeth took great care to design visually appealing screens throughout the course (see Figures 34–3 and 34–4).

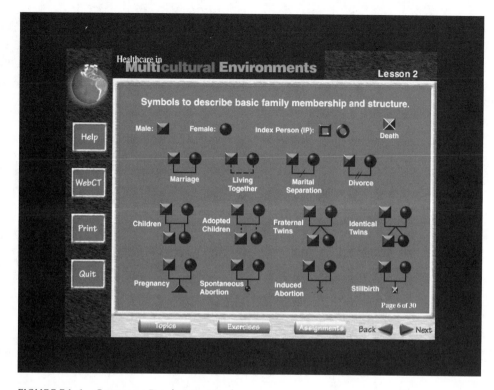

FIGURE 34–1 Genogram Development Tool

However, because of the large, digitized audio and video data files, and the graphically rich nature of the interactive course material, download times would be extremely slow if added to the Web-based course. Therefore, Elizabeth and Catherine decided to develop a CD-ROM. This was hyperlinked to the Web-based course, which also housed the text-based materials, the student discussion area, and course-management tools. Students could purchase the CD-ROM in the bookstore, just as they would buy a textbook.

Elizabeth was quite pleased with the progress toward the redesign of the course, which was renamed Healthcare in Multicultural Environments. However, she still had a few things to resolve. One of the shortcomings of the face-to-face course, as it was taught in prior semesters, was lack of exposure to, and participation in, real-world, cross-cultural issues faced by nurses. Elizabeth wanted to make up for that deficiency when redesigning the course and believed that information about current issues could be accessed on the Web. However, harnessing all of the information on the Web into something meaningful to clinical practice would be a challenge. As with planning for the video conference delivery of the course, Elizabeth was concerned about facilitating a psychological connection among the students and between the students and herself. On a broader scale, she wondered if she

FIGURE 34–2   Video of Cross-Cultural Patient Encounter with Interpreter

would be able to create a learning environment in which students could truly experience the affective elements of the course.

Elizabeth also knew that an understanding of the health care practices of other cultures begins with understanding one's own cultural heritage. For this reason, the redesigned course had an early emphasis on the student's journey of self-discovery. She recognized, however, that this could be dangerous if a student discovered painful family facts while isolated from a supportive group of peers or a supportive teacher. Also, Elizabeth worried about what to do if a student used the discussion forum as a soapbox to express a new found personal cultural identity.

Another concern centered on the school's shift to performance-based, competency assessments of learning. Elizabeth needed evidence of students' ability to communicate cross-culturally to satisfy the school's new requirements. This meant finding a way to evaluate students' performances in cross-cultural patient encounters.

Pondering all this, Elizabeth developed a list of questions to ask Catherine when they next met. Although she was not sure how to solve all the potential problems, she certainly felt excited about the possibilities ahead.

FIGURE 34–3   Course Title Screen

PRELIMINARY ANALYSIS QUESTIONS

1. Given Elizabeth's passion for teaching and her expert knowledge of the course content, how is this course redesign likely to affect Elizabeth's interaction with her students?
2. What support could you provide in this environment to protect students who might make painful discoveries about themselves? What strategies could be used to deal with inappropriate and excessive disclosure of personal information?
3. Given the content and the learners, develop a course outline that will enable learners to achieve the course goals.
4. Suggest appropriate methods for assessing learner performance.

IMPLICATIONS FOR ID PRACTICE

1. What are the advantages and disadvantages to using the Web to deliver a course with a high level of affective subject matter?

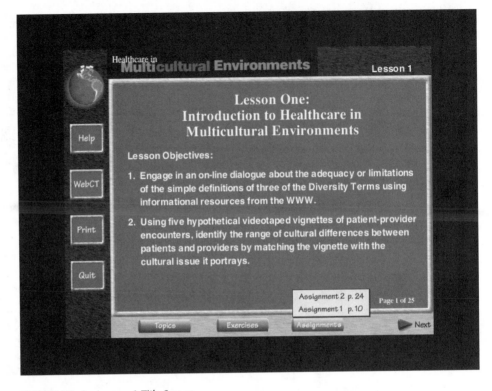

FIGURE 34–4 Lesson 1 Title Screen

2. What are the benefits and challenges of offering a course in cross-cultural communication via the Web?
3. Discuss when and how it might and might not be appropriate to use the Web to implement authentic assessment strategies.

Brent Wilson and May Lowry: The COMET® Modules

BY BRENT G. WILSON, MAY LOWRY, AND JOE LAMOS

THE INTERVIEW

Brent Wilson and May Lowry stepped into Joe Lamos's corner office. Joe was head of distance learning in the COMET® Program, a cooperative agency funded principally by the National Weather Service, with support from the air force and navy, charged with linking forecasters with weather scientists through on-site and distance-based training programs. Joe had stepped out, so Brent and May parked their bags and sat down at the roundtable beside Joe's computer. Within a minute, he arrived.

"Thank you for waiting." After pleasantries, Joe initiated the conversation. "Let me give you some background. The COMET® Program was started here in Boulder in 1989. UCAR—the University Center for Atmospheric Research— has a cooperative agreement with its sponsoring agencies to provide education and training in the application of the latest atmospheric science to weather fore- casting. The program uses teams of university professors, scientists, working forecasters, and instructional designers to design a program to provide profes- sional development to weather forecasters. This education and training both sup- ports the modernization activities of the weather services and provides a resource for the larger meteorological community.

"The program we want evaluated is our DL—distance learning—program. The National Weather Service, air force, and navy have about 5,000 forecasters all over the world, including in small local offices and on overseas bases and ships. It is usually too expensive and time-consuming to send those folks to a training center, so we are asked to provide on-station learning materials. What we have tried to do with the distance learning is to provide high-quality science information and forecast training, using state-of-the-art multimedia, first on videodisc and now on CD-ROM.

"You've been contracted to evaluate our series of multimedia modules. We have nine modules out now, distributed to all forecaster offices in the National Weather Service, air force, and navy. The modules run 4–12 hours in length and provide fairly comprehensive training on a variety of topics—the forecast process, marine meteorology, and so on. After turning out modules for five years, we're ready for a comprehensive evaluation of their quality. We want you to find out how they're being received and used out in the field."

May was listening intently. "Joe, tell us more about the module design."

"The modules are built around engaging scenarios depicting problems faced by forecasters," Joe responded with enthusiasm. "Learners are encouraged to describe how they would approach the problems. They're provided with help in the form of information, advice, quizzes, animation, and video clips of experts discussing the particular weather topic and forecasting techniques. We've put a lot of work into our designs; they've won awards, and we think they're generally very sound."

Brent asked, "What leads you to look at evaluating the program now? Is there something in particular you're looking for?" Joe responded, "Our designers and staff meteorologists get out in the field occasionally. They're expected to write up and share a short trip report for every site visit they make. Lately, these field reports have indicated a lack of use of the modules. We're hearing, word-of-mouth, that some offices don't have workstations operating correctly—or forecasters just aren't taking time to go through the material."

Joe continued, "That's why you need to get out in the offices to see how forecasters are making use of the training. I also think that a written survey will help you triangulate your office observations and interviews."

"It'll be loads of work, but I think it'll be worth it," May agreed. "You don't do a comprehensive evaluation very often; it's best to do it right."

Joe pulled out a summary sheet containing some key information about the COMET® Program and the modules (see Figure 35–1). "Here is the basic information you requested earlier. I've tried to lay it out clearly and succinctly; ask me if you have further questions."

Brent took the sheet and glanced down at the information. "Looks great, Joe. We'll take it from here."

FIELD INTERVIEWS

Over a 30-day period, Brent and May traveled to various corners of the country, observing office conditions and interviewing forecasters. The following field notes present essential findings of those visits.

Brent's Field Notes: Southland Air Force Base

The weather office is located within the main flight terminal building. The forecasting work area is directly connected to the pilot briefing area—not divided or

---

COMET Program Summary Sheet

Mission. To provide training that shows forecasters how to apply the latest scientific findings to their everyday forecasting work.

Primary clients. Three government agencies: The National Weather Service (NWS) and the weather-forecasting divisions of the air force (AWS) and navy (NMOC). There are more NWS personnel to train; they tend to have more formal education than navy and air force forecasters.

COMET modules. Nine modules have been developed and disseminated to forecast offices. The modules are funded through a cooperative agreement between the COMET Program and its sponsoring government agencies and are automatically sent free of charge to all forecast offices. Each office has a COMET workstation, comprised of a videodisc player attached to a computer.

Field support. The COMET Program has a telephone helpline, which allows forecasters to call in with questions. Most questions have to do with setup and software problems. The workstations are supposed to be devoted to COMET modules, but many offices install other applications, causing occasional conflicts and bugs in the running of the modules.

FIGURE 35–1

separated in any way. Eight or nine forecasters are assigned to the office, with three or so on-shift at a time. The COMET® modules have been moved alongside a wall in the hall just outside the forecasting area, close to traffic between rooms. There seems little room to view the modules without being in the way.

Stan, senior airman: The system keeps crashing. The main module that we use is for the Doppler radar. I just came out of school; I didn't know how to use Doppler. Pretty much, that's what we use. The other modules are not used.

Celia, master sergeant, forecaster, 13 years forecast experience: I did the Doppler series. It was interesting. They were good. To be honest, if I have to think about it, I cannot remember any other ones that I've done. About three-quarters of the time it doesn't work. But Stan's in charge. Now we'll get it going. How do we get trained? Around here, it seems as if they just hand us new stuff to do, and it's kind of osmosis—I just learn to do it. You just pick everybody else's brain. Someone comes right out of school and says, "Hey, how come you're not using this?" So I learn how to use a new tool or database by picking other people's brains. We share ideas.

May's Field Notes: Westcoast Forecast Office, National Weather Service

The Westcoast Forecast Office is located in a beautiful new facility. Like the other NWS offices, the hub is a ring of computer workstations, where the forecasters spend their time developing the weather products. This is a large office, with 40 forecasters and interns and a large support staff.

Group Interview

In an interview, the group talked about the NWS as a "fair weather service"—that is, they operate on the premise that there will never be a weather emergency and that no one will ever be out sick or take a vacation, so there is no slack at all in the staffing. This is a problem for training, because someone must be pulled off his or her shift to complete the training, which they are loathe to do. "Our ethic is that you shouldn't leave your station. You must maintain a presence at your desk."

Mark, a training officer, stated, "Training is something you do continuously. It does not fit for us to go down the hall and around the corner and carve out time for a module. Training for a forecaster is apprenticeship, and the problem always is a lack of time. Forecasters are individually trained—OTJ."

Others in the group agreed that there wasn't enough of Mark to go around. A big help would be for the COMET® Program to help Mark.

The group made some comments on the modules:

- The advantages of the modules are that they are self-paced, one can go back to get information if reticent to ask someone in the office.
- The hardware is not sufficient.
- We need relatively small and discrete chunks of information (e.g., 30–50 minutes).
- We really need instantaneous training on essential information.
- Shorter chunks: "We would love to have an hour on icing, an hour on turbulence, and so on."
- The modules need to be application-based—something we can use.

One group member commented: "COMET® can help us best by helping us frame local information, so that we can use it to train our own." He gave the example of the 1986 flood in their area. "It is an important weather event to us, and we have knowledge of it in our heads. How can we best use it to teach our forecasters? We need an electronic three-ring binder."

Brent's Field Notes: Old Town Air Force Base

The forecasting office is located in one of the hangars near the airfield, presently used by a fleet of vehicles. The office appears to be in serious need of remodeling. A divider separates the forecast area from the briefing area. When a pilot comes in for a briefing, the forecaster leaves the forecast area, walks around the divider, and offers the briefing. Five forecasters are available for shift scheduling at this office. That averages about one forecaster in the office at any given time. Professional interactions are usually limited to shift changes.

Pete, master sergeant, station chief/superintendent, 12 years forecast experience: We all know there's something in the modules to listen to; it's just different from what our focus is. We have never had the luxury of really forecasting the weather. What we've had to do is put together a forecast usually as fast as we can. Were talking to airborne air crews, and it's real easy to get into a reactive mode. We make the forecast quickly. An hour later, the forecast is already blown. It doesn't take much for things to go downhill quickly—what happens is we have to issue amendments. We have to answer telephones, issue briefings, and deal with a number of clients at once; we don't really have time to do a thorough analysis, as we'd like to do. If it were just forecasting, we could do a better job.

Brent's Field Notes: South River Office, National Weather Service

About a half-dozen forecasters are working. The COMET® workstation is in the main room, partially partitioned yet close to the circular forecasting area. I observe a good amount of collaboration in the office, with forecasters occasionally consulting together.

Jim, forecaster, 18 years forecast experience: I like being able to move around and interact with the material. I like the practices on the material. You're able to learn that way. The material is good, good techniques. An index would be useful for the modules. That way, let's say I'm dealing with a recurring situation here that doesn't seem to fit any model. I could try and look up similar cases in the modules or look for ideas that might also account for what's happening. I'd also like an opportunity to raise some of these problems to the scientists and get them to help us.

Blair, lead forecaster, 25 years forecast experience: The location of the COMET® workstation is separate from the work area. It's physically inconvenient for me to be walking over to the COMET® workstation, work a few minutes, then have to go back to answer a phone. I feel disconnected over there. I get an extra shift about once every two to three months where I can work on a COMET® module.

Pat, union steward, 33 years forecast experience [on requiring completion of the modules]: It's tough to get too regimental in an operational environment. You can't dictate requirements because you have to allow people to be fairly flexible in doing their jobs. From a union perspective, you probably could encourage individuals to complete certain modules, as part of their performance appraisals—you would want to negotiate that with them. But I don't think it would work as a national policy. I'm sure a national policy like that would require some kind of union approval.

May's Field Notes: Windy Point Office, National Weather Service

The Windy Point office is located in a somewhat remote area near the water with a view of the mountains. The heart of the office is a ring of computer stations. The middle of the ring is a work area with phones and rows of three-ring binders and other kinds of well-thumbed notebooks. Around the perimeter of the office are smaller cubicles for the forecasters and support people, a conference/training room, a break room, storage rooms, and a cubicle devoted to the COMET® workstation.

I arrived during a shift change. It reminded me of shift changes in hospitals during morning report or night report. The shifts overlapped, so that the departing forecaster could brief the arriving forecaster. The weather had been quite mild, but the forecasters still took about 30 minutes to exchange information.

In addition to the formal briefing at the change of a shift, I was struck by the amount of informal talk and exchange. It seemed that everyone was talking to someone else most of the time. Forecasters would sit at a station for a few minutes but would inevitably call someone over to look at the screen or would go over to another forecaster's station to compare notes. The norm seems to be collaboration with others and coordination of the work almost constantly.

Later, when I asked them about this coordination, the marine forecaster told me that no "weather product" goes out of the office without several people checking it and concurring. In addition, the marine forecast must be compatible with the public forecast and the aviation forecast, so that the office forecasts are consistent. Several people reminded me that forecasting is inexact, and two good forecasters can look at the same data and come up with different conclusions. They have to come to a consensus before the forecast goes public. I held an interview with a small group of forecasters; some comments included:

- "Give us something we can use at our workstations."
- "Smaller topics! [enthusiastic agreement all around] We have two hours to look at modules on a really good day. Thirty-minute to one-hour chunks would be best."
- "The index is missing; include a guide in the modules called 'Dr. Raindrop' [office joke]."
- "Give a time estimate on each section, so that we can plan when to use it."
- "Give me something I can finish; otherwise, I tend to go to sleep."
- "Give us something we can pull up—just in time—when we need it."
- "Good source of information. I like the self-paced strategy."

Jack, the lead forecaster, wasn't there for the group interview. Nevertheless, the same themes came up in conversation with him. Jack seems to be the grand old man of the office and everyone's mentor. This seems to be the norm in the forecast office—more examples of collaboration in forecasting and the apprenticeship style of training in the office.

One of Jack's main jobs is coaching. He spends about 30 to 45 minutes "on the fly" with a forecaster. His materials are in binders he has collected over the years, including materials from COMET® classes, which he thinks are great. He grabbed a binder and enthusiastically flipped through it. He said that every trainer has a binder like that one, full of their favorite maps, handouts, and so on. It is their personal cache, and they refer to them all the time—"the most useful training tool."

RESULTS OF THE WRITTEN SURVEY

In addition to site visits, the research team administered written surveys to a sample of forecasters across all three agencies. The findings from the surveys were mostly consistent with reports from site visits, focus groups, and interviews. The modules generally have a good word-of-mouth reputation among both users and potential users but a low rate of use.

Module Use

Forecasters were asked which of the nine modules they had used or completed. Module use followed a distinct trend, with older modules used more heavily than newer modules. This declining use rate partly reflects less opportunity by the forecasters to review the modules. Use rates by the NWS are substantially higher than for either the air force or the navy.

Module Design

The survey asked forecasters to rate the modules on the appropriateness of the content and the effectiveness of the instructional strategies and media. Overall, the forecasters reported that the modules are well designed. They especially appreciated the multimedia format, interactive instructional strategies, and the self-paced learning. Eighty-one percent reported that the COMET® modules contain information that is useful to them in their jobs. A quarter of them felt that there is too much emphasis on scientific information and not enough on the everyday skills of forecasting. The most frequent complaint was not having enough time to complete the modules.

PULLING IT ALL TOGETHER

After four months of gathering information through site visits and written surveys, it was time to make some sense of it. It was clear that the forecasters approved of the module design and sometimes used the modules but that they were not getting full use out of them. Why not?

Brent and May knew that there were issues of time, hardware/software, relevance to the job, accessibility, and compatibility with the routines of work and training. Now it was time to formulate recommendations and help the COMET® Program decide its course of action.

PRELIMINARY ANALYSIS QUESTIONS

1. Review the codes Brent and May used for categorizing the evaluation data, reflecting factors that seemed to have some effect on the use rate of the modules:

   T: time issues

   S/H: software/hardware issues

R: relevance to the forecasters' work

A: accessibility (Could the forecasters get to the modules to use, and, once they got to them, could they successfully navigate inside the lesson?)

C: compatibility (do the modules fit with the work and training routines of the office?)

What other codes would you add to this list? Would you modify or delete any? Provide a rationale for your decision.

2. Make a list of barriers to the successful use of the modules. Which of these barriers seem most important? Develop a conceptual scheme for organizing these barriers into a meaningful framework (e.g., individual vs. group factors; motivational vs. information; performance context vs. training context) in order to understand the problem better and to develop appropriate interventions.

3. List some possible interventions or changes that would address the identified barriers. Classify interventions in terms of cost (expensive vs. inexpensive) and time (short-term vs. long-term).

4. Consider the value implications of various interventions. How radical should interventions be? For example, one intervention is to rethink the COMET® Program's fundamental mission, emphasizing work performance over the application of scientific knowledge. Such a change may have far-reaching consequences for the organization, including some unforeseen negative consequences. How do you decide a best approach?

5. Develop a set of recommendations to present to Joe and the COMET® Program's staff for improving the effective use of the modules in the field. Be prepared to defend your recommendations with data and reasoning that link your recommendations to likely improvements.

IMPLICATIONS FOR ID PRACTICE

1. Discuss the importance of contextual factors in the implementation of instructional design products.

2. What kinds of information can instructional designers collect to determine the level of use of instructional materials by the intended learners?

3. What can instructional designers do to optimize the chances that instructional materials will be used effectively by the intended learners?

36

Jay Winzenried

BY TRISTAN JOHNSON, DORIS CHOY, WENHAO HUANG, AND MATTHEW F. ROSE

CORPORATE PLAN ANNOUNCEMENT

Seated around the conference table at InfoTech Inc., a cutting-edge information technology (IT) company that had grown to 150 employees since it incorporated six years ago, John Abersold, the company's president and CEO, looked around at the group of investors present. "InfoTech is looking to create and control a niche in the IT market involving a unique IT security assessment service for businesses," stated John. "To best deliver this service," he continued, "we are planning to train certified public accountants (CPAs) nationwide to provide information security assessments. This plan will help us expand our IT services using our existing CPA client base. It will also help the CPAs initiate and maintain IT support for their current clients, thereby further developing client trust. It is a win-win situation. As I see it, the CPAs are ideal for this plan because they have a pre-existing relationship of trust with their clients. The only difference is that previously our CPAs had been dealing with financial security; now they will deal with information security."

John continued to explain that, in order to offer this new IT security assessment service, InfoTech needed to train the CPAs. Although the CPAs were very familiar with financial auditing procedures, the core content for the IT security assessment would be almost entirely new to this financial service group. After completing the IT assessment training, CPAs would be in a position to recommend any needed networking and information technology services, which InfoTech could then provide.

WEEK ONE

While the senior management employees of InfoTech were working on the strategy for co-ordinating this service plan, they turned to their newly hired manager of training, 45-year-old Amy Sears, to work on the logistics and planning for the training portion. As an experienced trainer, Amy was hired specifically because of her previous experience developing instructor-led training for various Fortune 500 companies.

In the planning meeting with John, Amy realized that, although John was the president and CEO, he had surprisingly little technical experience with information technology. "Since I don't have the technical background," John stated, "I don't know exactly what will be involved in the training for this assessment service, but upper-level management thinks we will need about 15 hours worth of training in order to prepare the CPAs adequately to conduct the security assessment."

"As I am thinking about the overall project timeline," Amy responded, "the first thing I will need to do is to obtain content. I need to know who I should contact to get help with this." John listed the various support resources and recommended that Amy contact both the systems and the network technicians for help with the content.

Amy felt confident in her ability to spearhead the training effort but was somewhat taken aback when John indicated that InfoTech needed the CPA training in a mere eight weeks to meet a contractual obligation with some local CPAs. He told Amy, "We already have CPAs from several firms signed up for scheduled training, so it's important that we meet the deadline. You will have a sufficient amount of financial resources available, but we have to prepare this in just eight weeks."

WEEK TWO

In her interviews with InfoTech's 15 systems and network technicians, it became clear to Amy that, although the content was embedded in their practices, for the purposes of the training, it was unorganized and essentially ethereal and inaccessible. Amy realized that, although the InfoTech technicians were extremely knowledgeable about the technical aspects of their jobs, they were not able to articulate the basics in a way that could help create the CPA assessment training. Moreover, due to current corporate growth, all of the current technicians were extremely busy, just keeping up with the new business.

Now, 10 days into the project, Amy was feeling the pressure, especially since no one at InfoTech could provide her with a content outline for the training. She thought that, if she had some content to start with, making modifications would be a reasonable way to complete this project on time. Amy went back to John to see if he knew of anyone else who would be able to help with the content. John mentioned that he did not know of anyone within InfoTech but that he had some university contacts who might be able to identify relevant existing materials or perhaps even serve as subject matter experts.

After a few phone calls, John gave Amy the names of some contacts at Lamar University. Amy immediately called Sue Baird, director of Lamar University's Center for

Information Technology Research (CITR), and scheduled a meeting for the following week. Given the tight deadline, Amy was able to convince John to attend the meeting with Sue.

WEEK THREE

Sue was unaware of the project constraints that Amy faced, but she was willing to help. She invited a colleague and friend, Jay Winzenried, to attend the meeting the next day as a potential resource for InfoTech. Jay, an employee of WebIDS (a small design firm that specialized in Web-based IT training solutions) had spent the past six months working as an instructional design contractor on an educational project with CITR. Jay was happy to accompany Sue; he was always on the lookout for new business opportunities.

9:15 A.M.

Just prior to the meeting, Jay met with Sue to try to determine some of the basic needs of the client. Sue quickly mentioned, "I don't have any specific details about InfoTech's needs, except that they are trying to develop some training for CPAs. The center is interested in helping them because of several business opportunities from which we may benefit." So, although Jay was going into the meeting with very little information, he was excited to have the opportunity to consult with InfoTech and to help out his friend, Sue.

9:28 A.M.

Sue greeted John and Amy in the foyer of the conference room. She led them inside and introduced them to Jay. After a few minutes of easy conversation, she turned to InfoTech to ask about the specific purpose of the meeting.

9:35 A.M.

John began by presenting the big picture of what they were trying to accomplish. He shared the general details about InfoTech's plan to focus on a niche in the IT market by working with CPAs to provide information security assessments. Amy indicated that the main purpose of the training was to give CPAs the skills needed to conduct an IT security assessment for clients. "Ideally, the 15 hours of training will help the CPAs increase their conceptual understanding of how electronic information security impacts their clients' businesses. We want to be able to cover the basics of an IT assessment; however, it will be tough to give them practice on the step-by-step procedures of an assessment during that 15 hours of training. It is also important to keep the content current. To reflect the latest IT security methods, we will probably need training revisions every four to six months."

Jay asked, "Do you want this training to be delivered to CPAs across the country?" Amy responded, "Yes. In fact, we envision eventually providing this training to CPAs all over the world."

As Amy continued to discuss the training needs, Jay began to see how his instructional design expertise would enable him to assist InfoTech. He started in with a few ideas. "It seems to me that there would be advantages to using Web-based training. One of the biggest advantages is your ability to deliver this training to a geographically distributed audience. Also, this training could be delivered without the constraints of a single instructor, so ideally CPAs could participate in this training at their convenience. Additionally, a Web-based solution would be useful because of the content revision cycle. Various changes could be made and disseminated quickly and without running into distribution issues. Web-based training would be particularly attractive to audiences who are interested in professional development. Further, one of the biggest advantages is the ability to create a Web-based electronic performance support system (EPSS), which would allow CPAs specific, just-in-time support tools to conduct an assessment. CPAs could have the EPSS right there with them during an assessment. This would be a tremendous support to the CPAs as they perform the assessment."

Amy jumped in, "And this tool would be part of the training that InfoTech could create. I really like the idea of an EPSS. This would allow us to deliver training and to help support CPAs in an efficient manner. This has a lot of potential."

9:57 A.M.

Amy mentioned, "OK, it seems as if there are a lot of possibilities to all of this. Still, one of our most immediate challenges is that we need to see if the center or any faculty member has some related content, perhaps based on an existing course. We have looked internally to meet this immediate need, but we do not have the resources available to produce the content." Jay indicated that he had some experience with IT content, but he didn't think that he could personally provide the content for the InfoTech course. However, he thought he could help them with some of the design and development.

"I would imagine that someone here at Lamar would be able to help," stated Sue. "Our outreach coordinator, Vanessa Fea, will be here shortly. She probably has some ideas for you." Sue went to see if Vanessa was available to join the meeting.

10:10 A.M.

Returning with Vanessa, Sue quickly presented the various ideas that were previously discussed in the meeting. "One immediate concern is that InfoTech needs content to put into the training," stated Sue. Vanessa indicated that there was not an existing course similar to the one that InfoTech was proposing to develop. "But I might be able to help you. I have created a series of *PowerPoint*™ presentations for undergraduate students to try to recruit them into the field of information security. These materials would probably be able to provide an outline of the content you need for your CPA training."

"That would be great," exclaimed Amy. "It might be for students, but we would be really interested in taking a look at your materials. I don't see why we couldn't repurpose the content for the CPAs." For the next 10 minutes, Amy and Vanessa discussed how the materials might be reworked to meet InfoTech's needs. Amy and John thought that the materials would be an excellent starting point for their content needs. Vanessa agreed to deliver the various electronic files to InfoTech, so that they could get started immediately.

10:28 A.M.

Just as everyone was pleased to see that InfoTech's content needs were being resolved, Amy brought up the fact that she was faced with a tight timeline. "One thing that we need to consider is that our managers are thinking about leader-led training, and we need to get our training together for the first session in six weeks. We promised a group of local CPAs that we would have our training up and running by October 1."

Jay proposed, "We could begin working immediately on the development of Web-based instructional materials, but there is no way that we would be able to meet the six-week deadline. Is there any way you could move out the deadline?" Jay wondered why the six-week deadline was not brought up earlier. "If InfoTech really liked the idea of Web-based training," thought Jay, "why didn't they mention the time constraint earlier? Don't they realize how much time it takes to develop Web-based materials?"

However, John remained firm, "InfoTech has made a commitment to offer the training in six weeks. We already have people signed up." Sensing Jay's disappointment, Amy responded, "I do not have much experience with Web-based design and development, but I do believe that the Web-based solution would be appropriate in the long run. However, it is critical for us to deliver some training to the first group of CPAs. What can we do here? Can't we come up with some creative options? Our reputation is on the line!"

PRELIMINARY ANALYSIS QUESTIONS

1. What might Jay have done to avoid the challenges that he encountered in the InfoTech meeting?
2. What are some recommendations that Jay might present to meet InfoTech's needs?
3. What would be your suggested timeline for the next six weeks?
4. What should Jay suggest to his client regarding the long-term needs of the project?

IMPLICATIONS FOR ID PRACTICE

1. What design issues do instructional designers face in attempting to balance the short-term and long-term instructional needs of clients?
2. What other issues (e.g., ethical, communications, project management) do instructional designers face in attempting to balance the needs mentioned in question 1?
3. Develop a set of questions that instructional designers could use to assess quickly a client's short-term and long-term needs.

Part **III**

Case Learning: Reflections and Future Possibilities

Taking Stock of Your Learning: Setting Your Sights on the Future

BY PEGGY A. ERTMER

This book would not be complete without asking you, as a novice instructional design professional, to step back from your experiences with the cases in this book and to reflect on the entire case-learning process. Indeed, one of the primary purposes for using case studies as an instructional approach is to facilitate your growing ability to think like designers. This can be accomplished more readily if you take time to reflect, not only on *what* you learned (the case content) but *how* you learned it (the strategies you used while learning—your case-analysis approach).

REFLECTION ON THE CASE-LEARNING EXPERIENCE

"Experience alone is not the key to learning" (Boud, Keogh, & Walker, 1985, p. 7). The learning that results from the types of situations presented in this book depends not only on your *experiences* with these problem situations but also on your *reflections* on and evaluation of how you analyzed the design situations. Although you may never encounter the same situations as the designers in this book, you will continue to encounter messy problems that require problem-solving skills similar to the ones you used while analyzing these cases. Reflection on the case-learning process will enable you to more readily apply what you have learned from these cases to other contexts and other problems.

Dewey (1933) argued that we learn *more* from reflecting on our experiences than we do from actually having the experiences. As mentioned in the introduction to this book, reflection plays an important role during every stage of the learning process—before, during, and after. Reflection *prepares* us for learning; helps us monitor and adjust effort, strategies, and attitude *during* learning; and increases understanding and sense-making *after* learning. According to Wilson and Cole (1991), reflection helps bring meaning to activities that might otherwise be rote and procedural. Furthermore, reflection can help us learn how to think about our work and the work of others in order to understand it, learn from it, and eventually contribute to new conceptions of it.

To maximize your case-learning experience, consider the following series of questions regarding *how* you learned from the cases in this book:

- What was it like trying to learn from case studies?

  - How interesting, valuable, and relevant was the case approach?
  - How motivating was it?
  - How challenging and/or frustrating was it? What features contributed to the challenge level? Should these features be altered, and, if so, how?
  - How would you describe your attitude toward using case studies as a learning tool?

- Describe your case-analysis approach.

  - What strategies did you use to analyze each case? Did you use a systematic approach, or was it more hit and miss?
  - Did your approach change over the course of the semester, and, if so, how?
  - What did you do when you hit a "snag"? (Did you give up? Did you consult other resources? Did you talk to other students?)
  - Compare the effort required to analyze and discuss a case with that required to complete other instructional activities, such as writing a paper or completing textbook exercises.

- Reflect on how you can improve your approach to case learning.
- Now that you have completed a series of cases, what advice would you give to other ID students who are just beginning a course or book like this?

REFLECTION ON THE USEFULNESS OF THE CASE METHOD AS A TEACHING STRATEGY

Now that you've spent some time grappling with case studies as a learner and have considered the relative benefits and challenges of learning in this way, I'd like to ask you to change hats—to take the perspective of an instructional designer, rather than that of a student. (This shouldn't be too difficult—you've been wearing a variety of hats throughout the cases in this book.)

The designers in the cases you've analyzed were confronted with many difficult decisions. Often, they had to decide how to present critical information in an interesting and relevant way. Selecting instructional strategies is one of the most crucial steps in the design process. Yet educators continue to complain that "teachers teach the way they were taught," meaning that they tend to use traditional, didactic methods to present information, often without even considering whether a lecture would be the most effective means. Instructional strategies often are not selected purposefully. I once had a colleague (an ID student) tell me that, whenever she was asked to teach something, her first thought, in terms of strategies, was always a lecture. This was how she remembered learning; this was what she was comfortable delivering. She admitted that she had to force herself to consider a wide range of available strategies and to choose one that best fit the goals, learners, and context of the situation.

Hopefully, this book has given you a good sample of a very different approach to learning—case-based instruction. You've just spent some time thinking about what that experience was like, in terms of both the benefits and the challenges. Sometimes when I use this approach in my courses, I ask my students to *develop* a case as part of their coursework. There are additional benefits for students/designers when they attempt to describe a design situation in such a way that it captures the attention of their peers without leading them to their own preferred solution. This can be a valuable experience, extending the case-learning experience. Furthermore, it gives students the chance to assume the role of both designer and instructor.

Now that you are on the road to becoming an instructional designer in your own right, think about how you might be able to use this instructional strategy in the courses you design and the workshops you facilitate. Do you know of any situations that are particularly appropriate for such an approach? Can you think of situations where this approach would not be appropriate? Are there any specific types of learners who would or would not benefit from this approach? By reflecting on these questions, I hope that, when you begin designing or teaching your own courses and workshops, you will feel comfortable using an approach other than the traditional stand-up lecture. Perhaps your first thoughts, when asked to teach, will be, "How can I incorporate case studies into this instruction?"

REFLECTION ON THE FUTURE OF CASE-BASED INSTRUCTION IN THE ID FIELD

Judging by the responses we've had from reviewers, peers, instructors, and students, the use of case-based instruction in the ID field has started to take hold. Yet, given that there are no other casebooks currently available in this field, we were surprised by the number of people who indicated that they already use cases in their courses. The *ID CaseBook* now provides an outlet as well as an impetus to share our design experiences with others.

Text-based cases are the norm in other professions—business, law, medicine, and, more recently, teacher education. They are relatively inexpensive, accessible, and portable. In addition, some disciplines are beginning to experiment with other methods of delivery. Interactive hypermedia video cases have been used in teacher education (e.g., Abell, Cennamo, & Campbell, 1996; Lacey & Merseth, 1993), medical education (Williams, 1993), and public health education via interactive museum kiosks (Bell, Bareiss, & Beckwith, 1993–1994).

With the explosion of the use of the World Wide Web for instructional purposes and with the introduction of Web-based ID cases by Kinzie and her colleagues (Kinzie, Hrabe, & Larsen, 1998), a new and exciting vehicle for ID cases is now available. This method of delivery will make the dissemination and use of cases in our field even more likely and must be considered seriously by all who intend to use cases in their future work. Although the Web makes new instructional approaches and new pedagogical features readily available (e.g., video, audio, graphics), it brings with it additional pedagogical issues and concerns. These benefits and concerns are addressed in the remaining chapters of this book.

REFERENCES

Abell, S. K., Cennamo, K. S., & Campbell, L. M. (1996). Interactive video cases developed for elementary science methods courses. *Tech Trends, 41*(3), 20–23.

Bell, B., Bareiss, R., & Beckwith, R. (1993–1994). Sickle cell counselor: A prototype goal-based scenario for instruction in a museum environment. *Journal of the Learning Sciences, 3,* 347–386.

Boud, D., Keogh, R., & Walker, D. (Eds.). (1985). *Reflection: Turning experience into learning.* New York: Nichols.

Dewey, J. (1933). *How we think: A restatement of the relation of reflective thinking to the educative process.* Boston: Heath.

Kinzie, M. B., Hrabe, M. E., & Larsen, V. A. (1998). An instructional design case event: Exploring issues in professional practice. *Educational Technology Research & Development, 46*(1), 53–71.

Lacey, C. A., & Merseth, K. K. (1993). Cases, hypermedia, and computer networks: Three curricular innovations for teacher education. *Journal of Curriculum Studies, 25,* 543–551.

Williams, S. (1993). Putting case-based instruction into context: Examples from legal, business, and medical education. *Journal of the Learning Sciences, 2,* 367–427.

Wilson, B., & Cole, P. (1991). A review of cognitive teaching models. *Educational Technology Research and Development, 39*(4), 47–64.

Constructing ID Case Studies for Use via the World Wide Web

BY ANN KOVALCHICK, M. ELIZABETH HRABE,
MARTI F. JULIAN, AND MABLE B. KINZIE

The use of the World Wide Web to support and deliver instruction has gained broad appeal since its introduction as a viable Internet technology in 1993. The use of the Web for case-based teaching in instructional design was first explored at the University of Virginia's Curry School of Education, with the introduction of *The Trials of Terry Kirkland* (Hrabe, Larsen, & Kinzie, 1996), designed for the 1996 Instructional Design Case Competition. In 1997, we presented two more web-based ID cases: *Harvesting Cooperation* (Kovalchick, Kinzie, Julian, & Hrabe, 1997) and *Prescription: Instructional Design* (Hrabe, Julian, Kinzie, & Kovalchick, 1997). In 1998, we presented *The Chronicles of Rocket Boy* (Julian, Kinzie, & Larsen, 1998). These cases can be accessed at the following URLs:

- *http://curry.edschool.virginia.edu/go/ITcases/Site/Casebook/book.html*
- *http://curry.edschool.virginia.edu/go/ITcases/Site/Casebook/caseevent.html*

As the ID case-development team designed and developed each of these cases, we modified our approach according to what we learned about using the Web to deliver case-study instruction. Although problematic aspects of using the Web remain, we believe that it offers a flexible and sustainable mode of instructional delivery, as well as opportunities for strengthening the pedagogical underpinnings of the case-study method. In this section, we briefly discuss the advantages that the Web offers, describe how to exploit these advantages when developing for Web delivery, and provide a framework for pursuing the development of a Web-based case study.

WHY DESIGN WEB-BASED CASE STUDIES?

When we use the World Wide Web for case delivery, we can incorporate two significant features into our cases: the ability to suggest real-world complexities through the use of hyperlink/ hypertext navigation features and the ability to use multiple media to present simulated and authentic case evidence and to provide varied sensory experiences.

Realism and Hypernavigation

Our desire to consider the Web format for case-based instruction grew out of our recognition that, to effectively simulate practice in the ID profession, the complexities of real-world events need to be represented accurately in case materials. Print materials, although familiar and easy to use, essentially lack explicit interactive properties. They allow us to present a description of ID scenarios but require learners to comprehend events in a more or less sequential manner. Still, it is possible to design print materials to be more discursive, as in the use of case overviews, case objectives, and the preliminary analysis questions used in the cases presented in this book.

In designing Web-based cases, the aim is to reinforce the generative processes that good narrative facilitates. Presenting material via the Web enhances students' comprehension of text-based descriptions by contextualizing the attendant conditions of events and by explicitly prompting links among events described within the text. Consequently, real-world events can be presented nonhierarchically. This was achieved in *Prescription: Instructional Design* through the use of a floor plan metaphor and in *The Chronicles of Rocket Boy* through the use of a movie marquee, with scenes from the story as an organizing design principle tied directly to the selected case site.

Given that a primary feature of case-based teaching is its ability to foster connections between an individual's knowledge base and his or her experience, media that facilitate dynamic thinking are especially useful. The efficacy of hypermedia is that ". . . information can be rearranged, analyzed, shifted, and molded to suit the needs of each individual and the context in which material is learned and/or applied" (Borsook & Higgenbotham-Wheat, 1992, p. 10). This is significant, given that the range of problems that instructional designers face requires that they consider multiple points of view and predict alternative courses of action, often in ill-structured and unpredictable contexts. Web-based instructional materials can recreate these aspects of professional practice.

Instructional designers are often called on to create order and coherence out of less than optimal conditions. The ability of the Web to prompt links among ideas, events, and artifacts via hypertext and hyperlinks can direct learners to perceive and construct patterns of meaning among disparate sources of information. In this way, instructional designers gain practice in the use of analytical processes to both generalize and discriminate. Hypernavigation through a web of data relating to an instructional design problem will foster both inductive and deductive strategies of discovery, thereby expanding the instructional designer's toolkit of methods. For example, proven principles of instructional design methods can be systematically analyzed as they are woven into (or found lacking within) the case narrative. In this way, ID students can deductively test a variety of ID models and processes through the logical application of their constituent parts. Although designers often face a range of instructional conditions, it is important for novice designers to recognize the utility of formal models as a starting point for mapping out what is known and unknown about a given design scenario.

Used properly, hyperlinks also offer the possibility of providing various levels of scaffolding based on student needs. Although an advantage of Web-based cases is the abundance of information surrounding an ID scenario that can be provided, this may be an overwhelming amount of information for novice designers. Depending on the instructor's goals, navigation though the information may be chronological, teacher-led and highly directed, or student-centered, such that students are permitted to explore independently or in small groups. Hyperlinks can also allow the instructor to regulate the presentation of material by presenting the design scenario in small, incremental steps. The instructor may anticipate student difficulties with certain aspects of case specifics, or of an ID model used to analyze the case, and, increase the level of task difficulty as necessary. Instructors and students can model the analysis of the case and think aloud about choice-points and decisions relevant to ID problem solving. Depending on how hyperlinks are navigated, instructors may use various prompts, from checklists to open-ended reflections, to determine student mastery over both concrete and theoretical aspects of instructional design.

Multiple Media and Sensory Engagement

A second key aspect of Web-based cases is the ability to present content materials in multiple media formats. In practice, this remains a problematic aspect of using the Web and can be exploited most effectively if case materials are designed for local use at a specified level of technical capacity. As Web technology continues to develop, the ability to present audio, video, and animated media will be simplified. However, concerns for the responsible use of limited bandwidth will likely prevail for some time. Nevertheless, it is worth exploring options for using multiple media sources within Web-based cases. Often, it is the ancillary materials, such as interview clips, simulated documents, and relevant graphics, that lend authenticity to case scenarios. Providing an environment that is rich in artifacts that support the case issues and objectives allows students to simulate the processes of considering hypotheses and applying theories based on empirical evidence, as in an actual design scenario. In addition, ancillary materials provide a point of contact for collaborative processes, prompting students to weigh the importance of secondary information and to articulate their individual arguments for or against its inclusion in defining the design solution.

Perhaps most important, the presentation of case materials in multiple media formats ensures that case users and learners are prompted to engage with the case, using a range of sensory styles. Visual learners will likely focus on points presented via graphic and image formats, whereas aural learners will benefit from an audio clip that reveals a character's tone or speech cadence. Via a collaborative process, learners can develop and practice the skills that they are less inclined to rely on as a matter of preference, as well as learn to integrate insights and analyses by colleagues with learning styles different from their own.

Although the skills and knowledge of formal reasoning used to problem solve a design situation are essential aspects of professional practice, designers must also develop the insights and sensitivities to recognize particular conditions. Faced with a complex design problem, ID students can define given aspects of the problem and consider how local knowledge (the resources, talents, and skills represented by the fictionalized case characters) can contribute to developing a design solution. The rich context provided in Web-based cases can be especially useful for prompting novice designers to look beyond the obvious in cases where the application of common ID assumptions appears to have failed. In this way, ID students can learn to generate "grounded theory" to guide their decision-making processes in unique situations.

For example, in *The Trials of Terry Kirkland,* the designer, Terry Kirkland, has not conducted an adequate analysis of the sociocultural context in which the instructional design is developed and implemented. Had Terry understood the history of the group of individuals who had been developing the training, she may have recognized that key individuals were reacting to events that preceded her involvement. Although students who have used the case have provided thoughts on how Terry's design might have benefited from a contextual analysis, they were also prompted to cite specific ways in which she could have made use of this local knowledge, had a more thorough contextual analysis been done. Consequently, it would not be enough for ID students to recognize that a contextual analysis is necessary; they should also be able to determine how the findings can influence the parameters of the given situation.

As an instructional tool, Web-based case studies offer the possibility for a deep and sustained learning experience. The collection of experiences in a web-based case have the potential to transport the learner into the real-life drama that professional practice presents. To the extent that learners can observe the competing needs, desires, and worries present in the situation, experience the personalities involved, and feel the level of effort and thinking required, the more closely they can participate in an actual professional practice experience.

DEVELOPING CASE MATERIALS FOR THE WEB

As is often the case in materials development, designing Web-based cases requires an iterative cycle of concept development (identification of setting and issues), the design of the user experience (including the selection of media), and the development of prototypes and final case materials. Each stage overlaps and informs other stages. Given this integrative style, our approach to the development of Web-based cases has benefited from a team approach, with roles and responsibilities shifting for each case.

Concept Development

The lead writer begins developing the case by identifying a professional practice setting, proposed characters, and a list of possible practice issues an instructional designer might encounter in that setting. Then the team meets to discuss and flesh out these conceptual elements. Our settings to this point have been those that we have had personal experience with, for it is actual experience that we feel helps us create a realistic case environment. For example, to build *The Chronicles of Rocket Boy,* we began by conducting needs assessments in the selected case environment. Based on the past experiences of the lead author's work in the film industry, we selected performance support as a primary issue. The lead author then conducted a needs assessment with 10 companies, ranging from "mom and pop" film production shops to large, corporate production houses and talked with a range of personnel in line and supervisory positions, owners, and trainers/designers. We conducted multiple interviews of stakeholders at various levels across several organizations. This process ensured that we could create a realistic portrayal of a digital animation facility, the process, the interpersonal issues, and the personalities of the case characters. Our aim was to obtain stakeholders' perspectives on the environment and current ID issues and to reconstruct contextual factors that an instructional designer would encounter in the selected case environment. This needs assessment, as well as our own experiences as instructional designers and teachers of instructional design, informed the list of issues. We know that some of the biggest lessons we learned in practice were not necessarily things for which our ID training prepared us. We also know the kinds of experiences and issues that are difficult to recreate within the context of an ID "class project." We then selected one or two specific instructional design issues to guide the case development and ultimately to serve as key issues for the learners to assess. Before the lead writer and other team members can begin writing the case materials, however, design decisions must be made about the kinds of user experience we hope to create and the case media that we plan to use to help create these experiences.

Design of the User Experience

The user experience is influenced by several additional related factors: the organization of case information (see Shedroff, 1994, for a description of possible organizational methods), the interactivity provided (Laurel, 1990), and the types of media likely to be the most complementary to the organizational structure and interactivity. In addition, foremost in our minds is that the case is an instructional tool. Therefore, we take care to adhere to the principles of Web-based instruction that have been identified as supports for learning effectiveness (Bannan-Ritland, Milheim, & Harvey, 1998; Khan, 1997).

When we consider ways to organize the case, and the interactive possibilities the users will be presented with, our deliberations are directly informed by the themes reflected in the case setting, characters, and issues. For example, the organizational method for the initial Web-based version of the case *Harvesting Cooperation* is a timeline. Since the case has an agricultural theme, we felt that a timeline would mirror the importance of the passing of seasons, planting, and harvesting within a farming community. Time also plays a key role in the instructional design process, with expected completion dates and project management requirements figuring prominently. Perhaps most important, a timeline would allow case users to discover sequentially the case artifacts, much as they would were they actually to conduct information-gathering activities over the course of a needs assessment (the focus of the case). This allowed us to create an interactive experience that complemented the instructional design process.

The organizational method and type of interactivity, along with the setting and issues to be reflected in the case, lead to our media selection. We want the users' focus to be on the experience of analyzing the case, rather than on the technology used to present it. For Web delivery, this means making sure the target audience is capable of receiving and displaying the media files we provide, as well as attempting to make the media files as small as possible, so that download times are minimized. In *Harvesting Cooperation,* we used the timeline, the needs assessment issues, and our knowledge of our users' media capabilities to determine the best media for the case. We decided to provide the case information and experiences over time, through the use of journal entries (from the instructional designer's journal), e-mail communications among case characters, an interview transcript, and a variety of supporting documents (proposals, overhead transparencies, etc.). We selected static media (text and illustrations), as we had confirmed from a previous case evaluation (Hrabe et al., 1996) that a portion of our target audience did not have access, at the time, to the audio and video capabilities provided by the Web.

Development of Prototypes and Final Case Materials

During this stage of the case design and development process, a number of concurrent activities take place. In the process, modifications are made not only to the case setting, characters, and issues but also to the organizational strategies, interactivity, and choice of media.

The lead author now begins writing the case materials, assisted by members of the team, who write supporting materials under his or her direction. Since our focus has been on creating a discovery experience for users (as opposed to simply describing the case issues), we attempt to make this writing dramatic and evocative of the situation. Successive drafts of these materials are produced, reviewed, and revised.

A team member designated as graphic designer produces prototypes of the graphical interface, which are critiqued and revised. We try to create a graphical appearance that is attractive and enticing enough to arouse curiosity in the learners and to draw them into the experience. At the same time, we are aware of the need for a simple and easy-to-navigate graphical interface. Conventional interactive design suggests that user discomfort tends to increase with the number of hierarchies of information. For this reason, we attempt to provide all case information within two steps of the main page. Since some computers still have only 13-inch monitors (480×360 pixels), we try to present critical information within this area and to make it evident that additional information is available if users scroll down the page. When possible, we exploit the graphical interface to add realism to the case study. For example, e-mail correspondence between characters can be formatted to look as if it is from a UNIX® account, and newspaper and journal articles are arranged to look as if they have been copied from a publication, with appropriately stylized headlines and headers.

CREATING A CASE STUDY FOR THE WEB: PRELIMINARY DESIGN ANALYSIS

To help readers develop an understanding of the possibilities inherent in using web-based case studies for discussion, we provide a "Web Case Design Analysis Worksheet" (see the appendix). The use of this analysis worksheet assumes either that (1) case authors are considering transferring an existing text-based case to the Web or (2) case authors are writing a new case with the intention of using a Web presentation. In either situation, it is important that outcomes and expectations arising out of a web presentation are delineated very clearly. We believe that the use of this worksheet may be of help to authors in analyzing proposed Web case designs and clarifying goals. In particular, the worksheet will be useful after completing initial data collection on the case environment and issues, and after having substantially developed the content. Additionally, case authors can use the worksheet as one way to consider the costs and benefits of making the transition from a text to a Web format.

In order to carry out a Web case design analysis, authors for both new and existing cases should complete a preliminary plan identifying how the case will be presented on the Web and what multimedia components (video, audio, or animation), if any, should be included. Initial design decisions in the preliminary plan include determining how the theme of the case is to be integrated into a visual presentation that will focus the audience on the case issues. This should include the development of a simple site plan. At this stage of development, the site plan need not be very formal or complete but should provide an overview of how the case materials will be organized across the multidimensions available on the Web. The site plan may also incorporate an organizing metaphor (such as the hospital floor plan in *Prescription: Instructional Design*) or a theme (such as the timeline in *Harvesting Cooperation* or the marquee in *Rocket Boy*) although a simple, straightforward layout can be just as effective, particularly if the case is to be used by beginners. The design plan specifies each proposed Web page in the site plan and is used to document page content, page layout, hyperlinks, media (graphics, video, audio), and instructional intervention points. The design plan is most useful if created on paper and used as a prototype of the proposed Web design to be evaluated by content experts, colleagues, and members of the target audience.

The "Web Case Design Analysis Worksheet" is intended to encourage case authors to consider (and reconsider) the following questions in the preliminary design of a case:

1. What are the instructional purposes of the case?
2. How is the case structured to fulfill those purposes?
3. How does a case design that incorporates web presentation features enhance those purposes and structures for the intended audience?

It is our strong feeling that text cases and Web-based cases are not in competition. Each design has a different set of purposes and functions that facilitate understanding. Consider an important observation based on our experiences in designing multimedia case studies for use by students in the classroom and by participants in a case competition: Sooner or later in the case analysis process, Web-based cases *become* text-based cases. As you have probably observed, it is difficult to read text documents presented on a computer monitor. Thus, all of our users have indicated that they download and print out the cases for closer reading (Kinzie, Hrabe, & Larsen, 1998). Why, then, have multimedia Web-based cases, if students revert to reading text versions of them? In the following section, we describe what we have found to be some of the unique contributions the use of Web-based cases have made to facilitate learning in the instructional design classroom.

USING WEB-BASED CASES IN THE CLASSROOM AND IN THE COMPETITION ENVIRONMENT

How can instructional design students make greatest use of multimedia Web-based cases? We have explored the use of such cases with students in two widely dissimilar environments: in the classroom and in two national instructional design case competitions (see Kinzie et al., 1998, and Julian, Kinzie, & Larsen, 2000). Our experiences with students in both venues suggest that there are several instructional benefits to innovative uses of Web-based case studies.

Active Immersion into the World of a Case Study

Multimedia cases may best be suited to presenting multilayered, complex, ill-defined situations in which a variety of issues face an instructional designer against a background of subtly revealed political, cultural, and personal influences. Students may then take several class periods to "live with" the issues presented in such a case. Teachers can flexibly accommodate the needs of the class by choosing which issues to pursue in-depth. Through the use of class activities and leading questions during class discussion, the instructor can guide students through a complicated case, suggesting possible directions for exploration, adjusting perceptions, and raising contrary ideas when needed. More advanced students may be able to take these leaps independently.

Collaboration

Our experiences with these large, diffuse case studies suggest that they are most useful when analyzed by students working in teams. Teams of four or five members appear to be most effective. Smaller groups may lack the wealth of internal resources derived from pooling the experiences and expertise of individual group members, whereas larger teams tend to become unwieldy. Students have expressed enthusiasm for the dynamic process that often develops during such collaborations. Students perceive that the presentation of multiple perspectives during team deliberations and the act of coming to consensus are useful in their development as professionals (Kinzie et al., 1998).

The success of team collaboration within classes has led to frequent requests for collaboration across sites. Students enjoy sharing case responses with teams from other institutions. We have attempted to further such communication asynchronously through e-mail and the posting of comments and responses to the Website. Other possibilities for cross-site collaboration include the use of newsgroups or such synchronous communication provided by video conferencing or chat rooms.

Role Play

The availability of this technology, which can facilitate communication over distance, together with the interactive nature of the multimedia Web cases, have led to students' desire to overcome the static nature of the case-study model by interacting directly with characters from the case. Just as instructional designers in practice have the ability to ask questions of stakeholders and others, so students involved in a case analysis wish to have the ability to speak with important characters in the case. Certainly, the possibilities exist for such role play. The available technology could permit experts from the field or even instructors to answer student questions by taking on the perspective of a case character, either in online real-time or in a mailing list format. We explored such interactivity with *Harvesting Cooperation,* and our experiences confirmed what is known about developing online interaction—namely, that active facilitation by case authors is critical to maintaining online interaction among case learners (Pallof & Pratt, 1999). Consequently, as case authors, we need to be prepared to remain involved in the case development beyond its initial authorship and presentation.

Multiple Perspectives

In addition to the case analyses shared among teams within a class and across sites, the Web allows us the ability to present expert opinions from professionals in instructional design or from fields represented in a particular case. These can be made available at the case Website. Thus, in *The Trials of Terry Kirkland,* it is possible to hear from a public school administrator and an instructional designer who works in a school setting, and, in *Harvesting Cooperation,* we can hear from an extension agent as well as a designer connected to a large university. These expert perspectives provide other perspectives on the case and widen students' understanding about resources and contacts for developing professional knowledge in real-world situations.

Web-Based Research

Finally, instructional designers need to be aware of a multitude of resources and materials they will need for research and design development when they are hired to create content for areas in which they lack expertise. It is possible to embed links within a Web-based case study that lead to Internet resources that can aid students in creating their own design solutions to a case. Rich content materials are available on the Web, as are sources for expert contacts. Pointing students toward the Web as a significant resource can enhance their learning experiences. In *Harvesting Cooperation,* we endeavored to do this by including within the story a list of URLs that provided content information about the theme of integrated pest management.

The availability of new media delivery systems offers additional possibilities for using case-based teaching in instructional design. Hypermedia technologies, such as the Web, can enhance case-based teaching by providing a means of introducing authentic contextual cues, by prompting students to actively use analytical and organizing skills as they navigate through the Web-based case, and by presenting information in multiple media formats. In doing so, Web-based cases offer an additional means of closing the gap between theory and practice.

Appendix

Web Case Design Analysis Worksheet

PART I. CHARACTERISTICS

1. *Case Title:* _____

   _____

2. *Audience:* _____

   _____

   a. Who is the intended audience?

   b. How experienced is the intended audience in using cases?

   c. How experienced is the intended audience in using multimedia/Internet?

   d. What kind/how current is the technology to be used by audience in working with the case?

   e. Who else may use the case?

3. *Instructional Purposes*

What are the instructional objectives?	*How do the design and format function to support each of the instructional objectives?*
a. _____	a. _____
b. _____	b. _____
c. _____	c. _____
d. _____	d. _____

4. *Design Theme and Organization*

   a. Does the web design include a theme that communicates the focus of the case? If so, describe the theme.

   b. Describe the organizing site plan.

c. Does the design make use of a metaphor that supports the theme and facilitates user comprehension and navigation with the case materials? If so, describe that metaphor.

d. How does this organizing site plan facilitate comprehension and ease of navigation?

5. *Design Features*

List the features (text, graphics, hyperlinks, video, audio, off-site links, live interactive components, etc.).

Indicate how each feature facilitates content comprehension.

a. _____   a. _____

b. _____   b. _____

c. _____   c. _____

d. _____   d. _____

e. _____   e. _____

f. _____   f. _____

6. *Scaffolding*

What are the instructor intervention/ support strategies planned?

How is each intervention strategy integrated into the Web design or the instruction?

a. _____   a. _____

b. _____   b. _____

c. _____   c. _____

d. _____   d. _____

7. *Design Costs* to designer in creating Web-based case (requirements in time, technical expertise, equipment, site maintenance)

a. _____

b. _____

c. _____

d. _____

e. _____

PART II. EVALUATION

8. **What do you see as *strengths* of the design structure?**

   a. _____

   b. _____

   c. _____

   d. _____

   e. _____

   f. _____

   g. _____

   h. _____

9. **What do you see as possible *weaknesses* that may result from the design structure?**

   a. _____

   b. _____

   c. _____

   d. _____

   e. _____

   f. _____

   g. _____

   h. _____

References

Bannan-Ritland, B., Milheim, W. D., & Harvey, D. (1998). A general framework for web-based instruction. *Educational Media International, 35*(2), 77–81.

Borsook, T. K., & Higgenbotham-Wheat, N. (1992). *The psychology of hypermedia: A conceptual framework for R & D.* Paper presented at the Annual Meeting of the Association for Educational Communications and Technology (AECT), Washington, DC.

Hrabe, M. E., Julian, M. F., Kinzie, M. B., & Kovalchick, A. (1997). *Prescription: Instructional design.* Web-based case available at: http://curry.edschool.virginia.edu/go/ITcases/Site/Casebook/book.html

Hrabe, M. E., Larsen, V. A., & Kinzie, M. B. (1996). *The trials of Terry Kirkland.* Web-based case available at: http://curry.edschool.virginia.edu/go/ITcases/Site/Casebook/book.html

Julian, M. F., Kinzie, M. B., & Larsen, V. A. (1998). *The chronicles of Rocket Boy.* Web-based case available at: http://curry.edschool.virginia.edu/go/ITcases/Site/Casebook/caseevent.html

Julian, M. F., Kinzie, M. B., & Larsen, V. A. (2000). Compelling case experiences: Performance, practice, and application for emerging instructional designers. *Performance Improvement Quarterly, 13*(3), 164–201.

Khan, B. H. (1997). Web-based instruction (WBI): What is it and why is it? In B. H. Khan (Ed.), *Web-based instruction* (pp. 5–18). Englewood Cliffs, NJ: Educational Technology Publications.

Kinzie, M. B., Hrabe, M. E., & Larsen, V. A. (1998). Exploring professional practice through an instructional design team case competition. *Educational Technology Research and Development, 46*(1), 53–71.

Kovalchick, A., Kinzie, M. B., Julian, M. F., & Hrabe, M. E. (1997). *Harvesting cooperation.* Web-based case available at: http://curry.edschool.virginia.edu/go/ITcases/Site/Casebook/book.html

Laurel, B. (1990). *The art of human-computer interface design.* Reading, MA: Addison-Wesley.

Paloff, R. M., & Pratt, K. (1999). *Building learning communities in cyberspace: Effective strategies for the online classroom.* San Francisco: Jossey-Bass.

Shedroff, N. (1994). *Information interaction design: A unified field theory of design.* Web document available at: http://www.nathan.com/thoughts/unified/